Philosophical Encounters

LONERGAN AND THE ANALYTICAL TRADITION

The philosophical views of Bernard Lonergan often ran contrary to those of his contemporaries in the dominant analytical school. In *Philosophical Encounters,* Joseph Fitzpatrick examines the concepts and terms both Lonergan and the analytical school employed and shared in order to map out clearly where they agreed and where they differed, and indicates where fruitful possibilities exist for dialogue.

Fitzpatrick's approach is unique as he sets up direct encounters between representative topics and themes from the analytical tradition and those from Lonergan's extensive philosophical corpus. The result is a spirited battle of ideas. One notable feature is the level of agreement found between Lonergan and Wittgenstein where both depart from the philosophical pathway marked out by Descartes.

Philosophical Encounters defends Lonergan from the kind of attacks typically made against his position and reflects on the deep influences on his thought that help to account for its distinctiveness. Accessibly written and supplemented by a glossary of key terms, this book will be useful not only to those wishing to familiarize themselves with Lonergan's thought but also to anyone wanting to develop an acquaintance with some of the leading lights of the analytical tradition, such as Wittgenstein and Russell.

(Lonergan Studies)

JOSEPH FITZPATRICK is an independent education consultant and school inspector living in West Yorkshire, England.

JOSEPH FITZPATRICK

Philosophical Encounters

Lonergan and the Analytical Tradition

UNIVERSITY OF TORONTO PRESS
Toronto Buffalo London

© University of Toronto Press 2005
Toronto Buffalo London
Printed in Canada

ISBN 0-8020-3844-1 (cloth)
ISBN 0-8020-4884-6 (paper)

Printed on acid-free paper

Lonergan Studies

Library and Archives Canada Cataloguing in Publication

Fitzpatrick, Joseph
  Philosophical encounters : Lonergan and the analytical
tradition / Joseph Fitzpatrick.

  (Lonergan studies)
  Includes bibliographical references and index.
  ISBN 0-8020-3844-1 (bound).   ISBN 0-8020-4884-6 (pbk.)

  1. Lonergan, Bernard J.F. (Bernard Joseph Francis), 1904–1984.
  2. Analysis (Philosophy)   3. Critical realism.   4. Philosophy, Comparative.
  I. Title.   II. Series.

  B995.L654F58 2005   191   C2005-900864-4

University of Toronto Press acknowledges the financial support for its
publishing activities of the Government of Canada through the Book
Publishing Industry Development Program (BPIDP).

University of Toronto Press acknowledges the financial assistance to
its publishing program of the Canada Council for the Arts and the
Ontario Arts Council.

Contents

Philosophical Encounters

LONERGAN AND THE ANALYTICAL TRADITION

Introduction

It was apparently George Bernard Shaw who observed that the United States and Great Britain are two nations separated by a common language. Something similar might be said of the two systems of philosophy that are the focus of attention in this volume – Anglo-American analytic philosophy and the Thomist critical realism expounded by Bernard Lonergan. For these are two philosophies separated by a common set of terms. Each of the two, for example, speaks of idea, logic, existence, data, introspection, and the correspondence theory of truth, but each attaches a quite distinct and differing meaning or role to each of those terms. Both emphasize experience and truth conditions but attach different functions to each notion. Above all, both speak of the foundations of knowledge, but they disagree emphatically on what such putative foundations might be.

In these essays I have assigned myself the role of clarifying the difference in the meaning or function of some of these terms for these two philosophical systems. If we can achieve clarity, we might begin to understand what the other philosopher is saying. Philosophers are natural empire builders in the field of knowledge, for they feel themselves bound by the principle of self-consistency to defeat their opponents by means of arguments from within their own philosophical systems, on the basis of arguments drawn from their own vision or perception of what constitutes philosophical legitimacy.

This, it seems to me, is the inevitable consequence of having a system or a position in the first place, and is a perfectly legitimate form of philosophical procedure. It can, however, lead to mutual incomprehension and a tendency to assimilate your opponent's position to one that your particular philosophy can easily deal with, on the basis of verbal similarities and the like, and result in a failure to appreciate what is specific or distinctive about that position, how it might differ from other positions. One might presume, for example, because philosopher A speaks of the correspondence theory of truth and philosopher B also speaks of the correspondence theory of truth, that each philosopher must mean the same thing, when in fact it is quite possible that each means something quite different. My major objective in the chapters that follow is to overcome this kind of mutual distortion by setting out as clearly as I can the understandings and meanings that underlie various philosophers' verbal statements and claims: to get under the words to the underlying assumptions and intentions of their claims, so that each side has a clearer grasp of the other, a better take on what the other side is up to. The cause of philosophy will have been well served if this kind of mutual incomprehension can be reduced or eliminated. What is more, it is by means of this kind of procedure, I believe, that basic realities are uncovered, enabling a genuine comparison of the merits of each position. Like other philosophers, I shall be arguing from within my own philosophical perspective, which is that of critical realism, but in comparing my position with others' I shall employ the usual tools of the philosopher, examining which of two positions is stronger in terms of self-consistency, economy of explanation, and sheer explanatory power.

If I succeed in my mission, the analytic philosopher should have a better idea of what is being claimed by Lonergan's critical realism and the critical realist should have a better understanding of what the analytic philosopher is saying and of her mode of working or thinking. One difficulty that should be faced right away is that, while the critical realism referred to in these essays issues from the philosophy of one thinker, and has the virtue of being relatively unified, there is no such unity or agreement about what is meant by analytic philosophy or even the analytical *tradition*. As a term of convenience, 'analytic philosophy' has come to mean the dominant philosophy within the Anglo-American tradition throughout the twentieth century. It has outgrown its initial meaning whereby the primary task of philosophy was conceived to be the analysis of propositions, since that task was established within a philosophical enterprise – Logical Atomism – that the analytical tradition has for the most part left behind. Nevertheless, analytic philosophy has held on to the notion that philosophy is about language, and has extended its notion of language beyond its use in propositional statements. That the term 'analytic' has survived is due, I suspect, to its preoccupation with precision, clarity, and logical rigour – qualities the analytical tradition most admires and acclaims. We might say, then, that while it would not be possible to define the analytical tradition in philosophy by reference to specific themes or procedures, there is a set of *qualities* that the tradition has held up as the ideal to which philosophers should aspire. Along with these qualities, as a consequence of its admiration for these qualities, we can appreciate the ongoing concern the analytical tradition has with mathematics and logic. In this way, a rough-hewn understanding of what is connoted by the term analytic in modern philosophy begins to emerge: it is a tradition devoted to upholding high standards of logical argument alongside clarity and precision of expression that has a long-standing interest in logic, which it considers to be essentially linguistic. Strange to say, much of this could also serve as a rough-hewn account of the philosophy of Bernard Lonergan, although Lonergan is eventually more impressed with scientific method than with logic. While Lonergan's philosophy has not taken the 'linguistic turn' that to an extent defines the program of analytic philosophy, his writings reveal a long-standing interest in mathematics and logic and in the relation of logic to judgment. Furthermore, I shall argue for a broad similarity between Lonergan's response to the Cartesian tradition in philosophy and that of Wittgenstein, one of the begetters of the analytical tradition.

How far the particular philosophers I have brought into 'encounter' with Lonergan might be counted members of some so-called analytical division or grouping in philosophy is another potential source of contention. That Russell and Wittgenstein fully qualify for membership as analytic philosophers is not a claim that anyone is likely to gainsay, I suspect, since these two – along with their fellow Cambridge philosopher, G.E. Moore – have strong claims to be the supreme architects of the tradition. In so far as contemporary philosophers make positive use of the kinds of arguments and positions first set forth by Russell, Moore, and Wittgenstein, notwithstanding the differences between the three, they can be accounted members of the analytical tradition. Hume, of course, antedates the use of the term analytic as a description of a philosophical movement or grouping, but, again, few would contest his association with such a grouping since his influence on twentieth-century empiricism – an undisputed component of the tradition – has been profound.

Rodney Needham, whose method of philosophizing is thoroughly linguistic, is the only one of the philosophers encountered here who in a sense throws down the gauntlet to Lonergan, claiming as he does that Lonergan's notion of belief is not only wrong but also harmful and even dangerous. Dealing with Needham requires me to bring Lonergan's philosophy into contact with one of the most distinguished philosophers of his generation, the late Stuart Hampshire, whose *Thought and Action*, published in 1959, is widely considered to be one of the high-water marks of the first wave of post-war Oxford philosophy, along with Gilbert Ryle's *A Concept of Mind*, published a decade earlier. Michael Polanyi might be considered to stand apart from the majority tradition and to be undeserving – in whichever way one chooses to interpret the word – of the label *analytic*. But as a former scientist and a noted philosopher of science, he has the characteristics of an analytic philosopher, and a strong case can be made for his inclusion, at least as an ally of Lonergan's, albeit there are important differences between the two that it will be profitable to explore.

Perhaps stronger arguments could be adduced for the exclusion of Richard Rorty from the analytical tradition: in many people's minds, Rorty is a postmodernist whose end-of-Philosophy philosophy runs counter to the analytical tradition's 'core commitments to objectivism, realism and cognitivism.'[1] If one takes a more pragmatic view, however, as Rorty would doubtless encourage one to do, it could be argued that Rorty's *affiliations* are analytical. For Rorty is a particular kind of postmodernist, and his philosophical position rests on arguments first set forth by members of the analytic movement; his pragmatism, as he himself makes clear, can be seen to be an extension and continuation of the positivist and behaviourist strands in the analytical tradition. In this way, Rorty has the only minimal associations that one could stipulate, since very clearly the analytical movement in philosophy is far from being a cohesive set of principles or beliefs, or even a consistent way of doing philosophy, and membership can only be decided on the basis of certain lines of continuity and development.

In the 1998 Aquinas lecture, John Haldane, professor of philosophy and director of the Centre for Philosophy and Public Affairs, at the University of St Andrews in Scotland, urged Thomist philosophers to become better acquainted with analytic philosophy, the better to take part in the debates occurring in the mainstream of Anglo-American philosophy. This is a sentiment with which I wholeheartedly concur, for the reasons set out clearly by Haldane:

> The effects of neoscholastic hostility to analytical thought have generally been bad ones. Without open and informed exchange between conflicting positions there is no growth, and in the life of the intellect without growth there is stagnation. For its own self-definition and benefit a philosophy needs to test itself against rivals; but any activity ordered towards truth also has a responsibility to respect the same search when it is evidently pursued by others. Avowedly Catholic philosophers in general, and Neothomists among them, are largely isolated from the mainstream. In consequence, their intellectual standards are generally lower, and they are still not

1 I have borrowed this phrase from Hayden Ramsey, one of the contributors to the broad range of responses collected by the journal *New Blackfriars* to the lecture by John Haldane, referred to below. See *New Blackfriars* (Oxford) 80 (April 1999), 197.

sufficiently learning from nor contributing to the main debates pursued in the wider world. This latter failing is particularly ironic since some of the central themes of contemporary analytical philosophy, such as intentionality, normativity, causality and explanation, holism and reductionism, and realism and anti-realism, have also been prominent in Thomistic and neoscholastic thought from the middle ages onwards. Opportunities for productive engagement have been missed too often and for too long.[2]

Among the range of Thomist philosophers invited to respond to Haldane's lecture, a surprising number dwelt on the difficulty of simply using Aquinas in contemporary philosophical debate. A major part of the difficulty resides in the fact that Aquinas worked and wrote in an intellectual climate quite different from our own. Is it possible simply to 'mine' Aquinas for his ideas? This, as one respondent affirmed, 'would look to a historical scholar like a combination of exploitation and destruction, the intellectual equivalent of strip mining. Scholars routinely protest,' she continued, 'that analytical philosophers have no genuine desire to understand Thomas's thought, only a desire to use it. In the course of using it, they often attribute to him opinions he never held or even clearly rejected.'[3] In a not dissimilar vein, another respondent pointed out that '[b]efore we try to answer questions about the relationship between Aquinas' thought and the thought of Frege or Wittgenstein or Russell or Putnam or Quine, we must get a good hold on Aquinas' own thought, as he expressed it in terms no longer easily understood by us ... Moreover, it is exceedingly difficult to understand Aquinas well. It takes years to get a decent grip on his basic arguments and their interconnections.

'Before passing judgment on fragments of his thought, the scholar must see his reasoning unfold across a vast corpus of writings.'[4] Considerations such as these led Lonergan, a Thomist scholar who devoted eleven years to the study of Aquinas, to separate his historical studies of Aquinas from his own practice as a philosopher. As he put it, 'The first concern of historical scholarship is not to set forth and convince readers or hearers of the profundity of an author's thought, the breadth of his vision, the universal relevance of his conclusions. That sort of thing may be allowed to pad a preface or to fill out a conclusion. But the heart of the matter is elsewhere. It is a long journey through variant readings, shifts in vocabulary, enriching perspectives – all duly documented – that establishes as definitively as can

---

2 'Thomism and the Future of Catholic Philosophy,' *New Blackfriars* 80 (April 1999), 170.
3 Bonnie Kent, Columbia University, ibid., 186.
4 Thomas D. Sullivan, University of St Thomas, St Paul, ibid., 203.

be expected what the great man thought on some minor topic within the horizon of his time and place, and with no great relevance to other times or places. Only from a long series of such dissertations can the full picture be constructed.'[5] At the very end of his *Verbum: Word and Idea in Aquinas*, described by Anthony Kenny as the best book in English on Aquinas's philosophy of mind,[6] Lonergan observes: 'One can aim at understanding Aquinas; one can aim at a transposition of his position to meet the issues of our own day; but to aim at both simultaneously results inevitably, I believe, in substituting for the real Aquinas some abstract ideal of theoretical coherence.'[7] While there is only one definitive theoretical exposition of Aquinas, he argues, namely that which came from the hands of Aquinas himself, there are and must be many developments of his thought.[8] Therein lies the problem: the Thomist philosopher attempting to engage with analytic philosophers is unlikely to remain unchallenged when claiming that such and such is Aquinas's definitive opinion on a topic; and so the argument is liable to get bogged down in questions of interpretation and textual exegesis.

Though deeply influenced by Aquinas, Lonergan's philosophy is very much his own, starting as it does from an empirical inquiry into the nature of knowledge rather than, like Aquinas's, from a metaphysics with its basis in *principia per se nota* – so-called self-evident principles. Rather than beginning with metaphysics, which viewed as a starting point presents serious difficulties to the modern mind schooled in philosophy as it has developed since Descartes, Lonergan grounds epistemology in cognitional theory and cognitional theory in a descriptive account of cognitional practice: what is it we do when we make a knowledge claim in mathematics, science, history, or any of the other intellectual disciplines? When we have discovered the answer to that question, we can go on to ask the epistemological question, Why is doing that knowledge? and from there go on further to the ontological question, What is it we know when we do that? The problems to which Lonergan attempts to find solutions in the course of his efforts to answer these questions are the very problems shared by the practitioners of analytic philosophy referred to by Haldane: intentionality, objectivity, normativity, realism, and so forth. Indeed, Lonergan is fairly prolific in his solutions to the long-standing problems of modern philosophy: How can we reconcile subjectivity and objectivity? What is the relation between *is*

---

5 Bernard J.F. Lonergan, 'The Scope of Renewal,' *Method: Journal of Lonergan Studies* 16 (Fall 1998), 84.

6 Anthony Kenny, *Aquinas* (Oxford University Press, 1980), 83.

7 Lonergan, *Verbum: Word and Idea in Aquinas* (Darton, Longman and Todd, 1968), 220.

8 Ibid.

propositions and *ought* propositions? How can we claim to know reality? What is the criterion of objectivity? and so on. Lonergan, whose radical reflections on the post-Cartesian tradition bear a remarkable resemblance to Wittgenstein's, shares with Wittgenstein something of the engineer's approach to philosophical problems: let us set out the problem as meticulously as we can manage; now let us go about methodically finding a solution. As with Wittgenstein, philosophy in Lonergan's hands has the feel of a very practical activity. Of course, Lonergan was only one thinker and he was not right about everything; elsewhere I have offered serious criticisms of his views on aesthetics and on ethics. On the central questions of epistemology, however, as well as on the history of philosophy, he does have powerful insights to offer that are well worth sharing with a wider audience.

It is with this wider audience that I wish to dialogue and debate by comparing and contrasting Lonergan's views on a range of issues with those of some central and not-so-central representatives of the analytical tradition. The age-old method of contrast and comparison, beloved of generations of examiners, will, I trust, allow me to bring out the similarities of Lonergan's views with those of the analytic philosophers under consideration as well as to point up the differences. From the viewpoint of the analytic philosopher, there are also basic drawbacks in Lonergan's approach to philosophy, basic stumbling blocks that can prevent his philosophy from being taken seriously. I have attempted to confront these difficulties head-on at appropriate points in these chapters, mainly by demonstrating the deep differences between critical realism and empiricism, and the radical implications of these differences. Analysis was one of Lonergan's major philosophical tools: in his later period he took to calling his philosophy 'intentionality analysis' – the analysis of our conscious *intentional* operations. That, in a nutshell, is what he was about, and that very fact, together with the empirical nature of his starting point, may suffice to attract the analytic philosopher to find out what he has to say.

While contrast and comparison are the basic method of operation in this book, for the sake of clarity, in the opening chapter I present Lonergan's central ideas in a fairly straightforward and non-comparative way, deliberately adopting a rather popular style of exposition. My intention or hope is that this will help the reader to get into Lonergan's thinking more readily, free from the distraction of specific comparisons, so that a clear grasp of his central ideas will assist in the work of comparison and contrast that comes later. Because the various chapters were originally written as occasional essays, a certain amount of repetition inevitably occurs; but in revising the essays for publication in the form of consecutive chapters, I have attempted to ensure that repetition rarely occurs without some extension and deepening of the point made earlier. My intention is pedagogical: that by repeating a point while extending, deepening, or refining it, I might help readers to consolidate and deepen their grasp of its meaning and application. In setting out the essays, I have attempted to familiarize the reader with some central features of Lonergan's thought before moving on to wider considerations and viewpoints. Thus, the chapters can be read consecutively, with each succeeding chapter extending and deepening what the reader has learned in previous ones. Readers can, however, feel free to begin at the back or the middle or wherever they choose.

A few years ago I was struck by the remarks made by a colleague when he first learned of my interest in Lonergan's philosophy. He told me of a North American university, not a Catholic foundation, where scientists working on artificial intelligence were taking a great deal of interest in Lonergan's theory of cognition. This surprised me and I protested that Lonergan did not belong to the large and growing band of philosophers bent on convincing us that the human mind is some kind of glorified computer. My friend agreed; it turned out that I had taken his remarks the wrong way. What the scientists were interested in was finding the best model of human intelligence they could so that they could use it when attempting to construct an 'intelligent' computer. They had no wish to claim that the human mind is a computer and every wish to make a computer that was like the human mind, a computer capable of following the operations and procedures of human intelligence when successfully achieving knowledge. This explained their interest in Lonergan. I have often felt that there is a wide body of opinion on the subject of how human beings think, understand, and know that is in fundamental agreement with Lonergan (albeit Lonergan's name is by no means always explicitly connected with this opinion, nor should it be); only it is to be found not in the ranks of philosophers but in the ranks of educationists and teachers – of those whose business it is to know, empirically, how children and all of us learn so that they can adopt the best approaches to teaching. Philosophers might learn a lot from a study of pedagogy. This is why I start this series of essays with a straightforward and rather popular exposition aimed at providing the reader with a basic and easily accessible account of Lonergan's theory of cognition.

It simply remains for me to say that there is only one definitive edition of Lonergan's thought and that is to be found in his Collected Works, published by the University of Toronto Press.[9] What I have to offer here are my interpretations and, on occasion, developments of what Lonergan has to say on a limited range of issues. It goes without saying that any shortcomings in the views and arguments offered are mine and mine alone.

9 The general editors of the Collected Works of Bernard Lonergan, being published by the University of Toronto Press in 25 volumes, are Frederick Crowe and Robert Doran.

PART ONE

The Basic Position

1

The Structure of Cognition

I shall begin by saying what we are doing when we come to know something and then go on to explain why doing that is knowing. The first task is largely descriptive, taking note of the process we go through when achieving knowledge. It is something that teachers in particular – people who are professionally involved in the business of helping others to achieve under-standing and knowledge – should recognize fairly easily. The second task is explanatory. As explanatory it becomes prescriptive, because once we have achieved an explanation of why something constitutes knowledge it is possible to discriminate between legitimate and illegitimate knowledge claims, to tell the genuine from the fake. A true explanation has the capacity to be normative, and norms and what constitutes normativity in human knowing and doing play a large part in this book.

The Process of Coming to Know Something

To begin to understand the process of knowing let us look at a simple example:

If x − 4 = 20, what does x equal?

This extremely simple example tells us quite a lot. First of all, it makes clear something that is not always clear, namely, exactly what it is we do not know – the value of x. To come to understand something new, we usually have to identify the unknown. Once we have done this, we have what Lonergan terms a 'known unknown.' We still do not know, but we know what it is we do not know, and that is very important if we are ever going to know. In the second place, this example helps us to see what we do in order to come to know the unknown. To gain access to what we do not know we create what Lonergan calls a 'heuristic structure,' a structure of inquiry. We line up what we know and use it to attack the unknown. So, in the simple example, we put x on one side and everything we know about it on the other: $x = 20 + 4$. That enables us to find out the value of x.

Let us look at another example taken from the process of reading.

> When I ___ to ___ shops,
> I always have to t___ my croc___ with ___.
> He ___ pleased to g___ for a walk.
> He waves his t___ ___ smile___ at every___.
> Not ___y p___ple smile b___ck.
> They j___ blink and ___re.

The blanks are the bits we initially do not know – they are the 'known unknown' – and because we are not clear about them we do not know the full meaning of the text. But we use what we do know in order to make sense of the passage. To fill in the blanks we use what is already given in the passage, the clues on the page. But we go further than this and use a lot of knowledge we already carry about with us in our heads: knowledge of crocodiles and of human reactions to crocodiles; and also knowledge of the structure of language, of tenses, of spelling, of pronunciation, of singulars and plurals, of normal word order in English. We even make use of our knowledge of the white bits in the text in order to perceive that the bits of black ink are the words. Without that habitual knowledge – knowledge that as a rule we hardly advert to – we would not be able to make sense of the passage at all. That is why it is right to say that we do not just get meaning *from* the text but we bring meaning *to* the text. We do not invent the text, but we use our habitual knowledge in order to re-create it. But it is not only previous knowledge that has helped us to make sense of the passage.

We have also developed a number of active strategies. When we were stuck we read on and then returned to see if we could now make sense of the passage; we reread particular parts in the light of the whole passage; we tried out some words, only to eliminate them before we found the right word; we asked questions of the text and struggled to get the right answer; we were all the time looking for textual and semantic *cohesion*, and in order to achieve that we experimented, hypothesized, eliminated unlikely guesses, and used what we already knew in order to understand what we originally did not know. The need to achieve cohesion acted as a guiding thread in all our attempts to understand the passage: before we were even aware of such a thing as textual or semantic cohesion, the need to establish cohesion acted spontaneously as a spur to fill out and complete what we already knew. The effort to understand this simple text illustrates the spontaneous dynamism and structure of human inquiry and tells us how we come to learn anything.

It is exactly the same process that the scientist goes through. Questions arise when something puzzles us, when something unexpected happens. For example, it is initially surprising that if we pour five fluid ounces of alcohol onto five fluid ounces of water we get something less than ten fluid ounces of liquid. Why should this happen? If we pour equal amounts of alcohol onto alcohol or of water onto water, we get exactly double the amount of liquid. Why should mixing water with alcohol result in less than the anticipated double amount of liquid? To achieve an answer the scientist frames a hypothesis and then tests it. Just possibly the answer lies in the different molecular structures of water and alcohol: if we were to pour a volume of small pebbles onto an equal volume of large pebbles, for ex- ample, we would end up with something less than double the volume of pebbles. The scientist frames his hypothesis and then tests it by means of observation and experimentation.

What is clear from this account is that acquiring understanding and knowledge is not a passive process: it is not a matter of sitting back and waiting for atoms of meaning to enter our brains through our eyeballs. We achieve understanding by asking questions. Having asked the question, we work at an answer. This might give rise to a hypothesis. But a hypothesis is not the answer, only a possible answer. We hear a bang next door, in the next room. 'What is that?' – something might have fallen off the shelf, the wind might have blown open the window, our infant son might have hit something with a hammer, the gas fire might have exploded. All sorts of possibilities run through our mind, some of them worrying. We run next door to find that it is in fact the wind that has blown the window from its catch and the window is moving vigorously to and fro. One of our possible explanations has emerged as the correct one. We make the judgment, 'It's all right. Only the window.'

What actually are we doing at the point of judgment? We are basically confirming our understanding – or one of the possible understandings that we initially put forward. We are determining that one of our hypotheses is correct, is true. How do we do this? In the example quoted, the answer is deceptively simple: we go and take a look. The noise came and went. I needed an explanation. I went and looked. But something rather more than mere gaping or gazing was going on. I looked because attached to each possible answer were certain conditions: if my infant son had hit something with a hammer or some such implement, then the hammer or some similar implement would have been there, and so would my son; if the gas fire had exploded, there would have been clear signs of damage, and so forth. The fact that the window was off its catch and was being moved about violently by the wind, and that there was no evidence of damage to the fire and that my son was asleep, etc. all helped to eliminate alternative explanations and confirmed that the wind blowing the window was the best of the possible explanations.

In scientific explanation judgment often requires more complex procedures, but it is essentially meeting the same demand for confirmation of a hypothesis and elimination of other possible explanations. We work out the implications of one of the hypotheses. If this hypothesis is true ('if' is an important word in science), then this and this and this would occur in the following circumstances. The circumstances are created by experiment and we wait to see if the predicted outcomes occur. If they do, the hypothesis is to that extent confirmed. If they do not, the hypothesis is to that extent weakened, and may have to be abandoned altogether.

Why Is Doing That Knowing?

Lonergan's theory of cognition consists of three steps: experience, understanding, and judgment. These three steps correspond with the scientific process of gathering the data, coming up with a hypothesis that explains the data, and carrying out experiments to check whether the hypothesis can stand. The object of experience is data, the given. Data in the first instance we might think of as simply the deliverances of sense, of acts of sensation – the content of seeing, hearing, touching, tasting, smelling. Lonergan's notion of data should not be confused with empiricist notions of sense data: data for Lonergan are not the building blocks of reality 'already out there,' stretched out in space and time. They are what we experience but do not yet know or understand. Data are what we ask questions about. They may be partially understood as we understood the words on the page of the crocodile passage, but did not initially understand the full text because we did not know what letters should go into the blanks; in the same way, the data are all the elements in the simple algebraic example, including the unknown 'x.' The data in the 'banging window' example are simply the noise in the room next door: an auditory sensation within a domestic context. Interrogation of the data gives rise to such questions as What is that? Why is that happening? How often does it occur? Data give rise to questions and questions, if we are successful, give rise to insights into the data. We fill in the blanks in a way that makes sense of the passage, we determine the value of 'x,' we discover the source of the noise. We interpret the data, we decipher it, make it meaningful. All of us in our inquiries into what is going on in the world behave like the scientist. For both scientist and layperson the data considered as data are not yet meaningful but are a source of potential meaning.

Meaning is what takes place at the second step in coming to know. We come up with a meaning to make sense of the data, we offer an explanation of something we experience but do not yet understand. Meaning, then, takes place when we make sense of our experience, when we achieve an understanding of the data. The kind of meaning we establish will depend on the kind of data that are puzzling us and the kind of questions we ask. What is that? might give rise, in the first instance, to a description: 'There is a dark patch on the carpet. It has a shiny, silvery texture. It is cold and wet to the touch.' Description helps us to understand the data by relating them to our senses – dark, shiny, cold, wet. Sometimes that is all we want. But I may want more than a description, I may want an explanation and in that case I ask, Why? Explanation consists of relating things to each other in a way that answers the question. There is a wet patch on the carpet: it is there because water is coming through the ceiling directly above the wet patch and falling onto the floor. The water is coming through the ceiling because there is a hole in the roof above the ceiling and it is raining outside. Explanation consists of relating things to each other (rain – hole in roof – ceiling – water on carpet), description of relating things to our senses (dark, shiny, cold, wet). In science, both are used. Through description we relate how things look, whether they are hot or cold, whether they change colour at certain points, whether things explode into flame, and so forth. Accurate sensory observation is crucial to science. But description does not provide us with explanation, and science wants explanation in addition (as indeed common sense does too on many occasions). Why do things look like that, why does this behave like that, at what temperature exactly does it ignite, and so forth? Explanation links things to things, often by means of numerical ratios or in ways that can be expressed by the use of numerical formulae.

If the questions leading to the formulation of meaning are What? and Why? and How often? the questions that lead to judgment are Is that so? Is it probably so or probably not so? These are questions looking for a different answer from the questions that give rise to understanding. These are questions looking for affirmation or negation, for a yes or a no. Positive judgment is the affirmation that the proposed meaning (description, interpretation, explanation) makes sense of the data. We can now go further in our account of judgment. Previously we said that in positive judgment we confirmed our understanding or hypothesis as correct or true. We can now see that the way we do this is by affirming that our understanding *fits the data*. Judgment is, in effect, a synthesis of the data and their meaning, a synthesis of step 1 and step 2. So step 1, experience of the data, leads to questions such as What is that? which take us on to step 2. Answers are proposed at step 2. These in turn give rise to questions seeking confirmation (or negation) of the proposed answer in the form of Is that so? Is it probable? These new questions take us on to step 3. And step 3 consists of ensuring that step 2 matches (or fails to match) step 1. What is affirmed is the data as bearing this meaning – the data become a something. It is no longer a mere auditory sensation giving rise to a question but a fact – the window is being blown by the wind. It is through judgment that we know the truth and through the truth that we affirm what is so, that we affirm the real, that we know reality. 'The true is the real' might be understood as a shorthand way of expressing this point. The same point is expressed more precisely by saying that the truth is what is intelligently understood and reasonably affirmed in judgment. Judgment is the third step in knowing and results in the knowledge claim that something is or is not the case. In judgment we are done with hesitation, with hypothesizing, and take a stand on what is the case, on what is so or probably so – or on what is not the case, is not so or is probably not so. In judgment we answer yes or no to the questions Is that so? Is it probable?

Why is doing that knowing? In what exactly does the normativity of this account of knowing reside? How does it help us to distinguish between genuine and fake knowledge claims? The answer to each of these questions lies in the coherence achieved between the proposed meaning or explanation and the data. It is this coherence that licenses the subject conducting the inquiry to move to a positive judgment and make the knowledge claim. Discovery of an incoherence between the proposed explanation and the data – the discovery, for example, that the window is still firmly held by its catch – leads to a negative judgment: the blowing of the window by the wind is not the explanation of the noise. Coherence and incoherence between explanation and data constitute an objective standard for the validation of judgment. While it is true that meaning is supplied by the subject, the data are not; the data are what are given and explanation, to be valid, requires that it meets and matches the data. When explanation fails to match the data, then a negative judgment can be validly made, such as that it was not the wind blowing the window that caused the noise. Whatever the case, the standard of objectivity is the achievement of coherence or incoherence between the account offered by the inquirer and the data that have to be accounted for.

How do we know if coherence or incoherence of this kind has been achieved? We know this by knowing if and to what extent the conditions attached to any explanation have been fulfilled. The proposed meaning, or hypothesis, or solution to the problem is a conditioned. For it to be true, certain conditions have to be fulfilled. When these conditions are fulfilled – when, for example, certain predictions are realized, or when we are able to move to the scene and can see for ourselves – we no longer have a conditioned, but a conditioned whose conditions have been fulfilled. Lonergan calls that a *virtually unconditioned* – a conditioned knowledge claim whose conditions have been satisfied. Again the fulfillment or non-fulfillment of the conditions is not a matter for the subject to decide but something that occurs independently of the subject. This account of knowing acknowledges the role of the subject in asking and answering questions and suggesting answers; but it also accounts for the objectivity of knowing by insisting on the indispensable role of the data, the given, and on the role played by the need to fit the data in verification.

The Coherence and Correspondence Theories of Truth

This fairly simple and straightforward account of what knowing consists of helps, I believe, to answer a lot of the questions that are current in contemporary epistemology. Let me advert to only one such problem, but one that will take us on to a consideration of some of the *deeper elements* entailed in Lonergan's model of cognition. This is the conflict between the correspondence theory of truth and the coherence theory of truth. The coherence theory is probably the dominant one in philosophy today – things are true if they hang together. The correspondence theory, by contrast, finds that things are true if what I claim to be the case corresponds with reality. The correspondence theory is in many ways the commonsense view: things are true if they correspond with what is already out there. For example, if a proposition corresponds to the reality it supposedly depicts or expresses, it is correct; if it does not, it is wrong. The trouble with this version of the correspondence theory is that we can never line up propositions on the one hand and reality on the other and see if they match. We only get at reality, we only access reality, through ideas expressed in propositions and so we are never able to stand above the idea and see if it matches reality. This version of the correspondence theory of truth is impossible to verify.

For this reason scepticism becomes a problem in epistemology. If I can only know reality by virtue of ideas, through the medium of what I carry around in my head, and, moreover, if I can never be sure that what I carry around in my head matches what in fact is the case in the world, then can I ever claim to know anything? It would appear that reality in fact – or what I call reality – is just a screen of perceptions or ideas that I have in my brain. I can never get beyond the screen to reality itself. What I claim to know is not reality at all, but my ideas. I can never get out of my own head, so to speak, to a reality – the reality – which exists independently of me. We are into solipsism, subjectivism, scepticism, idealism, fideism, and all the other problems that dog traditional epistemology. How does Lonergan's cognitional theory deal with these problems?

To find the answer we must first recognize that when we speak of what knowing is we usually have in mind a particular model. The later Wittgenstein said that philosophers were bewitched by a particular picture of language; Lonergan believes they have been bewitched by a particular picture of knowing. Philosophers frequently fail to advert to the model they are using, to the *model of knowing* that is being assumed; they simply take that first step for granted, presuming that the model of knowing they entertain is what knowing must be. Lying behind the problem of ideas as an impenetrable screen is a model of knowing that considers knowing to be a kind of seeing or a kind of looking. This understanding of knowledge has been subjected to brilliant attack by Richard Rorty in his book *Philosophy and the Mirror of Nature*[1] and is the main object of Lonergan's attack in his book *Insight*.[2] According to the ocular version of knowing, correct knowing is looking and seeing what is there and incorrect knowing is looking and seeing what is not there. Ideas in the ocular model of knowing represent reality out there: the idea of a chair or table or desk, for example, is some kind of inner representation or copy of the realities that lie out there in space. But, as we have seen, this understanding of idea, this idea of idea, runs into the problems of scepticism and solipsism we referred to a moment ago: the problem of how we can ever know reality independently of what we carry around in our head. The notion that knowing is a kind of looking or seeing, that it is analogous to an act of ocular vision, and that the mind is some kind of inner or spiritual eye or mirror, is the notion that Lonergan most heartily repudiates. And with that repudiation goes the correlative idea of *reality* and of *objectivity* – the idea that reality is what is out there already, spread out in space and time, and that objectivity is reaching out to that reality with our senses. The idea of idea as an inner depiction or representation of an outer reality accompanies the notion of knowing as looking. What is more, the idea of idea as an inner representation of what lies out there gives rise to a notion of the *mind* as some kind of inner space in which these inner representations dwell. The mind is the inner space in which dwell the ideas that represent the realities located in the universe of space and time that lies outside the mind. So it is that the model of knowing as looking gives rise to distinctive notions of reality, of objectivity, and of the mind. Lonergan rejects this model of knowing, and so he rejects each of these other notions.

What does Lonergan put in place of the ocular model of knowing? The answer is the three-step model described above. In that version looking or

1 *Philosophy and the Mirror of Nature* (Basil Blackwell, 1980).
2 *Insight: A Study of Human Understanding* (Longmans, Green and Co., 1957).

seeing or any form of sensing is not what knowing is, but only a first step in the process of coming to know something. Beyond that first step there are two other steps that have to be taken. Lonergan famously said that those who think that knowing is like looking find what is most obvious in knowing and conclude that that is what knowing obviously is. So, if knowing is not like looking, ideas are not like inner pictures or representations of reality; reality is not what is already out there spread out in space and time; objectivity is not reaching out to that reality with our senses; and the mind is not some inner space in which ideas dwell. The trouble with the notion that knowing is like looking is that it leads us to recreate the world, and the notions at the heart of cognition, in concrete, pictorial form. But if knowing is not like looking, what are ideas? Ideas are intelligibles, they are the answers to our questions. They are the answers to the questions What? Why? How often? They are the accounts we give of the data we interrogate.

Ideas

Let me explain this rather subtle point. Plato was struck by the problem of *universals*. How is it that when we see a particular chair we apply to it the universal notion of chairness? We could not grasp this in a particular thing because that would be to take from a particular what a particular cannot give, namely, something that is universal, something that can be applied to any number of chairs, to any number of particular objects in the world. The idea of chair – as opposed to particular chairs we come across – is indifferent to time and place, and can be applied universally. It must, Plato believed, exist prior to the particular as an Ideal Form of which particular chairs are an instance, things that partake of the universal Form of Chairness. When we recognize something as a chair we are simply recalling our knowledge of the universal Form. Lonergan sees this version of idea put forward by Plato as a myth that has had an influence on *conceptualism*. Conceptualism, Lonergan contends, is the major intellectual error of our age against which he pits his own *intellectualist* theory of knowing. Conceptualism would have it that what are first in knowledge are concepts or ideas, universal ideas that we apply to the world in order to understand it. The problem with conceptualism is that it leads on to scepticism or solipsism or idealism, because if ideas come first how can we ever claim to know the real? The idea is always intermediary between the knower and the known. We are back to scepticism and the problem of the screen of percepts we can never get around in order to make immediate contact with the real.

Lonergan's idea of the idea is the Thomist one, which is also Aristotelian, that what comes first is not ideas but understanding. *Ideas come out of understanding.* What is more, understanding is not applying a universal concept, it is grasping the idea or the universal in the particular. In trying to understand what an eclipse of the sun is, I grasp what it is that causes an eclipse – the passing of the moon between the sun and the earth. In the same way, in order to understand the general concept of a chair, I need to grasp first what it is that makes something a chair. In doing that I am not making an internal sketch or visual representation of the particular object, but I am grasping what it is that makes this thing a chair. I am grasping, if you like, the design or plan of this chair, what it is that makes these bits of wood or metal into a chair. To turn it around the other way, if I were making a chair I would need to make it according to a design; this design would make the materials into a chair. The materials have the potential to become many things – it is the design or idea that makes them into this chair. It is by grasping the design or plan or idea that is in a thing and is not independent of the thing that I understand the kind of thing it is, its uses, its function, the relations it has with other things in the world. The idea does not represent the thing, it does not stand for the object in the world; it is that which *makes something an object*, a particular thing. By grasping the idea I grasp not something in the mind but something in the object: the idea I have intentionally in my mind is identical with that which exists causally in the thing. Idea is not separate from reality, it is not something in inner space that stands over against the real world of concrete things our senses bump up against. The idea belongs to *ousia*, to the being of the thing. It is that which causes this to be the thing it is: it is a cause of being. It is important to grasp this if we are to avoid idealism, representationism, and all their attendant problems. However, this is not the whole of knowing. Lonergan is at one with Aquinas in going beyond Aristotle and beyond the level of ideas to the level of verification and judgment.

As we have seen in our consideration of the three-step model of coming to know, the idea has to be confirmed, has to be tested and checked out to make sure that it is truly the idea that makes this the thing that it is. So long as we remain at step 2 we remain at the purely conceptual level and there is no knowing if our idea or hypothesis corresponds to anything in the real world. The question Is that so? or Is that probable? propels the subject from the purely intellectual or conceptual level to the ontological level of judgment. But in this version judgment is not achieved by attempting to compare my idea with reality already out there but by investigating to see if my idea fits the data. So in the traditional detective story any ideas or guesses as to the identity of the murderer have to be matched against the available evidence, the clues the author has provided. The match is not of the idea with some pre-existent reality – as the ocular metaphor of knowing as looking suggests – but of the idea with the evidence, with the data. In the detective story, if we come up with the right idea, the data fall into place;

the right idea or supposition brings everything together – the observations of witnesses, forensic evidence, motivation all come together to form a cohesive, unified explanation.

Let us look at an example drawn from real life. Alongside a large photograph of a lifeless dolphin lying on some rocks, and under the headline 'Was this dolphin and 15 others killed because they failed as deep sea US spies?' the (London) *Observer* told the story of the mysterious death off France's Mediterranean coastline of twenty-two dolphins, sixteen of which had a wound on the underside of their necks:

> 'It's a graveyard,' said a spokesman ... 'One or two are natural deaths. But for the rest it's impossible to say. Something is going on, for sure, but we have no idea what.'
>
> There is no shortage of theories ... Some possibilities have been discarded: the dolphins are unlikely to have died from the trauma of being caught accidentally by fishermen because their skins seem to show no scars from a trawler's netting. A theory that they may be the victims of a band of twisted thrill-seekers has also been ruled out, since the wound found on 16 ... of the dolphins – a neat fist-like hole – is on the underside of their necks.
>
> 'The hunting hypothesis seems implausible because you would expect to find a wound on the upper part of their bodies, the most accessible to humans.' Full post-mortem tests have yet to be carried out but the possibility that the dolphins are dying of a virus such as the Moribilis disease ... has also been excluded for the time being, again because of that troubling wound.
>
> Some scientists have postulated, without conviction, that rising sea temperatures may be driving the mammals closer to the coast, where they have been battered on the rocks. Others have raised the possibility of a rogue 'killer dolphin.' But again, that neat, circular wound does not fit. Only one man has so far come forward with a theory, fantastic as it may seem, that could explain it ... Leo Sheridan, 65, an accident investigator of some renown ...
>
> 'I am convinced that these were dolphins trained by the US Navy, and that something went badly wrong,' he said ...
>
> The dolphins, fitted with harnesses around their necks and with small electrodes planted under their skin, were taught first to patrol and protect Trident submarines in harbour and stationary warships at sea ... Later, a more sophisticated system of two-way communications was developed to allow the control room to stimulate the dolphins – which work in teams of four – to attack an intruding diver ... If the dolphin went AWOL, which amorous males are prone

to do, or became overstressed, a small explosive charge in the harness, on the underside of the neck, could be detonated by remote control ...

'It seems to me no accident that these dolphins first began washing up in the middle of a military crisis when American warships and submarines were en route to the Gulf. Sixteen, in other words four teams, display this distinctive wound. And that wound is consistent with a small detonation.'[3]

Although not everyone accepted this hypothesis, what interests us here is not its truth or falsehood but the reasoning that led to its formation. It need hardly be pointed out that the scientists involved did not try to match some internal picture they entertained in some inner space called the mind to the reality of the dolphins 'out there.' The scientists assembled the data and asked questions in order to make sense of them by relating different features of the data to each other. The data consisted of a number of facts: dead dolphins in surprisingly large numbers, sixteen with a neat circular wound on the underside of their necks, washed ashore, off the Mediterranean coast of France, at a certain time.

A convincing hypothesis had to explain each of these facts without introducing guesses that would have required the data to be different from what they were. So the hypothesis that the dolphins had been killed by local fishermen was discounted because it would have required evidence of damage caused by the trawler's netting – the data that could have lent weight to this hypothesis were simply not there; the conditions imposed by that particular hypothesis were not fulfilled.

Likewise, the small, neat wound led to the discarding of the notion that the dolphins had been the victims of some marauding band of local hunters, since hunters would be much more likely to inflict a variety of wounds on the upper side of the dolphin's body and not one neat hole on the underside of its neck. The hypothesis had to 'fit' the data, to be 'consistent' with them – words actually used in the text; or, to put it another way, the conditions required for a hypothesis to fit the data had to be satisfied.

It is worth noting that one of the fulfilled conditions quoted by Leo Sheridan was the fact that the US Navy operated a training program for dolphins in San Diego – though remote from the bodies of dolphins washed up on the French coast, this fact becomes relevant once Sheridan has formulated his hypothesis.

3 *The Observer*, 1 March 1998, 7.

So the fit between the data and the hypothesis presents conditions that have to be fulfilled if the match between the data and any one of the hypotheses is going to be found to be satisfactory, leaving no part of the data unexplained. It was such a match that made Leo Sheridan's hypothesis convincing and led some of the scientists to make the judgment that the dolphins were probably killed by the US Navy. Verification consists in achieving or showing a match between idea and data; the more perfect the fit or match, the more that alternative hypotheses are convincingly ruled out, the stronger the verification.

In judgment we affirm that something is the case. Now, underpinning the three steps of knowing, driving them, binding them into a single act of knowing is the pure, disinterested desire to know. We have a natural desire to know things. Asking questions is not the primordial urge; rather asking questions is a manifestation of the primordial desire to know. This is a natural human desire. If you ask me if that is true, you are demonstrating the truth of what I am saying – questions are simply the unfolding or manifestation of this natural human desire. And what I want to know is everything about everything. There are no limits to human curiosity. It is this impatience with incompleteness, with what is only half true, with answers that are unsatisfactory, that drives us on, to ask more questions, to find better, more satisfactory answers. Lonergan calls the drive to know and the questions it gives rise to the 'operator': that which drives us onwards to seek ever fuller and better answers.

Now, what does all this have to do with the supposed conflict between the coherence theory of truth and the correspondence theory? Quite simply, for most philosophies, these two theories are seen as rivals: one is right and the other is wrong. They cannot both be right. Or can they?

Consider. If I subscribe to a confrontational model of knowing, believing that it is by looking out at the world and observing accurately what I see there, the notion of a correspondence theory of truth looks inevitable and convincing. The truth of my claims will, quite naturally, appear to be the accuracy with which they match what is, in reality, out there. A statement is true if it corresponds with the facts as they are; it is false if it fails to correspond with the facts as they are. The correspondence theory is the champion of the absoluteness of facts and the defender of the independence of facts within any belief system that I may subscribe to. You might say 'facts are facts' is the slogan of those who subscribe to the correspondence theory of truth. Facts do not depend on my say-so, but rather the truth depends on my statements being in conformity with the facts as they are. But, as we have seen, there are not a few arguments offered against this view.

There are many forms of the coherence theory, but its general basis is that it overcomes what Lonergan would call the *naive realist* component in many versions of correspondence. The naive realist says he knows something because he can see it, rather as G.E. Moore claimed to prove the existence of the external world by holding up his hands and saying, 'Here is one hand' and 'Here is another.' Against this the coherence theorist says we know something because we can fit certain things together.

The correspondence theorist tends to assert the objective nature of knowledge, to emphasize the objective pole in knowing. The coherence theory tends to emphasize the subjective pole in knowing, the putting together of various clues by the investigator, the subject carrying out the inquiry. One theory is empiricist, the other tends to be more akin to idealism.

Lonergan believes in both coherence and correspondence and, indeed, that one makes no sense without the other. Against the empiricist or naive realist he denies that knowing is taking a look at what is there, but with them he believes in the absoluteness of facts and the independence of facts from the knower. What justifies the independence of facts from the knower's say-so, according to Lonergan, is the *conditioned nature* of understanding at step 2. The proposed meaning or understanding, if it is to be affirmed as fact, must fit the data. That is a brute requirement; it is not something that I can determine by my volition or willpower or that depends on my say-so. The need for the conditioned to have its conditions fulfilled before understanding can be affirmed as true is the ground for facts being independent of the knower, of the one who makes the judgment. It is the givenness of the data and the need for understanding to fit the data that provide Lonergan with the grounds for rejecting subjectivism and idealism. For this reason his *critical realism* – the name he gives his epistemological position – agrees with the empiricist that truth is a correspondence between what I claim to be true and what in fact is so.

But against the empiricist and with the idealist, Lonergan argues that all facts have to be interpreted, that there is no such thing as an uninterpreted fact. We do not establish facts by bumping up against them with our senses. What we bump up against with our senses are data, and they are not yet meaningful. They are that which we interrogate in order to establish their meaning. If facts emerge at the end of this process, it is because we have shown that understanding fits the data, that these data bear this meaning or bear this explanation. And we do that by showing that so many things converge on this being the case that the conditions surrounding the knowledge claim can be considered to be fulfilled.

There are no such things as brute facts, only brute data. Humanly attained facts are always interpreted, always invested with meaning, and meaning emerges from a process of *fitting things together*, as we have seen in the examples we have considered. It is rather like a jigsaw puzzle where the convergence of the other pieces with the one we are attempting to place enables us to judge that we are placing it correctly. That is why the coherence theory of truth is also true. Far from being the opposites in the opinion of empiricism and idealism respectively, the correspondence theory of truth and the coherence theory of truth are held by critical realism to be two aspects of one process of knowing the real. The reason is that – to use the shorthand phrase I used previously – the true is the real. To find the truth, as we have seen, is a matter of fitting things together, of achieving coherence. But when the truth is affirmed the real is also being affirmed and the claim is being made that what is empirically true corresponds to the real world.

How can Lonergan espouse both a coherence and a correspondence theory of truth? The reason is that Lonergan does not subscribe to a confrontational model of knowing. And because he does not see knowing as confrontational, he does not see objectivity as the result of reaching out to reality already out there now, by sensory extroversion to objects already deemed to be out there. This repudiation of objectivity as a reaching out to what is already there should not be misunderstood. Lonergan's theory of knowing and of objectivity does hold that objects exist in the world independently of me. What he is opposed to is the commonsense belief – shared by some proponents of coherence as well as by most proponents of correspondence theories – that objectivity *in knowing* is reaching out *through our senses* to what is there. For Lonergan the truth can be objectively known, and it is by knowing the true that we know and affirm the real: his theory of knowledge allows him to restore to common sense the world in all its objectivity precisely by denying the commonsense assumption that knowing is like looking. He restores to common sense what common sense is in danger of losing – namely, the objectivity of facts – by repudiating the commonsense conception of objectivity as sensory extroversion. The strange paradox of common sense is that its starting point – that knowing is a kind of looking – often leads to the conclusion that its assumed finishing point – that facts are 'out there' independently of the knower – is impossible.

Objectivity

The pure, disinterested desire to know the truth is the ultimate criterion of objectivity. The desire or drive to know is something that arises spontaneously and irresistibly in human beings and is present in the reader who is attending to what is being said in this chapter, striving to understand it and asking if this understanding is true. It is this desire or drive that prompts the questions – What is that? and Is that so? – that in turn propel the process of coming to know something. Objectivity is being true to the human desire to know; it consists in being at one with this desire, in resisting our biases and personal preferences and, on occasions, the traditions we inherit, in order to remain faithful to this desire or drive. This is often hard to do. But while this striving for the truth is the overarching criterion of objectivity, each level of cognition has its own peculiar function to perform and so its own criterion of objectivity; or we might say that the quest for objective knowledge is manifested in different ways at the different stages of knowing.

At the first level of cognition, the empirical or experiential level, the criterion of objectivity is the givenness of the data. What is peculiar to the data of experience is their *givenness* – they are externally or internally present to us – and hence the criterion of objectivity at the level of seeing, hearing, and so on, is to see or hear what is there and not to see or hear what is not there. In the true spirit of empiricism, Lonergan maintains that at the level of sensation the subject must be submissive to the givenness of the data and not, for example, fabricate evidence or grounds.

At the second level of cognition, the intellectual or conceptual level, the criterion of objectivity is intellectual coherence – what is sometimes called internal coherence – allied to the logical ideals of clarity and rigour. The need for coherence in a concept, idea, or hypothesis is widely accepted. The mind has great difficulty in holding onto what is incoherent, what does not hold together, what is self-contradictory or intellectually unharmonious. Logical and mathematical judgments are based purely on attaining this type of intellectual coherence, for the truths of logic and mathematics are independent of any empirical facts in the world.

At the third level of cognition, the rational or critical level, the criterion of objectivity is the unconditioned. For judgment to be attained the conditions related to the suggestion or hypothesis put forward at the second level have to be fulfilled so that the suggestion or hypothesis becomes a virtually unconditioned. The achievement of the unconditioned means that the suggested idea or supposition fits the data encountered at the first stage of knowing, and this licenses the subject to move to the affirmation of the idea or supposition as true. Lonergan calls the three-step process of cognition, comprising experience, understanding, and judgment, *generalized empirical method* on account of the fact that it is the method that underpins all empirical investigation, whether it be in the realm of science or history or geography or accident investigation, or whatever.

These three basic steps are the steps taken in all investigations of the world; as such, they constitute the basic, invariant pattern or structure of cognition. They are the common core of all empirical knowing.

Consciousness

Consciousness is relevant to Lonergan's cognitional theory because it is a theory based on observation of what knowing is, of what one does when one comes to know something. That is why it is relatively easy to support this theory with so many examples, for unlike some other versions of knowing, critical realism is not simply one philosopher's response to what other philosophers claim knowing to be. It gets out of the philosopher's ivory tower and seeks to know what the mathematician, the scientist, the geographer, the historian, or the accident investigator are actually doing. What is more, since all of us are knowers in some sphere or other, Lonergan's cognitional theory claims to correspond to what *we* do when we come to know something. Where Wittgenstein advised that if we want to know what words mean we should look to see how they are used in the contexts that are their home, Lonergan advises that if we want to know what knowing is we should look at what mathematicians and scientists and historians and engineers and men and women of common sense do as they go about their business. But how can we claim to observe what knowing is? How – to test Lonergan's theory by its own standards – do we establish the data, which in turn we interpret in order to provide a theory of cognition? Lonergan's answer is that each of us can know what cognition is because the process of cognition is a *conscious process.* We are conscious when we are working out answers to questions, not unconscious. And because we are conscious, we can take hold of what we are doing, what it is we get up to, the various moves and manoeuvres we perform, when we come to know something. The data of cognitional theory are not hidden away in some secret recess; they are the data of consciousness.

Now we must take care when we talk about consciousness. As in all things to do with epistemology, there are traps for the unwary. Consciousness is not a kind of looking, it is not a kind of inward peering at what I am doing. It is not something that occupies some inner space where our ideas dwell – as we saw before, that notion of the mind derives from the notion that knowing is like looking, and if we interpret consciousness in that way we are back with all the problems that have afflicted the dominant epistemological traditions of the West. *Consciousness is self-presence*: it is being present to oneself as one does something. It is because I am present to myself when I experience something, when I strive to understand and when I affirm propositions as true, that I can know what knowing is. When I know something, I am aware that I know it. When I understand something, I am aware of my understanding. When I have sensory experience, I am aware of having this experience. It is almost tautological to say this, because without this awareness, there would be no experience, without this awareness there would be no understanding, without this awareness there would be no knowledge. Consciousness as self-presence is something I simply experience and not necessarily something I know or understand. It is a basic feature of human acts of knowing and understanding but need not itself be known or understood. Yet nothing can be present to me unless I am present to myself. I cannot experience pain, I cannot solve problems, I cannot arrive at judgments if I am comatose or in a dreamless sleep: if, in short, I am not present to myself.

When speaking of consciousness there is the danger that we will treat it as something *in addition* to the operations of thinking about something or doing something. But to be present to oneself because one is conscious is not an additional operation of this kind. If I am driving my car or writing a letter I attend to what I am doing, I concentrate on my driving or my writing. But to say that I attend or concentrate is simply another way of saying that these are conscious and not unconscious activities, because when I am conscious or aware of doing something I am also conscious of myself as doing them. Being present to myself is a necessary precondition for conscious activity as well as for retrospective awareness or memory. If I were not conscious when I drove or wrote I would not be able to recollect these activities and later to mention to someone: 'I went for a drive this morning,' or 'I wrote a letter this afternoon.'

Of course, such self-presence is not usually the focus of my explicit attention and in that sense is implicit rather than explicit. Even when I make consciousness the object of my explicit attention – as I am doing in this section – I am implicitly aware of myself attending to myself as the explicit object of my attention! In other words, *at the level of performance my self-presence is always implicit.* At the level of performance, consciousness is always non-reflexive, non-introspective, simply experienced. In the same way the reader who is attempting to focus on what is being said in this section is implicitly aware of her- or himself as inquiring into the nature of consciousness. Far from getting in the way of conscious activities such as driving or writing or inquiring, such implicit self-presence is crucial to these acts because without it I would not be able to attend to my driving or my writing or questioning, nor would I be aware that it was *I* who was driving or writing or raising questions. And without the 'I' there would be no driving or writing or inquiring at all. Consciousness is not only cognitive, it is also constitutive – it constitutes me as a person.

The Fourth Level of Consciousness

Each of the steps of cognition outlined above corresponds to a particular level or stage of consciousness. When I look and touch and taste, I am empirically conscious; when I inquire and understand, I am intellectually conscious; and when I make a judgment that this is so or is not so, I am rationally conscious. But beyond these three levels there is another level, the fourth level of consciousness, a level of freedom and responsibility, the level at which we make value judgments – judgments about right and wrong, good and bad, the level at which we make choices and decisions. Above all, it is the level at which we act. At this fourth level consciousness truly becomes self-conscious – we not only take a stand on what is so, but we actually stand up for what we believe in and make ourselves through our decisions and actions. At the fourth level of consciousness my self-presence is accentuated, as I truly put myself on the line.

It is rather artificial to talk about the first three levels of consciousness, the levels of cognition, without talking about this fourth level because, although we distinguish them, we cannot neatly separate the first three levels – cognition – from the fourth level, the level of value judgment and morality, the level of freedom and responsibility. It is, after all, at this fourth level that we live our lives, socialize, suffer, enjoy ourselves, and are motivated to seek for solutions to the problems that afflict us. That is one of the great truths in Wittgenstein's *Philosophical Investigations*: knowing and living in society cannot be neatly separated from each other. Knowing cannot be surgically removed from the situations and problems that prompt us to ask questions and motivate us to find answers. It was the modern academy and Enlightenment philosophy that attempted to separate knowledge from valuing and factual judgment from moral judgment, just as it attempted to cast the inquirer in the role of a solitary individual on his or her own, cut adrift from the rest of society.

As I hope to demonstrate in the chapters that follow, Lonergan's division of method into four stages corresponding to four levels of consciousness in the human personality helps to demonstrate exactly how each stage in the process has its own autonomy and yet is linked to the others, is at once continuous with and discontinuous from the other stages. Because of this, I believe it can be successfully argued that while knowing is distinct from valuing, valuing would not be possible without knowing. Furthermore, as I also hope to show, this form of argument leads in turn to restoring to our understanding of the individual person the notion that a person is only intelligible as a social being, as one who is both a product of and a creative member of society.

Intentionality

When Lonergan began calling his approach to philosophy 'intentionality analysis,' he meant that, in the context of coming to know, sensory acts such as seeing *are intentional acts*, acts that intend to bring the object before me in a particular way. Seeing is not just looking and it is certainly not just gazing or gaping. It has an intention to it: through seeing, the object comes before me as seen. Likewise, through understanding, the object comes before me as understood, as intelligible, as having meaning. Through judgment the object comes before me as what in fact is so. Binding together these different acts of seeing, understanding, and judging is the conscious intentionality to know. And to know is to know what is, to know being, to know the real. Human intentionality is unconfined, it is impatient with uncertainty and incomplete knowledge claims and it drives humanity onwards and upwards towards ever more satisfying and more complete explanatory schemata and viewpoints. All human knowledge in all fields of inquiry is driven by this basic desire to know, by this conscious intentionality of the inquiring subject. That is why Lonergan called his approach 'intentionality analysis' – it is not the analysis of our feelings or hidden desires, which the psychologist or psychiatrist might carry out. It is the analysis of the conscious intentional operations we perform when we engage in intellectual investigation.

The fourfold process of knowing and valuing, corresponding to the fourfold division of human consciousness, forms an interlinked set of operations, which all of us perform when we experience, understand, make knowledge claims, and form value judgments. This process constitutes the *common core* of all knowing and all instances of the human and natural sciences, thus expanding method beyond the three steps of 'generalized empirical method.' Lonergan calls this fourfold set of operations *transcendental method*, both in Kant's understanding of 'transcendental,' meaning that it is a method that provides the necessary but not sufficient conditions for the possibility of knowing any object in any field of inquiry, and also in the sense that it is a method that is common to our humanity, a method we operate and practise in so far as we are human. This fourfold structure, we shall argue in chapters to come, gives rise to an interpretation of the human person that runs counter both to the dualism stemming from Descartes and to unitary physicalist interpretations of personhood set up in opposition to Descartes today.

The fact that there is *nothing occult* in this theory of knowing and doing – that everything about it is open to inspection and scrutiny – distinguishes it from just about every other theory of knowing with which we are familiar. Hume talks about the hidden operations of Nature. Kant claims about the noumenon that it is completely unknowable. Russell speaks of 'simples' or atomic facts without being able to provide any convincing examples of what would constitute such a fact. And while the early Wittgenstein searches for the hidden essence of language, the later Wittgenstein rejects this quest for the hidden, for the occult, characteristic of his earlier philosophy.

Instead of trying to invent a language built on the principles of logical atomism that would replace ordinary language, the later Wittgenstein says we should be content with ordinary language and find reality revealed in that. Now Lonergan is not Wittgenstein, but there is something of the spirit of the later Wittgenstein in Lonergan's rejection of all attempts to solve the problems of epistemology by appealing to secret processes, in his total repudiation of any recourse to that which 'must' (it is alleged) underly our cognitional operations. Just take hold of your conscious processes, Lonergan urges us: note them, identify them, see how they relate to each other, and you will understand the structure of cognition. Do not try to reduce consciousness to something else, to neural impulses or the workings of a computer or any other hidden mechanism claimed to be what consciousness *really* is. Interpret consciousness in light of your own consciousness. Be true to consciousness and you will understand the structure of cognition.

In this opening chapter, for the sake of achieving a certain overarching clarity, I have presented many of Lonergan's central ideas rather starkly, without the distraction of footnotes. The reader may feel that the ideas have not been sufficiently tested or subjected to enough scrutiny. In the chapters to come, where I compare and contrast critical realism with other epistemologies, I shall test these ideas against what philosophers from the analytical tradition have to say. I shall also make up for the lack of footnotes in this opening chapter. This should provide the opportunity for some of these central ideas to be expanded and opened up, and allow the reader the chance to weigh them more carefully and see how far they do, in fact, correspond with the reader's own conscious processes when coming to know something or when forming evaluations of something.

PART TWO

Encounters, Comparisons, and Contrasts

2

Epistemology: Lonergan and Hume

Hume's Position

It is striking how the two philosophers Lonergan and Hume set out on similar enterprises and with remarkably similar tactics. On tactics, Lonergan quotes with approval Hume's remarks in the Introduction to *A Treatise of Human Nature* that 'one does not conquer a territory by taking here an outpost and there a town or village but by marching directly upon the capital and assaulting its citadel.'[1] Hume's intentions at the outset of his enterprise are clearly stated in the same Introduction:

> 'Tis evident, that all the sciences have a relation, greater or less, to human nature; and that however wide any of them may seem to run from it, they still return back by one passage or another. Even Mathematics, Natural Philosophy, and Natural Religion, are in some measure dependent on the science of Man; since they lie under the cognizance of men, and are judged of by their powers and faculties. 'Tis impossible to tell what changes and improvements we might make in these sciences were we thoroughly acquainted with the extent and force of human understanding, and could explain the nature of the ideas we employ, and of the operations we perform in our reasonings.[2]

---

1 *Insight: A Study of Human Understanding* (Longmans, Green & Co., 1957), xxx.
2 *A Treatise of Human Nature*, ed. L.A Selby-Bigge (Clarendon Press, 1888).

Lonergan's ambition is not dissimilar:

> Thoroughly understand what it is to understand, and not only will you understand the broad lines of all there is to be understood but also you will possess a fixed base, an invariant pattern, opening upon all further developments of understanding.[3]

It is in their manner of understanding understanding that the two philosophers differ. Hume states his with his customary clarity: 'And as the science of man is the only solid foundation for the other sciences, so the only solid foundation we can give to this science itself must be laid on experience and observation.'[4] Hume never questions this basic method, and when he speaks of 'experience and observation' he understands these terms in a very strict and narrow sense. Where Locke before him had wished to examine the understanding in order to discover 'the utmost extent of its tether,' but had never doubted that knowledge can signify an extramental reality, Hume conceived the problem in a bolder and logically more rigorous manner. All we have knowledge of, he says, are our perceptions, and these he divides into (a) impressions and (b) ideas. Impressions, which derive from 'unknown causes,' are the immediate data of sense, and Hume frequently speaks as if they were images that reveal their nature immediately.

Ideas are copies or 'faint images' of impressions and there can be no idea without a corresponding impression. The acid test of the validity of an idea for Hume, therefore, becomes, 'from what impression is that supposed idea derived?' It is by means of this test that he gets rid of Locke's notion of material substance and Berkeley's notion of spiritual substance: we have no sense impression of either. We can see that for Hume knowing is highly analogous to sensation, since ideas, which make up what we know, derive from sensation and have their validity tested by reference to sensation. Indeed, so frequently are we struck by the pictorial character of Hume's examples that we might be allowed the oversimplification of saying that he comes close to suggesting that knowing is 'taking a good look': correct knowing is looking and seeing what is there; incorrect knowing is claiming

---

3 *Insight*, xxviii.
4 *Treatise*, xvi. As has been frequently noted, Hume is here involved in something of a *petitio principii*. On the one hand, he suggests that the other sciences need as a basis the fundamental science of man; on the other, the method by which he aims to tackle and unfold the science of man is what he understands to be the method of those other sciences.

to have an idea of something that looking does not reveal to be there, the mistake made by Locke and Berkeley.

For Hume the world is basically a manifold of impressions, the mind a bundle of perceptions, and one of the problems that faced him was to explain the unity that we perceive in the world. If each sensory impression is 'loose and unconnected,' as he maintains, why do we not experience the world as a chaos or disjointed flux? (This was the same problem faced later by Kant, which Kant overcame by means of the synthesizing power of his a priori forms and categories.) Our seeing ideas in certain familiar patterns, Hume explains, is due to the power of the association of ideas that gives rise to beliefs and habits that guide the imagination to impose a unity on the manifold of impressions. In performing this operation the imagination is particularly guided by the qualities of resemblance, contiguity in time and place, and cause and effect. The association of ideas, then, supplies the 'cement' that binds together the Humean world in place of the discarded notion of substance. But there is a distinction to be drawn between the relations of resemblance and contiguity and the relation of cause and effect. Whereas resemblance and contiguity are given in sensation, causality is not. What do we mean, Hume asks, when we say that one thing is a cause and another its effect? In sense perception we have an impression of flame and an impression of heat, but we have no impression of a cause linking the flame with the heat, nor could the idea of cause arise from a simple comparison of the idea of flame with the idea of heat. Hume's answer is that causality is nothing more than temporal and spatial succession, on the part of the object, and, on the subject's part, an expectation that when A happens B will follow.

This account of causality entails grave problems for science, not only because the causal explanations of modern science frequently lead to the postulation of unobservable entities, but also because the inferences of modem science are grounded on their explanatory power, while Hume's account of causality as spatial and temporal contiguity leaves explanation out of account. Perhaps a more serious difficulty for Hume is that, having made sense impression the touchstone of valid knowing, he has thereby imprisoned knowledge within a screen of percepts, since it is impossible to get behind the screen and see whether the percepts correspond to objects in the world. ''Tis vain,' he says, 'to ask, whether there be body or not? That is a point which we must take for granted in all our reasonings.' His scepticism becomes complete when, having reduced the external world to an impenetrable screen of percepts, he flattens the ego itself into the same screen. Hume clearly sets out with a profound belief in the efficacy of scientific method as he conceived it – experience and observation – but ends up sadly unconvinced that science has any rational foundation. But apart from a number of inconsistencies that tend to arise in the effort to establish some kind of unity on the flux of impressions, Hume's work is remarkably systematic and true to his initial decision to rely only on experience and observation. The many philosophers who have tried to get round him have generally failed so long as they have stuck to the same basic method of operation. Hume has been over the ground very thoroughly and blocked most possible routes of escape.

Lonergan's Response

Lonergan does not accept Hume's premises. He advances on his capital and assaults his citadel. In particular, he attacks Hume's basic contention that all valid knowing is built up from impressions or what twentieth-century philosophers call sense data. Lonergan's reply to Hume is that knowledge does not consist of sensation alone or of images of what we sense; rather, the process of coming to know is a structured activity, the three main moments of which are experience, understanding, and judgment. By experience he means the deliverances of sense and the deliverances of consciousness (a notion I shall return to later). By the deliverances of sense is meant that which is given when we see, hear, touch, smell, taste. But sense experience does not by itself constitute knowledge. I cannot see, smell, or taste what happened in the past, what you are thinking, or the mass or electrical discharge of a proton. Experience simply provides the material for inquiry that leads to understanding. It leads to such questions as 'What is that?' 'How does it work?' 'Why did it happen?' and so on, the questions that promote the intelligent subject from the level of experience to the level of understanding. I cannot, for example, experience an electron. But I can experience, by seeing it, a streak on a photographic plate; and I can think of various ways of accounting for it, including the passage of an electron. Experience gives rise to questions that, if successful, yield insight into the nature or meaning of an object, of words, of an activity.

Insights are not like Humean ideas, which remain loose and unconnected except in so far as they are bundled together by the power of association. Insights occur under the pressure of the inquiring subject who wants to know something. To take another example, the prisoner wishing to escape sees a few loose bricks, a plank of wood, and a piece of rope and says, 'An escape route!' Sherlock Holmes calls this kind of thing a 'deduction,' but it is clearly not a logical deduction from given premises. Rather it is what Lonergan calls an insight, an act of understanding that unifies the data (a bit of rope, a plank of wood, etc.) by placing them in a single explanatory perspective. As this small example illustrates, the concept of an escape route does not drop ready-made out of the sky; nor is it normally grasped in one single insight, but emerges at the end of a number of insights that coalesce to yield an answer to the question of the search. Over a period of time insights accumulate and cognitive dispositions and habits are built up enabling us to 'read off' facts or situations without apparent effort; or we commonly take over the insights of others and these become part of our habitual mental furniture. But most of us on occasion move from ignorance to answer through original insights of our own and it is the structure of these that Lonergan develops in expounding his cognitional theory.

Once insights are formed we do not spontaneously remain at the level of concepts and hypothetical conclusions, and there remain the questions that promote the subject from the level of understanding to the level of judgment: 'Is it so or is it not so?' 'Is it probable or improbable?' These are questions looking for a definite answer, asking for affirmation or negation, moving the subject from the strictly conceptual level to the ontological level. By a series of tests the prisoner may be able to check whether his belief in an escape route is well founded or illusory; and the scientist can perform a whole battery of tests and experiments to discover whether the passage of an electron is the most satisfactory of available accounts. For it is only by testing our understanding that we can distinguish fact from fiction, proof from fancy, reality from wish-fulfilment and reach the truth and, through the truth, reality. Reality is known through the truth and the truth is what is intelligently understood and reasonably affirmed in judgment.

Although Hume ends up by doubting the reality of the physical world,[5] his notion of the mind at the outset of his investigations is that of a passive system receiving impressions from 'out there.' The world is a given, reality is already-out-there-now and objectivity is a matter of seeing the world as it is and not seeing what is not there. Lonergan does not conceive of reality as already out there, nor of knowing as taking a good look at what is already there. For the same reason, objectivity for him is not sensory extroversion to what is already there. What is already there is not reality but data: sounds in the air, marks on the page, the contents of acts of seeing, hearing, touching, smelling, tasting. Any significance attaching to data comes from understanding. It is understanding that allows us to say that what is seen is a typewriter or tape recorder, what is heard is a symphony or a scream, and so forth.

Unlike Hume, who speaks as if impressions were pictorial images that reveal themselves immediately, and who appeared to believe that certain relations between ideas, such as resemblance and contiguity, were revealed by sensation, Lonergan contends that mere looking or mere hearing tells

5 *Treatise*, 187.

us nothing. There are no brute facts and no bare facts and no epistemologi-cally privileged facts in Lonergan's cognitional theory to act as building blocks for the construction of further facts. There are no non-interpretative descriptions of so-called literal facts. There may, it is true, be levels or degrees of interpretation: two people seeing the same object may agree that it is made of copper; one may go further and say that it is a coal scuttle, while the other reserves judgment on this point. But even the agreed opinion that the object is made of copper is not a given, but emerges from an act of interpretation. All that is given are data and data in so far as they remain data are not yet meaningful.

Consciousness and the Self

This is Lonergan's cognitional theory in very summary outline. He has been able to work it out because experience refers not only to the deliver-ances of sense but also, as I said above, to the deliverances of consciousness. The notion that besides experience as sense there is experience as con-sciousness is crucial to Lonergan's claim that we can analyse the process by which we come to know something. For if consciousness is not something we experience there is nothing on which to ground an analysis of knowing. When he considers the question of personal identity, Hume considers the claim that we are in all our activities 'at every moment conscious of what we call self,' and then places his objections.

> For from what impression could this idea be derived? This question
> 'tis impossible to answer without a manifest contradiction and absur-
> dity; and yet 'tis a question, which must necessarily be answered, if
> we would have the idea of self pass for clear and intelligible. It must
> be some one impression, that gives rise to every real idea. But self or
> person is not any one impression, but that to which our several
> impressions and ideas are supposed to have reference. If any impres-
> sion gives rise to the idea of self, that impression must continue
> invariably the same, thro' the whole course of our lives; since self is
> supposed to exist after that manner. But there is no impression
> constant and invariable.

Hume continues:

> For my part, when I enter most intimately into what I call myself, I
> always stumble on some particular perception or other, of heat or
> cold, light or shade, love or hatred, pain or pleasure. I never catch
> myself at any time without a perception, and never can observe

anything but the perception. When my perceptions are removed for any time, as by sound sleep; so long am I insensible of myself, and may truly be said not to exist. The mind [he concludes] is nothing but a bundle or collection of different perceptions, which succeed each other with an inconceivable rapidity, and are in a perpetual flux and movement.[6]

Throughout his cogent analysis Hume takes consciousness to be perception (which he interprets as knowledge). Lonergan, in answer to Hume's objection, would agree with Hume were consciousness simply equated with perception. For 'if consciousness is knowledge of an object, it can have no constitutive effect upon an object; it can only reveal its object as it was in its proper reality prior to the occurrence of the cognitive act or function named consciousness.'[7]

Lonergan continues:

if without consciousness John has no other psychological unity beyond the unity found in the objects of his knowledge, then by consciousness John is merely manifested as having no psychological unity beyond the unity found in the objects of his knowledge.[8]

This far Lonergan is in agreement with Hume. But he goes on to drive home even more rigorously than Hume the consequences that follow from an identification of consciousness with perception:

Again, if without consciousness John cannot possibly be the conscious subject of physical pain, then by consciousness John is merely manifested as being incapable of suffering. Similarly, if without consciousness John cannot be the consciously responsible principle of his own intelligent, rational, free, or responsible acts, then by consciousness as knowledge of an object John merely knows himself as neither consciously intelligent, nor consciously rational, nor consciously free, nor consciously responsible.[9]

The notion that consciousness is nothing more than perception, Lonergan continues, 'overlooks the fact that consciousness is not merely cognitive but also constitutive. It overlooks as well the subtler fact that consciousness is

---

6 *Treatise*, 251–2.
7 *Collection*, ed. F.E. Crowe (Darton, Longman & Todd, 1967), 176.
8 Ibid.
9 Ibid.

cognitive, not of what exists without consciousness, but of what is constituted by consciousness.'[10]

The point to grasp is that what is known is known to be known. Were it not, Hume could not begin to talk about perceptions, since unless consciousness not only allows me to perceive but allows me further to be aware of myself as a perceiver (constitutes me as a perceiver), it would not be possible for me to know that I had perceptions. On strictly Humean terms it would be impossible to be aware of perceptions at all. From what impression could the idea of perception be derived? This question ''tis impossible to answer without a manifest contradiction and absurdity.' Man's consciousness is, if you like, raised to the power of two: it is because he is present to himself that anything else can be present to him; and when he is not present to himself, as for example when he is in a deep sleep, nothing else can be present to him. It is by attending to this presence-to-himself and affirming it that Lonergan seeks to fashion a theory of cognition. The awareness that accompanies sensing, understanding, and judging supplies the data on which such a theory can be based. To deny such data is to remove the basis for philosophical inquiry, as happens when it is declared that only what is reducible to the data of sense can be considered meaningful or valid; philosophical propositions are not normally about sensibly observed matters of fact. By recognizing the data of consciousness as well as the data of sense Lonergan makes possible a cognitional theory that is at once empirical and coherent. It is the task of philosophy to think systematically about what is already going on, to seek to understand what we are doing when we claim to understand or to know something and to make explicit and objectify this understanding. Mathematical, scientific, and common-sense knowing are already occurring. By examining these forms of knowledge, or more precisely by discovering ourselves as subjects who understand and know in any of these fields of inquiry, we will grasp the pattern of the process of coming to know. Lonergan invites each of us to practise introspective awareness, to catch on to what we are doing when we claim to come to know something, and in that way to test the validity of his analysis.

The Desire to Know

What binds together the three steps or stages in Lonergan's theory of knowledge – experience, understanding, judging – and makes them into one dynamic activity, is the pressure in the inquirer to discover the truth, what Lonergan has called 'the eros of the mind,' the free, unrestricted desire to

10 Ibid.

know. Knowing is a conscious, intending activity and what is intended is the truth. It is this intention to know, this psychic drive or thrust, and not sensory extroversion to what is presumed (as in Hume) to be 'already out there now,' that is the overarching criterion of truth. What is known is related immediately to this self-transcending nisus; understanding and judgment are simply answers to the questions generated by the desire to know. Put another way, the questions leading to understanding and judgment are an unfolding of this basic intentionality. The desire to know is something that arises spontaneously and irresistibly in human beings and is present in the reader who is attending to what is being said in this chapter, striving to understand it and asking if this understanding is true. But while this striving for the truth is the overarching criterion of objectivity, each level of cognition has its own peculiar function to perform and so its own criterion of objectivity; or we might say that the quest for objective knowledge is manifested in different ways at the different stages of knowing.

What is peculiar to the data of experience is their givenness – they are there – and hence the criterion of objectivity at the level of seeing, hearing, and so forth, is to see or hear what is there and not to see or hear what is not there. At the level of sensation the subject must be submissive to the givenness of the data (and not, for example, fabricate evidence or grounds). At the level of understanding the criterion of objectivity is coherence allied to the logical ideals of clarity and rigour. The need for coherence in a concept, theory, or factual account is widely accepted. Lawyers, for example, insist that their client's account of events 'hangs together,' while opposing lawyers spend much of their time trying to 'punch holes' in this account. The mind, it would appear, has great difficulty in holding on to what is incoherent, what does not hold together. As Kai Nielsen says apropos of the notion of God, 'But if a concept is incoherent, one ought not, even as an article of faith, to take it on trust that the concept in question has application. If the concept of God is incoherent ... we have decisive grounds for not believing in God.'[11] But if the need for coherence receives almost universal recognition, the asymmetricality of its application for or against a theory's validity is something of a puzzle. On the one hand, if a theory lacks coherence it is considered to be defective to that extent; on the other, the fact that a theory is coherent does not prove that it is true. Michael Polanyi, who considers coherence a mark of rationality, nevertheless points out that '[c]oherence as the criterion of truth is only a criterion of stability. It may equally stabilize an erroneous or a true view of the Universe.'[12] Lonergan's treatment of coherence helps to solve this puzzle.

11 Nielsen, *Contemporary Critiques of Religion* (Macmillan, 1971), 115.
12 Polanyi, *Personal Knowledge* (Routledge & Kegan Paul, 1958), 294.

The three basic principles of formal logic are (1) the principle of identity – a thing is what it is; (2) the principle of non-contradiction – a thing is not what it is not; and (3) the principle of excluded middle – there is no alternative to affirmation or negation. The reason why logical coherence is ruled by these three principles, according to Lonergan, is that thinking, conceptualizing, defining, supposing are all preparatory to the act of judgment and anticipate that act. In judgment we can either affirm – it is so – or deny – it is not so – but cannot both affirm and deny the same thing in relation to the same – there is no third way. (We can, of course, and commonly do, decide that we do not know enough to judge and postpone our judgment; but then judgment does not take place.) It is because knowing is a unified structure consisting of understanding and judgment that, at the level of understanding that is preparatory to judgment, the same three principles obtain. In other words, under the pressure of the desire to know understanding is heading for judgment and anticipatorily submits to its laws.

Lonergan's theory, therefore, throws light on the universally acknowledged sway of logical coherence at the level of understanding. It also has the effect of placing logic within the movement from ignorance to answer and refuses to consider philosophy to be 'a department of logic,' the view put forward, for example, by A.J. Ayer in *Language, Truth and Logic.*[13] It also explains why coherence has a strong negative value, since at the level of understanding a proposition or concept is simply en route to judgment, and what is found incoherent at this level will be rejected on purely logical grounds. But since beyond understanding there remains judgment, the positive value of coherence is reduced, since mere logical coherence does not prove that a situation obtains in the real world. Coherence is a necessary but not a sufficient condition of truth.

Beyond coherence there remains the question 'Is it so?' Attached to every prospective judgment of fact are certain conditions; verification or validation consists precisely in ascertaining whether these conditions are satisfied. Before the inquiring subject can legitimately be promoted from the level of understanding to the level of judgment, the hypothesis, concept, or supposition supplied at the level of understanding has to be put to the test. And this is done when the subject reverts to the givenness of the data. It is precisely the givenness of the data that will test the bright idea put forward to explain the data. This is a further rational demand before anything can be affirmed as fact; it is, if you like, a further demand for

13 Ayer, *Language, Truth and Logic* (Gollancz, 1946 ed.), 57.

coherence, though the coherence in question at this stage is not logical coherence but the coherence involved in the suggested explanation or interpretation fitting the data, cohering with the data. And so it is that to test an explanation or idea we go back to inspect the data to see if the data confirm or weaken the explanation or idea. In the case of the prisoner who believed he had discovered an escape route, a number of 'givens' have to be taken into account.

There is the plank of wood, but is it strong enough, propped against the wall, to support the prisoner's weight? Are the loose bricks removable and at the right height to allow the prisoner to scale within a few feet of the top? Finally, is the piece of rope long enough and strong enough for the prisoner to loop it round the spikes surmounting the wall and haul himself to the top? These are the conditions that have to be fulfilled before a secure judgment, 'There is an escape route,' can be made. In the case of science it is frequently the case that a hypothesis has the power to predict the behaviour of phenomena in certain circumstances; the circumstances are made available; if the phenomena behave in the manner predicted, the hypothesis is confirmed to that extent. We spontaneously seek out relevant given or established qualities, attributes, or happenings in order to test a supposition or hypothesis.

When it is achieved, knowledge is the affirmation of the subject's coherent interpretation combined with the givenness of the data; it is a synthesis of the givenness of the data and the subject's cognitional processes. When the conditions attached to a judgment of fact are fulfilled, it becomes an unconditioned. The criterion of objectivity at the level of judgment is the unconditioned. The value of this analysis is that it shows that reality, in Lonergan's critical realism, exists independently of the knower. The fact that conditions independent of the subject have to be met before judgment can be made validly indicates that there is an impersonal, detachable quality about what is affirmed in judgment – it is independent of the subject who affirms it. Since what is known is not relative to the subject, is not something that simply appears to him or seems to him or appeals to him, knowing is a self-transcending activity, and what is known is potentially public and can become a shared possession. In denying that reality is 'already out there now' Lonergan is simply denying that reality is, as the naive realist believes, a non-interpreted fact we bump up against with our senses; he is not denying that facts exist independently of the subject or his knowledge of them.

Philosophy, as here presented, is concerned with three questions: What am I doing when I am knowing? To answer this question is to provide a cognitional theory. Why is doing that knowing? The answer to that question is an epistemology. What do I know when I do that? The answer to this third question is an ontology or metaphysics, a general theory of what constitutes reality. To use the preferred vocabulary of analytic philosophy, a cognitional theory is descriptive: it describes the processes of cognition. An epistemology is prescriptive: it prescribes the conditions necessary for valid knowledge; it discriminates between valid and invalid knowledge. Ontology is implied in epistemology since valid knowledge is knowledge of the real. Lonergan has met Kant's demand that all metaphysical terms be accounted for in terms of an intellectual or cognitional program. And like Kant's, Lonergan's philosophy is critical, since any alleged element of the real not grounded in cognitional activity is to be eliminated. But unlike Kant, Lonergan maintains that what is affirmed in judgment is the real, and unlike Hume there is no question for him of an unbridgeable gulf between the known and the real, since the real is isomorphic with cognition.

The Fourth Level of Consciousness

So far I have spoken of three steps or stages in coming to know: experience, understanding, and judging. But even within the process of coming to know there is a moral requirement, a demand for authenticity. The subject has to commit himself to the desire to know the truth against the pressures of laziness, bias, and self-interest; she has to submit willingly to the givenness of the data and the normative demands of her rationality. She must resist the temptation to overlook unwelcome data, to spin theories without regard to the data, to affirm judgments that exceed the scope of the data. Even in the process of coming to know, then, the subject is under the sway of the fourth level of consciousness, a level of freedom and responsibility. Beyond knowledge there is the question of what is to be done on the basis of this knowledge that involves deliberation, evaluation, decision, and action. As the subject formally moves into the sphere of evaluation and action, her commitment moves up a notch; she is not simply taking a stand, as in judgment, on what is or is not the case, but is determining what she stands for. At this stage consciousness is heightened and becomes self-conscious: it is not simply a state of affairs that is affirmed or denied; the subject's very personality is at stake. The notion of a fourth level of consciousness that presupposes the previous three but is quite distinct from them overcomes, I shall argue later, the Humean is-ought poser that has exerted enormous influence in modern Anglo-Saxon moral philosophy.

Transcendental Method

The method by which we come to know and act is, according to Lonergan, a normative pattern of recurrent and related operations that yields cumulative and progressive results. It is a transcendental method because it provides the conditions that make possible the determinate operations in any field of human inquiry, whether in science or history or mathematics or literary criticism or philosophy or whatever. The methodologies of each of these disciplines is different, but underpinning each is the need to attend to the data, understand them, and reflect critically on that understanding and judge its probability, and the need to proportion judgment to the evidence coupled with the conviction that to do so is worthwhile. Even the hypocrite pays tribute to this method by his efforts to suggest that he has performed each of these operations with exactitude, in the knowledge that detection of the omission of any one of them would incur condemnation. The method, therefore, is transcendental in the sense that any denial of it is susceptible to a kind of *reductio ad absurdum* in the form of a contradiction between the content of the denial and the intellectual performance that alone could make such a denial valid. For any denial would claim that certain data had been overlooked or misunderstood, or that a better explanation of the data was possible, or that the task of explaining was not worthwhile. The method is transcendental in that, while it is open to improvement and refinement, it is not open to radical revision, since any such revision would entail the employment of the method that is to be revised. We cannot, with consistency, revise the reviser.

There is a sense in which we are all born to practise transcendental method and another sense in which we most certainly are not. In so far as we are attentive, intelligent, reasonable, and responsible we are each of us practitioners of transcendental method. But the objectification and intellectual appropriation of the method is not something that we are born with, but rather something that is achieved only with very considerable effort and after prolonged and subtle analysis. But once achieved, transcendental method will prove to be a piece of intellectual bedrock on which all further intellectual exploration can be grounded. It will not only sustain and guide positions consistent with its precepts, but will also provide a vantage point from which other contrary positions can be viewed and assessed.

Looking back on Hume's theory of knowledge (and the Enlightenment notion of rationality that Hume epitomizes), one cannot fail to be struck by its colossal dependence on an apparently hidden but operative (and talked about) mechanical apparatus. Thus, the formation of simple ideas into complex ideas is attributed to mechanical association, the origin of beliefs (in, for example, the permanent existence of objects) is put down to unfathomable but irresistible operations of the mind; moral actions are deemed to follow from feelings of pleasure and pain. Mechanical beliefs and habits perform a compensatory role in Hume's theory of knowledge.

For Hume is aware that in our practical living we assume, for example, the relative permanence of material objects, we operate on the principle of cause and effect, and we understand similars similarly, but he can provide no rational justification for any of these activities. Hence he ascribes them to mechanistic beliefs and habits with which a beneficent Nature has provided us. In offering these explanations of human action, of course, he goes far beyond what his declared methodology – experience and observation – could possibly yield, but he is acting in the spirit of his methodology, which he sees as an attempt to bring philosophy into line with science. The predilection of Hume and the *philosophes* of the Enlightenment for mechanical explanations, which result in a mechanistic view of man, can be attributed to the enormous appeal of Newton, to whom Hume always refers with great deference. The influence of the explanatory power of Newton's mechanical laws would be difficult to exaggerate.

Perhaps the difference between Lonergan's philosophy and Humean empiricism can be made clearer if we refer to Karl Popper's 'three world' distinction. The three worlds comprise everything that exists in the concrete universe. World One is the world of matter and energy, including everything from subatomic particles to galaxies, from chemicals to human brains, from pens to skyscrapers.[14] World Two is the world of consciousness, embracing all our conscious activities from dreaming to evaluating. World Three is the world of objective knowledge, the world of language, culture, civilization, including all the expressions of human creativity and perversity that have been preserved and encoded in W1 objects such as books, paintings, films, buildings, and so on. Lonergan, who considers the data of philosophy to be the data of consciousness, offers an analysis and objectification of W2. Since all knowledge proceeds from W2, his analysis of W2 is presented as grounding all of W3, including the physical sciences and technologies that explain our relations with W1. Advancement in knowledge in the physical sciences is by way of the empirical verification of W3 in Wl. The enormous gains in knowledge that this method achieves are all the more impressive when set beside the method of medieval science under the influence of Aristotle. There the canonized structures of W3, in the form of Aristotelian metaphysical categories, determined the composition and movements of W1. When this form of reasoning was broken – and the overthrow of Aristotle was a major factor in the Enlightenment denigration of the medieval intellectual achievement - and W3 became dependent on verifica-

---

14 I am indebted in this paragraph, not only for the idea but for much of the language and the examples, to Matthew L. Lamb's fine article 'The Production Process and Exponential Growth,' *Lonergan Workshop 1*, ed. Fred Lawrence (Scholars Press, 1978).

tion in W1, the success of the new method led to its importation from the physical sciences into the human sciences. When this happened in philosophy, the activities of W2 were reduced to processes in Wl. Lonergan's analysis of W2 does not attempt to reduce either W2 to W1 or W3 to W2. Rather, by giving a verifiable account of the process of cognition, it offers a clear basis from which the reduction of W2 to W1 can be recognized for what it is, at variance with the factual processes going on in W2.

3

The Notion of Belief: Lonergan, Needham, and Hampshire

Human intersubjectivity, Lonergan argues, is something that occurs spontaneously in a variety of contexts.[1] I preface an account of his notion of belief with this remark lest the misleading impression be given that Lonergan believes all intersubjective communication to be rational and premeditated. More than most modern philosophers, he is aware of community-feeling and fellow-feeling, of psychic contagion and emotional identification – of forms of interaction that are not the object simply of choice or decision. Moreover, he is aware of the irrational forces that can inhibit or block the path towards the accumulation of insights and sound judgments.[2]

Lonergan's account of belief, which considers the act of belief to be based on a *rational decision*, is normative: it is not meant to exclude a priori the possibility of irrationally induced beliefs; it is a norm that can all too easily be broken. But it *is* a norm, and as such marks out certain uses of the word – what we might designate as 'true belief' or 'responsible belief' – against which any other use of the word can be measured. Finally, 'belief' is a word used in a wide variety of senses that are determined by context. Thus, there is the notion of 'belief' in the psychological sense of opinion that falls short of certainty ('I believe it might rain later'); and of 'belief' implied by knowledge ('I know I am writing at my desk,' implying that I also believe this); or there is belief in something as a desirable state of affairs that does not exist at present ('I believe in the equality of all men before the law'), implying some form of moral commitment. Lonergan's use of

1 *Method in Theology* (Darton, Longman and Todd, 1972), 57–61
2 *Insight: A Study of Human Understanding* (Longmans, Green & Co., 1957), 191–206, 218–42 on various kinds of bias.

the word 'belief' is a somewhat specialized use intended to bring out the social character of what we call knowledge. But it is not in any way an aberrant or exceptional use. As I hope to show, it is a primary or central use of the word, and other, more peripheral, uses can easily be accommodated by his theory of how judgments of fact and value are arrived at.

In his acquisition of the knowledge that informs his decisions and actions it would be absurd to think that the knowing subject confines his judgment to what he comes to know by and for himself. Our senses are confined to a very narrow strip of space-time and we perforce rely on the senses of others to learn about the world. Likewise, we depend on the insights of others and the formulation of these in concepts, hypotheses, theories, sayings, techniques, and so forth. And our judgment too of what is or is not the case is filled out by the knowledge learned from others. Further, the presuppositions upon which insights are built are taken for granted because they are commonly assumed, and even that knowledge we generate by ourselves is fused in symbiotic fashion with a far larger context of knowledge we take over from others. In other words, we exist and decide and act in a web of *belief*, and advancement in knowledge would be impossible if this were not the case. Like Michael Polanyi,[3] Lonergan believes that science is sustained and progresses by building on existing knowledge, which is not subject to constant revision, and by collaboration, by which is meant the contribution to a common plan or pursuit of the findings of a number of specialists. Knowledge is historical and social, and without belief not only science but common sense and common living would decline. ''Human knowledge, then, is not some individual possession but rather a common fund, from which each may draw by believing, to which each may contribute in the measure that he performs his cognitional operations properly and reports their results accurately.'[4]

We learn from others not only by repeating for ourselves the acts of understanding first performed by others, as, for example, we learn Euclidean geometry, but more commonly by taking someone's word for it. This account of belief finds inadequate a dispositional account that arises from the behaviourist's attempt to reduce inner states to observable behaviour. The arguments against the dispositional account of belief need not be repeated here. Let it suffice to say that although beliefs frequently correlate with particular forms of behaviour, the overt behaviour is not the belief itself, and it can be said without contradiction that one occurs without the other.

3 See, for example, *Knowing and Being*, ed. M. Grene (Routledge and Kegan Paul, 1969).
4 *Method in Theology*, 43.

The *possibility* of belief lies in the fact, observed in the previous chapter, that truth is not dependent on the mind of the knowing subject, that it has an essential detachable quality and as such can become a shared possession. The first step in belief is taken when someone communicates his knowledge to another. The second step is a general judgment of value, which recognizes that human beings are fallible but realizes that belief is the only means of advancement in knowledge and that the alternative is regression to primitivism. The third step is a particular judgment of value, which assesses the reliability of one's source, his intellectual acumen, his honesty, the coherence of his statements with each other and with what one knows from others, and so forth. The fourth step is a decision to believe based on the general and particular judgments of value. The fifth step is the act of believing, when I personally believe to be true the judgment of fact or value communicated to me.[5]

Lonergan's use of 'belief' is, as already noted, limited and has as its object that knowledge which is not immanently generated by the subject, but which he nevertheless accepts. Belief is distinguished from the subject's own immanently generated knowledge; it is the acceptance of another's knowledge claim that the subject is not in a position to make or to verify personally. It implies that what is believed is true or probably true, and the believing subject is willing to take someone's word for this. It is important to note that this notion of belief is not, in terms of how language is normally used, in any way odd or exceptional. The *Shorter Oxford English Dictionary* gives the following definitions of 'belief':

> 1. The mental action, condition, or habit of trusting to or confiding in a person or thing; trust, confidence, faith ... 2. Mental assent to or acceptance of a proposition, statement, or fact, as true, on the ground of authority or evidence ... 3. The thing believed; in early use, esp. a religion. Now often = opinion, persuasion ... 4. A creed ...

Lonergan's understanding of belief conforms, then, to some of the oldest uses of the word, conforming to the second of these definitions but embracing also the first. Other uses of the term to mean opinion or immanently generated knowledge can, moreover, be contained within Lonergan's notion of knowledge. His definition in no way violates the various uses of this highly protean word.

Lonergan's use of 'belief' presumes the truth of what is believed and combines trust with intellectual assent. It is the element of trust that makes it the case that the act of belief is based on a decision. This element of trust

5 Ibid., 41–7.

can be greater or lesser, depending on the believer's competence in the area of knowledge to which the belief appertains.

For example, what I decide to believe may so closely cohere with my own immanently generated knowledge or what I already believe from others that the decision is easily and swiftly made. Or I may have little lateral backing for the belief and decide to believe my source for other reasons – possibly circumstances may dictate a swift decision if certain consequences are to be averted. In either case, Lonergan is at pains to point out that, in the general case, belief is natural and necessary to the advancement of knowledge and, in particular cases, the decision to believe can also be founded on good reasons.

This is Lonergan's position. It does not meet with universal approval and Rodney Needham in particular treats it rather roughly in his book *Belief, Language and Experience*.[6] Referring to Hampshire's observation that in some societies 'a man's belief would be considered as much part of his responsibility as his behaviour to other men,'[7] Needham comments:

> An example of this outlook is the Catholic tradition, latterly expressed
> by Lonergan, that belief is a free and responsible decision of the will;
> and European history is notoriously replete with the consequent
> reprobation, oppression, and burning of men because of their wilful
> failure, or refusal, to believe. 'A particular moral outlook, connected
> with particular forms of social life, will show itself in the distinctions
> that are stressed in the forms of common speech' (Hampshire, op.
> cit.). Such linguistic usages survive, however, long past their practical
> relevance, and despite their unsuitability for the description of experi-
> ence; but so long as they are current they exert an insidious influence
> toward the conception of belief as a voluntary faculty.'[8]

Apart from the highly questionable insinuation that to consider belief to be founded on a free decision is to open the way for persecution and oppression, Needham's remarks amount to a rejection of the many common usages of the terms 'belief' or 'believe' which suggest that to believe is to act on a decision – such usages as 'I refuse to believe that,' 'I simply will not believe (that my wife is unfaithful),' 'After much thought and delibera- tion I made up my mind to believe what she said,' and so forth. The precise argument Needham raises against these usages I shall examine shortly. His general position, which he traces to Wittgenstein and supports by referring

---

6 *Belief, Language and Experience* (Basil Blackwell, 1972).
7 Stuart Hampshire, *Thought and Action* (Chatto and Windus, 1959).
8 Needham, *Belief, Language and Experience*, 85.

to Hampshire, is that the theoretical positions of the past have inevitably left their residue in our language long after their 'practical relevance' has disappeared, and hence no appeal to usage can settle the question of the meaning of words denoting 'human capacities.'[9] What Needham, as an anthropologist, is concerned with is the interconnection of forms of life and language. Since there are and have been many forms of life, it is not surprising that he finds any appeal to common linguistic usage in an attempt to settle philosophical disputes to be taking 'for granted what is in fact radically problematical.'[10] Although he seeks support from Wittgenstein, Needham's approach seems to be decidedly anti-Wittgensteinian. He seeks to argue his thesis by a detailed consideration of the notion of belief and asks if there exist criteria for the use of this word that would allow or enable us to define its meaning. Turning to European languages, he finds a great disparity of meanings attached to the word and concludes that the word 'belief' admits of no definable meaning.

As we have seen, Needham attacks the notion that belief is founded on a voluntary decision with considerable animus. Yet in dealing specifically with Lonergan's analysis of belief he in no way discriminates the precise sense in which Lonergan employs the term. Lonergan uses belief to indicate the social character of knowledge: not only do we learn from others, but we also rely for our judgments and our advancement in knowledge on the immanently generated knowledge of others. Nowhere does Needham advert to this feature of Lonergan's analysis of belief: anyone reading his book could be excused for concluding that Lonergan's use of 'belief' refers to any or all of the meanings attached to that word.

Needham's precise argument against the *voluntary basis* of belief is as follows:

> We say, for instance, that we 'cannot' believe something as though it were in our power to believe or not as we decided ...; but when we introspect in search of the exercise of that power we find that none of the philosophical dubiety is at all relieved – and, of course, if it were that easy a matter the dubiety could scarcely have survived. If, after saying that I cannot believe, I suddenly assert, 'Yes, I can,' I do not thereby switch from disbelief to belief, and I cannot by any firm intention alone bring myself to do so. This is a matter of common experience, testable on the spur of the moment, yet our language tends to persuade us to the opposite.[11]

9 Ibid. 63 and 187.
10 Ibid., 63.
11 Ibid., 83.

It is not at all clear in what sense Needham is employing the word 'belief' here. If he equates belief with immanently generated knowledge, then it is true that I cannot decide to believe or not to believe – that would be tantamount to saying that I can decide to know or not to know. If, however, by belief is meant a truth claim for which the intrinsic evidence is not available to me (for example, when I have not been present at an accident), or is not intelligible to me (such as in a great deal of science), then it appears that a certain element of decision is necessary. How otherwise can I come to accept the truth of something for which the evidence is *external* to the belief itself – such evidence as, the source is honest, is intelligent, his account is coherent, it accords with what I already know, and so on? All Lonergan is claiming is that an act of responsible belief (in the sense of that word he has designated and that the dictionary informs us is central) is at once rational and voluntary. It is true that so long as I remain committed to doing what is reasonable I sometimes cannot switch from belief to disbelief: but no more can the good man, so long as he remains committed to what is right and good, switch from doing good, and yet we consider his actions free and voluntary (otherwise we would not admire him). What is true of the good man in matters of action is true of the rational man in matters of belief. His commitment to follow the suasions of reason has to be constantly renewed; and while it may be habitual, the habit is the product of many voluntary acts of commitment. It is to entertain a desperately simple and distorted notion of human freedom to consider that what is done freely is necessarily done arbitrarily or 'at will': as if one could throw a mental switch and simply do the opposite.[12] Human freedom and rationality are interdependent: where reason is excluded in principle from certain decisions (as in the case of a compulsive alcoholic or a psychopath) we do not consider the relevant decision to be a free one – we say, indeed, that there was no decision, that the action was *irrational.* The possibility of a free decision presumes the possibility (though not always the actuality) of deliberating, of marshalling the evidence, of weighing the pros and cons – of reasoning, in short. Needham's argument operates on the premise that rationality and freedom are mutually exclusive, when in fact the opposite is the case. The notion of rationality entails the notion of freedom.

However, let me call attention to another serious deficiency in Needham's argument. When he turns to philosophers to find if they can supply any

12 This argument is not unique to Needham and is to be found in other authors claiming that belief is not the result of a free decision of the subject. Lonergan's distinction between 'essential' freedom and 'effective' freedom is relevant to this discussion. See, for example, Lonergan, *Understanding and Being*, ed. E.A. and M.D. Morelli, vol. 5 of Collected Works of Bernard Lonergan (University of Toronto Press, 1990), 230–3.

criteria for the use and understanding of belief, he at no time refers to how that notion operates within the general system of their thought, and in particular to how it integrates with their account of knowledge. We have already noted this omission in the case of Lonergan, and Needham is guilty of a similar failure in the cases of Hume, Kant, and Hampshire, each of whom he quotes at some length to demonstrate his thesis that the use of 'belief' is subject to no recognizable criteria. His technique is simply to quote the contrary philosophical opinions in isolation and conclude: 'This is typical of the issue. The best of minds are at odds, the most persuasive of arguments brings no resolution ... and linguistic usage provides conflicting and indecisive evidences. But at least it is sure that no readily discriminable act of the will can be assumed as a criterion of belief.'[13] But this kind of argument will not do. And the reason is that the notion of belief put forward by these philosophers is intimately linked to their understanding of the nature of knowledge. *As such it can be seen to have certain definite criteria defining its meaning.*

The meaning of 'belief' as these authors use it is not so arbitrary or wayward as Needham would have us think, and he is being not a little naive when he writes, 'It is an interesting feature of the major arguments, more-over, that they are not much directed against other interpretations ... but that each is an independent sally against the ground thought to be occupied by the subject of the problem. The span of time that they cover, also, stresses the equivocal character of the topic, for there is no decisive supersession of ideas from one theory to the next: Hume and Kant address us just as directly as do Wittgenstein and Hampshire.'[14] Furthermore, by providing us with no ac-count of the relevant theories of knowledge or meaning, Needham gives us no grounds for making a rational assessment concerning which position might be correct. This omission, of course, tends to support the relativistic thesis he is pursuing. But let me begin by looking at the case of Hume.

Hume's Notion of Belief

Hume writes that 'belief consists ... in something, that depends not on the will, but must arise from certain determinate causes and principles, of which we are not masters.'[15] Experience produces belief in us 'by a secret operation and without being once thought of.'[16] If we wonder at the secrecy with which beliefs arise in us (according to Hume), we might find

---

13 Neeedham, *Belief, Language and Experience*, 85–6.
14 Ibid., 61.
15 *A Treatise of Human Nature*, Selby-Bigge ed. (Clarendon Press, 1888), 624.
16 Ibid., 104.

the clue in the gaps that exist between what, on Humean terms, we can legitimately claim to know and what we in actuality claim to be certain of. For Hume was aware that in our practical living we assume the relative permanence and stability of material objects, we operate on the principle of cause and effect, and we understand similars similarly, but he could provide no rational justification for any of these practices. Hence he ascribed them to belief. *Belief performs a compensatory role in relation to Hume's theory of knowledge.* Experience or Nature are invoked to explain what Hume thought to be the irrational beliefs by means of which we live our lives, because reason cannot provide an explanation.[17] Hume was simply being consistent when he thought of belief as 'a certain feeling or sentiment,'[18] and considered it 'more properly an act of the sensitive, than of the cogitative part of our natures'[19] (although it is questionable whether, on Humean terms, even knowledge rises above 'the sensitive part of our nature'). It is surely misleading to approve Hume's understanding of belief without referring to its role within the whole Humean system, but Needham does this frequently.

Kant's Notion of Belief

In the same way, Kant's notion of belief follows on his understanding and description of knowledge. Strict knowledge, according to Kant, arrives at necessary and universally valid judgments by way of a priori forms and categories, but is limited to the area of sensible intuition. It is, accordingly, impossible to have *knowledge* of anything lying outside the sphere of sensible experience. In the area of behaviour, however, the absolute character of morality is forced upon us by the way in which reason affirms moral imperatives unconditionally and regards them as universally binding.

From this follows the postulate of human freedom and the further two postulates of the immortality of the soul and the existence of God. It would be wrong to term these three postulates knowledge, since pure reason is confined to sense experience. They are rather regulative ideas – ideas, that is, that regulate our behaviour. Their existence cannot be demonstrated (and neither can their non-existence): one does not *know* the objects corresponding to these regulative ideas; one can only *believe* in their reality; hence Kant's saying that he limited knowledge in order to make room for faith.[20]

---

17 Ibid., 187.
18 Ibid., 624.
19 Ibid., 183.
20 Lonergan, it is worth noting in passing, makes an important distinction between belief and faith.

Belief is not contrary to knowledge but continuous with it: Kant speaks of the three postulates as 'regulative principles only of speculative reason, which do not require it to assume a new object beyond experience, but only to bring its use in experience nearer to completeness.'[21] Kant's notion of belief falls between opinion, which is neither subjectively nor objectively sufficient, and knowledge, which is both subjectively and objectively sufficient. Belief is subjectively sufficient but not objectively; thus it gives rise to conviction, but not to certainty.[22] The conviction is not logical but moral: I cannot even say that *it is* morally certain that there is a God, and so on, but only 'that *I am* morally certain, that is, my belief in God and in another world is so interwoven with my moral nature, that I am under as little apprehension of having the former torn from me as of losing the latter.'[23] What this account points up is that, like Hume's, Kant's notion of belief is not some 'isolated sally against the ground ... occupied by ... the problem,' but is a corollary of his theory of knowledge and forms an integral part of the whole Kantian system.

As with Hume, by presenting Kant's notion of belief in isolation Needham gives the misleading impression that it is subject to no specifiable criteria. This, we can see, is wrong. The criteria governing Kant's use of belief are dictated by his theory of knowledge. Needham might respond that his comparative study of how belief is understood by major philosophers reveals a great disparity. This is undoubtedly true, and the reason why major philosophers have disparate understandings of belief is because they have disparate understandings of knowledge. Since Needham has chosen the use of the term 'belief' as a test case in his elaboration of a general thesis leading to extreme relativism, his omission of the *place* of this concept in an individual philosopher's system of thought must be seen as weakening his case. The appearance of arbitrariness surrounding the notion that his presentation implies is seen to be quite false once it is recognized with what care individual philosophers have integrated the concept of belief with their epistemological investigations.

Hampshire's Notion of Belief

Stuart Hampshire, another of the 'major philosophers' whose notion of belief is examined by Needham, is an interesting example of a British philosopher whose philosophy approximates in certain key areas to Lonergan's. Both Hampshire and Lonergan reject the 'mistake common in

21 *Critique of Pure Reason* (Longman 1963 ed.), 233.
22 Ibid., 469.
23 Ibid.

empiricist philosophy, to represent human consciousness in waking life mainly as a state of passive awareness, as opposed to a state of unawareness of the external world in sleep and unconsciousness.'[24]

The common rejection, which implies a rejection of Cartesian dualism, is based on the common acceptance of the role of intention in meaning and acting. Lonergan would welcome Hampshire's contention that the meaning of a statement cannot be reduced to a mere understanding of the words without reference to the variable intention of the speaker that lies behind the words.[25] And Hampshire's unification of thought and action in the same subject by means of the notion of intention would also be welcome. Yet in spite of the large degree of agreement between the two philosophers there are some major discrepancies (to be discussed later), not least in their respective notions of belief. Although he quotes Hampshire against Lonergan, Needham does little to discriminate the precise sense in which each uses the term 'belief,' though he does add much later in his book that Hampshire's use is 'exceedingly general and inclusive.'[26] I believe it is this highly generalized understanding of belief that explains Hampshire's disagreement with Lonergan.

Hampshire writes that beliefs 'constitute the unchanging background of his [the subject's] active thought and observation, and they constitute also his knowledge of his own position in the world in relation to other things.'[27] Clearly, Hampshire does not distinguish between belief and immanently generated knowledge. Of a piece with this is his presentation of the process of coming to believe as one of giving one's assent to a statement, where he fails to discriminate between the different conditions under which assent may be given.[28]

It is this failure to distinguish belief from knowledge that leads Hampshire to deny that believing is founded on a decision: 'But when a statement is brought to my attention and the question is whether I believe it or not, the decision that I announce in the words "Yes, I believe it" is not a decision to do anything; nor can these words constitute an announcement that I have attempted or achieved anything. I have not decided *to* believe; I have decided *that* the statement in question is true.'[29] But it is surely odd to speak of deciding that something is true. The truth of a statement is not something I *decide*. To claim that something is true is to claim to know, and

24 *Thought and Action*, 94.
25 Ibid., 200.
26 *Belief, Language and Experience*, 145.
27 *Thought and Action*, 150.
28 Ibid., 159–60.
29 Ibid., 158.

common linguistic usage does not allow me to say that I decide to know. I assess the evidence and, given my desire or intention to know the truth, I assent or withhold my assent on the strength of the evidence. Provided I remain committed to knowing the truth, assent follows by what Lonergan calls 'natural necessity.'

There is no positive intervention of the will in the assent I give in knowledge claims. But in cases where the evidence is not available to me or not intelligible to me – and these are the conditions that obtain, as we have seen, in cases of what Lonergan terms 'belief' – there can be no assent by 'natural necessity' and to assent to the statement in question demands the positive intervention of the will, or what is commonly called a decision. The source of Hampshire's disagreement with Lonergan would appear to be his failure to discriminate between different kinds of belief and, in particular between belief and immanently generated knowledge.

It might be worthwhile at this point running over some of the discrepancies between Hampshire and Lonergan, since Hamphsire is an example of a British philosopher working broadly within the Wittgensteinian tradition whose position in a number of instances comes close to that of Lonergan. These discrepancies might be enumerated as follows:

(1) Intention for Hampshire seems to be much closer to a self-conscious activity than is the case in Lonergan, for whom the intention to know the truth, for example, is spontaneous and irresistible and, while conscious, is not fully a self-conscious activity. There are, of course, self-conscious intentions, those namely that take place at the fourth level of consciousness, but not all intentions are formed at that level. 'Formed' is probably not the right word here; it might be better to say simply that not all intentions occur at this level.

(2) Hampshire, following Ryle and Wittgenstein, contends that mental actions are somehow shadowy and parasitic upon their expression.[30] While Lonergan would see mental acts as being aimed by the subject toward judgment and possibly decision and action, he would hardly describe them as shadowy or parasitic. Perhaps the metaphor of shadow reveals a vestigial relic here of the 'private' and the 'public' that can be traced back to Descartes. Rather than describe mental acts as parasitic on their expression, Lonergan would see a heightening of consciousness as the subject moves from experience through understanding and judgment to decision and action. There is no reduction or tendency to reduce the private to the public or vice versa, but there is a recognition that I become the person I am through my meanings, values, decisions, and actions. Authenticity re-

30 *Thought and Action*, 163.

quires a consistency between my knowing and my valuing, and my valuing and my doing. In that sense, then, there is frequently a moral requirement to act following upon a certain understanding of a situation; but at the same time, I may be inauthentic and refuse to match my action with my understanding and judgment. This is a position frequently found in life, yet Hampshire cannot admit it. Because he considers the private to gain its value from what actually occurs in public, so-called private intentions not endorsed by action are simply not credited. Insincerity cannot exist for Hampshire. Descartes's ghost continues to haunt modern philosophy!

(3) Finally, Hampshire identifies the subject with his will, which he seems to consider to be uninvolved, even in a negative capacity, with the process of coming to know.[31] Lonergan would not identify the subject with the will merely, but at the same time he would see the will – or the subject's willing – as involved in a negative capacity in the process of coming to know insofar as the intention to know frequently has to be sustained against other pressures and interests that give rise to bias.

From the point of view of this chapter, my criticism of Needham has enabled me to uphold Lonergan's position on belief against contrary positions, and this kind of dialectical confrontation is, I believe, of vital importance if a concept's validity is to be truly tested. It has also forced me to draw out and elaborate certain features implicit in Lonergan's notion of belief and this, it is hoped, will help the reader to a fuller and clearer grasp of his position.

The more massive thesis that Needham builds on his lengthy examination of belief, which has vital implications for anthropology, philosophy, and indeed all disciplines whose object is to understand human experience and behaviour – namely, that '[t]he solitary comprehensible fact about human experience is that it is incomprehensible'[32] – must be considered to have been seriously weakened by this examination of the flaws in his arguments.

31 Ibid., 153–4.
32 *Belief, Language and Experience,* 246.

4

Subjectivity and Objectivity: Lonergan and Polanyi

Reason must in all its undertakings subject itself to criticism; should it limit freedom of criticism by any prohibitions, it must harm itself, drawing upon itself a damaging suspicion. Nothing is so important through its usefulness, nothing so sacred, that it may be exempted from this searching examination, which knows no respect for persons. Reason depends on this freedom for its very existence.

Kant, *Critique of Pure Reason*, B 766 (in Michael Polanyi, *Personal Knowledge*, 271–2)

Objective Knowledge

The relation between subjectivity and objectivity is rightly coming under scrutiny in present-day studies in the humanities, since it brings critical reflection to bear on a split or fissure that has deeply affected European culture over the past three or four hundred years. This split undergirds further dichotomies such as mind-body, inner-outer, and spiritual-material as well as the individual-society. It is the philosophical ally of that elevation to paradigm status of the logico-scientific model of knowledge, which has called in question traditional forms of human knowledge and belief incompatible with its declared method of verification in the moral, the religious, and the aesthetic spheres. It is now widely acknowledged that the subject-object split has led to a mutilation of what can be credited as 'real.' The genesis and historical development of this split through Descartes, Hume, and Kant into twentieth-century logical positivism and the analytical tradition generally has been extensively examined and criticized. The demolition work is well in hand; the diagnosis of philosophical illness is widely accepted. What is not widely achieved as yet is a balanced understanding of what an alternative philosophical position might look like. A number of movements within contemporary philosophy compete for attention, but the crucial question facing each of them is, how can it be shown, without rhetoric and emotional pleading, that what is 'truly subjective' is also 'truly objective'?

An article in *New Universities Quarterly* draws attention to a number of objectivist features in the philosophy of Michael Polanyi,[1] one of the most eminent of modern philosophers who have attempted to reconcile subjectivity and objectivity in knowledge. The article defends Polanyi against the accusation of subjectivism, which 'has become the almost orthodox reaction to Polanyi's writings in the philosophy of science.'[2] Among the objectivist features of Polanyi's philosophy the author highlights are the following:

(a) Theoretical knowledge has greater objectivity than knowledge gained through the senses, because theory is explicit and open to public checks and tests.

(b) For Polanyi the objectivity of a theory is determined by two additional criteria: '(i) It should reveal an independent reality; (ii) It should lead to further discoveries.'[3] It is clear that Polanyi believes that there is an independent reality and that it is the task of the scientist to reveal this reality; that reality has a rational structure and a good theory can be considered objective because its own rationality reveals 'the rationality of nature.'[4]

(c) But how is the rationality of a theory to be recognized? The author itemizes several criteria – beauty, economy, simplicity, and coherence – picked out by Polanyi that 'stand for those peculiar intellectual harmonies which reveal more profoundly and permanently than any sense experience the presence of objective truth.'[5]

(d) How then can a set of 'intellectual harmonies,' how can the subjective state of mind of the scientist, be taken as a guarantee that what he claims to know is reality? At this point, the progressive nature of theory is stressed: it should yield further discoveries and shed light on a wide range of problems. This is adduced as a warrant for its veridical quality. 'Polanyi's

1 Robert J. Brownhill, 'Objectivity and Subjectivity in Polanyi's *Personal Knowledge*,' *New Universities Quarterly* 35 (Summer 1981), 360–72. I have chosen not to name Dr Brownhill throughout this chapter.
2 Ibid., 360.
3 Ibid., 363.
4 Ibid., 365.
5 Quoted from M. Polanyi, *Personal Knowledge* (Routledge & Kegan Paul, 1958), 16.

seemingly mystical answer is that the scientist's contact with reality reveals them to him, but he means by this that the theory allows the scientist to see a whole lot of problems begin to fall into place.'[6]

Now it seems to me that this article successfully and rightly points to a number of objectivist features in Polanyi's thought, features that would win the approval of those Popperian philosophers of science who accuse Polanyi of subjectivism. (There does, however, seem to be a gap in the reasoning between *c* and *d*: how are such criteria as economy and coherence – 'intellectual harmonies' – related to the *objectivity* of the scientist's claim?) It is perhaps understandable that such an article should focus on those features that Polanyi holds in common with his Popperian critics, but in doing so it tends to reduce the great importance Polanyi attributes to *subjective* elements in knowing: for example, the article states that '[t]he commitment of the scientist, as Polanyi clearly indicates, is not a criterion of truth although it is an indication that the scientist believes his theory to be true. The only criterion of truth is the theory's agreement with reality and this we cannot know, although we can have beliefs about it.'[7]

This, I submit, is flatly contradicted by the following forthright statements by Polanyi, which hold out commitment as *the* criterion of truth.

> Responsibility and truth are in fact but two aspects of ... commitment: the act of judgment is its personal pole and the independent reality on which it bears is its external pole ... No one can utter more than a responsible commitment of his own, and this completely fulfils the findings of the truth and the telling of it.[8]

Although Polanyi's analysis of commitment is regarded in this article as providing 'the ammunition for the critics who wish to designate his work subjectivist,' Polanyi actually intends it to *rebut* the charge of subjectivism. 'It is the act of commitment in its full structure that saves personal knowledge from being merely subjective.'[9] Polanyi does not understand commitment as arbitrary commitment following on the whims or predilections of the inquiring scientist, but as a *responsible* act, at once profoundly personal and yet with a universal intent bent on discovering the truth. As Marjorie Grene puts it, 'Polanyi is *not* suggesting, as Kierkegaard or Sartre would do,

6 Brownhill, 'Objectivity and Subjectivity,' 366.
7 Ibid.
8 M. Polanyi, *The Tacit Dimension* (Routledge & Kegan Paul, 1967), 87 and 77.
9 *Personal Knowledge*, 65.

that I seek in some isolated, empty center the self-sufficiency of my original choice of myself.'[10]

Polanyi maintains that what gives personal knowledge its objectivity is the free and responsible submission to the claims laid upon the inquirer by the truth he is seeking to discover – that is, his commitment as a form of self-compulsion.[11] Polanyi's notion of commitment, therefore, is more than a mere concomitant of truth-finding, something that is usually found in intellectual inquiry. Rather, it is commitment that gives intellectual inquiry its validity and objectivity.

Tacit Knowing

Perhaps the most startling omission in the article is any reference to Polanyi's notion of 'tacit knowing.' While Polanyi may have attributed greater objectivity to theory than to knowledge through the senses, he nevertheless claims that, like all knowledge, theory is founded on tacit knowing:

> Our whole articulate equipment turns out to be merely a toolbox,
> a supremely effective instrument for deploying our inarticulate
> faculties. And we need not hesitate then to conclude that the tacit
> personal coefficient of knowledge predominates also in the domain
> of explicit knowledge and represents therefore at all levels man's
> ultimate faculty for acquiring and holding knowledge.[12]

The point here is that tacit knowing is not critical: 'Tacit knowing cannot be critical ... [S]ystematic forms of criticism can be applied only to articulate forms.'[13] Polanyi posits a distinction between 'What we can know and prove' and 'What we know and *cannot* prove,'[14] and the former, he claims, is founded on the latter. 'All knowledge is either tacit or *rooted in tacit knowl-edge*. A wholly explicit knowledge is unthinkable.'[15] It is this feature of Polanyi's thought – the founding of theory and all explicit knowledge on a-critical tacit knowing – and not his notion of commitment that provides 'the ammunition for the critics who wish to designate his work subjectivist.'

10 M. Polanyi, *Knowing and Being,* ed. Marjorie Grene (Routledge & Kegan Paul, 1969), xi.
11 M. Polanyi, *The Study of Man* (Routledge & Kegan Paul, 1959), 62–3.
12 Ibid., 25.
13 *Personal Knowledge,* 264.
14 Ibid., 286.
15 *Knowing and Being,* 144.

Here Polanyi's philosophy is not merely open to the charge of subjectivism but practically invites it.

I do not wish simply to dispute this article's interpretation of Polanyi, however, but to provide a preamble for a more profitable exercise. First, I wish to safeguard a valuable ingredient in Polanyi's position, without which his very considerable achievement would be greatly reduced – namely, his forceful and convincing defence of the subjective pole in knowing. Second, I wish to draw attention to serious weaknesses or limitations in his account of knowing. Third, I shall offer corrections of these limitations by a philosopher who holds a great deal in common with Polanyi, Bernard Lonergan. It is, I believe, by modifying and amplifying Polanyi's thought through the insights of others, rather than by attempting a partial and somewhat reductive interpretation of it, that Polanyi and what he stood for will best be served.

It would be most fruitful first to develop further certain aspects of what Polanyi means by tacit knowing. This is the foundation of all explicit or formulated knowledge as set out in words or symbolic formulae. Its structure, Polanyi suggests, is most clear in the act of understanding, for understanding is essentially tacit: 'A process of comprehending: a grasping of disjointed parts into a comprehensive whole.'[16] In tacit knowing we rely on a *subsidiary* awareness of particulars in order to attend to a focally known object – we recognize a face, for example, through our subsidiary awareness of its features. We gain intellectual and practical control of our surroundings through the instrumental use of our body: we *attend from* our body in order to *attend to* those things that lie outside it.[17] And just as we extend the control of our body by the use of a probe or a tool, so we extend our person through the assimilation of the various symbolic forms (language, theories, etc.) our culture offers. Knowledge is not something that can be detached without loss to the knower; rather it is through the acquisition of knowledge and skills that we develop as persons.

Polanyi's observations on tacit knowing are among the most important contributions to philosophical thinking; they draw our attention away from the fixed and the formulated to the living process that underlies all intellectual achievements – the process of observing, thinking, selecting, understanding, reviewing, choosing, and so forth, which is hidden from public scrutiny. I believe a serious flaw in Polanyi's understanding of the tacit dimension that makes it difficult to rebut the accusation of subjectivism is his contention that tacit knowing is a-critical. For Polanyi criticism seems to mean a form of publicly formalized testing of articulate forms and operations. Since tacit knowing is pre-articulate and hidden from public scrutiny,

16 *The Study of Man*, 28.
17 *Knowing and Being*, 147–8.

it cannot be tested in this way; and so it is a-critical. Thus, Polanyi merges tacit knowing with belief and proclaims the fiduciary roots of all knowledge: 'All truth is but the external pole of belief and to destroy all belief would be to destroy all truth.'[18] If truth is ultimately founded on the subject's accumulated beliefs that are, in principle, closed to scrutiny, it does indeed become a wearisome business to maintain that Polanyi is not caught in the subjectivist net. At times there is an almost desperate defiance in Polanyi's utterances on belief, when commitment is less an impersonal dedication to truth-finding than a rock to cling to for the want of anything surer:

> I believe that the function of philosophic reflection consists in bringing to light, and affirming as my own, the beliefs implied in such of my thoughts and practices as I believe to be valid; ... that I must conquer my self-doubt, so as to retain a firm hold on this programme of self-identification.[19]

I have no wish to degrade belief, but Polanyi's use of the term is so broad as to render it virtually meaningless. Even 'our judgment as the paramount arbiter of all our intellectual performances' is 'itself a fiduciary act of my own.'[20] In the final analysis, all distinction between knowledge and belief breaks down and so, in Polanyi's hands, cognitive terms such as understanding and judgment lose their distinctive meaning and thus their reality. Belief may be a protean word, but common usage is against Polanyi here since it distinguishes what, on the one hand, we claim strictly to believe and what, on the other, we claim to know. Polanyi's too hasty retreat to belief appears to spring from his narrow definition of 'critical,' taken over from his empiricist opponents: carrying out systematic public tests. This understanding entails that the hidden realm of thinking and understanding – the tacit dimension – is a-critical. These non-explicit factors of knowing cannot be 'critical,' and so they are grouped together as forms of belief, as if knowing that is not explicit must be belief. Designating the tacit dimension as a-critical is, I believe, the fundamental weakness in Polanyi's philosophical system. It leaves him vulnerable to the accusation of subjectivism. Despite his many fruitful observations on the structure of tacit knowing, Polanyi fails to analyse adequately the process of *critical reflection* that leads the subject to judgment. Here Lonergan's systematic reflections on the structure and dynamism of our knowing can compensate for limitations in Polanyi's philosophical enterprise.

18 *Personal Knowledge*, 286.
19 Ibid., 267.
20 Ibid., 265.

Lonergan's Position

Like Polanyi, Lonergan has a high regard for the products of modern science and for the scientific method that produced them; and like Polanyi he judges the empiricist philosophies developed in response to the scientific revolution as a serious reductive distortion of the scientific method, in the sense of the processes the scientist goes through in moving from ignorance to knowledge. As in the case of Polanyi, Lonergan focuses on the living performance, the dynamic processes that underlie and underpin all formulated knowledge and systematic experimentation. He agrees with Polanyi that these processes are tacit and not available for public scrutiny, but maintains that they are nevertheless capable of analysis. In his major philosophical work, *Insight*, Lonergan moves through mathematical, scientific, philosophical, and common-sense inquiry and knowing; and he invites the reader to discover that the same invariant pattern of cognition occurs in each of these fields. It is not possible to give a public demonstration of the structure of knowing, but everyone who claims to have come to know something can reflect on the processes she went through in moving from ignorance to answer. In this way she can come to appropriate the dynamic structure of her knowing.

Hume conceived knowledge as the passive reception by the subject of internalized sensations. The analogy between knowing and sensation, the notion that knowing consists in 'taking a good look,' is what Lonergan considers to be empiricism's basic flaw; it is the residue of a *naive realism* that infects almost all modern approaches to the question of knowledge. It assumes that reality is 'already out there now' and that objectivity consists in reaching out to reality so conceived. The key objection to this view of knowledge and objectivity (and it is one to which Polanyi is vulnerable) is that reality so conceived can never be known, because we can never line up our knowledge on the one side and reality on the other side to see if they match. On these terms it is impossible to build a bridge between the known and the real, and so we are trapped in subjectivism or even scepticism.

Lonergan responds to this problem by claiming that the process of coming to know is a structured activity, the three main moments of which are experiencing, understanding, and judging. By experience, such as sense experience – our normal seeing, hearing, touching, smelling, tasting – we become aware, we attend to the data of the problem or situation. But sense experience does not by itself constitute knowledge. So long as I simply look at the clues in a murder mystery I cannot be said to know who the murderer is. Likewise, I cannot see, smell, or taste what happened in the past or the sum of the angles of a triangle. Experience simply provides the material for inquiry that will lead to understanding. It gives rise to questions such as What is that? How does it work? Why did it happen? How often does it occur? and so on, the questions that promote the intelligent inquirer from the level of experience to the level of understanding. Understanding takes us beyond what is merely experienced. As Polanyi observes, '[t]he process of understanding leads beyond – indeed far beyond – what a strict empiricism regards as the domain of legitimate knowledge.'[21] Inquiry, therefore, if successful, yields what Lonergan calls an insight and what he and Polanyi call understanding, a mental activity that unifies the disjointed data by placing them in a single explanatory perspective.

Though Polanyi has much that is illuminating to tell us about the nature and structure of understanding, and while he perceives that knowledge and understanding are distinct (since our understanding can be wrong), he does not take us beyond understanding. Consequently, his criterion of truth is dependent on the subject's responsible commitment. For Lonergan a third step is necessary for knowledge to be achieved. Once insights are formed, we do not spontaneously remain at the level of concepts or hypotheses; there arise the questions that promote the inquirer from the level of understanding to the level of critical judgment: Is it so or is it not so? Is it probably so or probably not so? These are questions looking for a definite answer, moving the inquirer from the strictly conceptual level to the ontological level. Understanding is not, as Polanyi believed, a-critical, because the inquirer must undertake critical reflection before she can affirm or deny her understanding as true. In particular, she must review the data and see if her explanatory hypothesis fits. Scientists conduct tests and experiments to discover whether their hypothesis is the most satisfactory of available accounts. And so, while for Polanyi and Lonergan the moment of insight, the flash of illumination, is pre-verbal and pre-conceptual, Lonergan maintains that the first insight – direct insight – has to be rehearsed and probed if second insight – reflective insight – is to ground a judgment for or against our hypothesis. Understanding is not the a-critical process that Polanyi took it to be, for it is by testing our understanding, by deliberately subjecting it to critical reflection, that we distinguish fact from fiction and reach the truth, and, through the truth, reality. Reality is not 'an already out there' that we contact by extroversion, but rather it is what is intelligently understood and reasonably affirmed in judgment. To the famous objection, in either its empiricist or its idealist form, that we can never know reality in itself, since all we have access to are sense data or appearances, Lonergan replies that this would only be so when reality is conceived as 'already out there now,' and objectivity as an achievement of sensory

21 *The Study of Man*, 21.

extroversion; it is not so if sensitive operations are only a first stage in knowing: 'It is just as much a matter of judgment to know that an object is not real but apparent, as it is to know that an object is not apparent but real.'[22]

Let me summarize what has been said so far about the cognitional process, using Lonergan's words:

> But human knowing is also formally dynamic. It is self-assembling, self-constituting. It puts itself together, one part summoning forth the next, till the whole is reached. And this occurs not with the blindness of natural process, but consciously, intelligently, rationally. Experience stimulates inquiry, and inquiry is intelligence bringing itself to act; it leads from experience through imagination to insight, and from insight to the concepts that combine in single objects both what has been grasped by insight and what in experience or imagination is relevant to insight. In turn, concepts stimulate reflection and reflection is the conscious exigence of rationality; it marshals the evidence and weighs it either to judge or else to doubt and so renew inquiry.[23]

What binds the three steps or stages in knowing together, making them one dynamic activity, is the pressure in the inquirer to discover the truth: knowing is a conscious, intending activity and what is intended is the truth. This *intention* to know, this psychological drive or thrust, and not extroversion to what is 'already out there' is, for Lonergan, the overarching criterion of truth. What is known is related immediately to this self-transcending thrust; understanding and judgment are simply answers to the questions generated by this desire to know. The desire to know, according to Lonergan, arises spontaneously and irresistibly in human beings. Like Polanyi, Lonergan notes a moral ingredient in coming to know, a requirement of intellectual authenticity. This takes the form of a commitment to upholding the unrestricted nature of man's desire to know the truth against complacency, laziness, bias, and self-interest. I am personally involved in my knowing. 'A judgment is the responsibility of the one that judges. It is a personal commitment.'[24] My acquisition of knowledge does not leave me personally unaffected, but in acquiring meaning about the world I am placing myself in relation to the world, making myself. This is the reason why Lonergan

22 B. Lonergan, *Collection*, ed. F.E. Crowe (Darton, Longman & Todd, 1966), 235.
23 Ibid.
24 B. Lonergan, *Insight: A Study of Human Understanding* (Longmans, Green & Co., 1957), 272.

berates 'The Principle of the Empty Head' in comments that bear comparison with Polanyi's remarks on the 'virgin mind' and the futility of a presuppositionless position.[25] It is in their respective elaborations of the subjective pole in knowing and in their recognition of the traditional and social dimensions involved in pursuing an academic discipline that Polanyi and Lonergan are most at one.

The notion of intellectual coherence as a criterion of truth was one that puzzled Polanyi. Certainly he considered coherence to be a mark of rationality, but he was also aware of its limitations as a guarantor of the truth of an idea or intellectual position. He said, 'Coherence as the criterion of truth is only a criterion of stability. It may equally stabilize an erroneous or a true view of the Universe.'[26] Lonergan's treatment of coherence helps to solve the puzzle. For Lonergan holds that the achievement of knowledge is a three-step process of which understanding is only the second step. According to Lonergan, intellectual coherence is a necessary criterion for the validity of this second step: we simply cannot understand what is self-contradictory or what does not hang together intellectually. But this second step does not complete the process of coming to know – hence it is that intellectual coherence is a necessary but not a sufficient criterion of truth, which is only discovered and can only be affirmed at the third step in the process of coming to know, the step taken with the judgment that something is the case.

Lonergan repudiates the notion of a pre-existent ego standing over against reality 'already out there.' For him the real is attained through the truth; in true judgments we affirm facts in the world. As an object of judgment, fact is rational; the notion of reality unmediated by acts of meaning is absurd. As an object of understanding, fact is intelligible, it is coherent and unified. The notion of a 'brute fact,' of a non-interpreted fact, is repudiated. Finally, as the object of sense, fact shares the givenness of the data in all its concrete particularity – it is not the subjective creation of the knower. (This, we might say, is the common sense understanding of 'object,' the object we encounter with our senses.) Subjectivity and objectivity are both retained, since the real is isomorphic with the structure of cognitional activity. Like Lonergan, Polanyi insists on the role of the subject in knowing; but unlike Lonergan, he never finally repudiates reality as 'already out there,' because he offers no analysis of critical judgment. His problem then becomes one of building a bridge between the known and the real; of showing how marks of rationality in theoretical knowledge –

25 See B. Lonergan, *Method in Theology* (Darton, Longman & Todd, 1972), 157–8.
26 *Personal Knowledge*, 294.

features such as economy, coherence, and so on – can be said to reveal reality; of substantiating the following:

> The discovery of objective truth in science consists in the apprehension of a rationality which commands our respect and arouses our contemplative admiration: that such discovery, while using the experience of our senses as clues, transcends this experience by embracing the vision of a reality beyond the impression of our senses, a vision which speaks for itself in guiding us to an ever deeper understanding of reality.[27]

In the end, Polanyi is forced to take refuge in belief and the fiduciary basis of all knowledge, a position that, if adhered to, would have disastrous consequences for many of his own finest insights.

Conclusion

Having said this, however, it must be added that what Polanyi and Lonergan hold in common is much greater than what separates them. In particular, each in his own way repudiates the notion that the human subject is a mere spectator before an impersonal universe; each insists that all knowledge is the product of human creativity and that science is one of humanity's greatest achievements, its theories and laws the constructs of the human mind by which we attempt to interpret and explain the universe. We are involved in our knowing. That theme leads on to the existential dimension, to what Lonergan calls the 'fourth level of self-transcendence, a level of freedom and responsibility,' and what Polanyi calls 'the higher principle of responsibility'; but to follow these mutually enriching philosophers in that direction would require another chapter, at least.[28]

27 Ibid., 5–6.
28 But see Walter E. Conn, *Conscience: Development and Self-Transcendence* (Birmingham: Religious Education Press, 1981), to which this chapter is indebted.

5

Problems and Solutions:
Lonergan and Russell

The reason for focusing on Russell in this chapter and on Wittgenstein in the next is that they above all have created the mould that has shaped the analytical tradition – they are its supreme architects. In this and the next chapter, I am going back to source. If we can understand Russell and Wittgenstein, we can begin to see where the analytic movement is coming from. Both men are giants of twentieth-century English-language philosophy, whose photographs, unusually for philosophers, would frequently be recognized by the average *homo academicus* if not by the man in the street. Russell's face looks out at us from just about every book that carries his name: emaciated, ascetic, the bright eyes alert and as cold as the logic to which he was so passionately, almost mystically, devoted. Then there is Wittgenstein's startled stare, confrontational, challenging, at once abrasive and anguished. Lonergan is much less well known, but we have the Karsh photograph of him as a comparatively old man, his face almost devoid of expression, his eyes turned inwards like a Greek statue, the master of interiority, of the inner side of human personality, which, he believed, holds the key to philosophy.

Lonergan's Notion of the Four Levels of Consciousness

Let me begin with Lonergan so that we can hold in our heads a picture of his central position when I come to Russell and Wittgenstein and their many followers. What is Lonergan basically saying? He is saying that as human beings we operate at four distinct but related levels of consciousness. First of all, we are conscious – this is something that philosophers in the analytic camp who have their roots in empiricism, behaviourism and pragmatism, or in Wittgenstein, have not always been willing to grant. Consciousness is a phenomenon that for various reasons behaviourists and pragmatists have not had much time for, and that Wittgenstein also found philosophically unhelpful, for reasons I shall explain later. You can begin to see why Lonergan, whose philosophy is wrapped up with consciousness in all sorts of ways, is regarded by members of the analytic school as philosophically strange, as methodologically beyond the pale.

Not only does Lonergan speak of consciousness, he also claims that we operate at four levels of consciousness. Let me explain once again this point, which I have outlined in previous chapters. In England before the arrival of the railways, under the pressure of the industrial revolution, a huge complex system of canals was developed. The narrow boats that still ply these canals normally travel along at a single level, but every now and then they have to go up or down hill. The problem arises of how you get a long, narrow boat up a hill, for example. The way it is done is by the creation of different locks at different levels – different steps of water, we might say, controlled by a gate at each end. The boat goes into the first lock and the gates close behind it. The water level in this lock is then raised to the level on the next lock, the gates separating the first from the second lock are opened, and the boat passes into the second lock. The lock gates are closed behind the boat and the water at this second step is raised until it is level with that at the third step. The gate is opened between the second and third stages and the boat passes through the open gate into the third level – and so it goes on.

Now if we compare consciousness to the water in a canal, we might think of the first level of the canal as empirical consciousness. This is a level at which we ask no questions, but simply drift along, enjoying the free flow of sensory representations and their images and all the various feelings we associate with them. Then suddenly we ask a question – something catches our attention and we ask, 'What is that?' Our mind is aroused, it stirs itself and begins to probe. And what we were previously lazily enjoying, the data of sense, are no longer vague, indeterminate, hazy, amorphous, free-floating, but become determinate, shaped, patterned, meaningful. They become invested with meaning as I answer the question: the data are transformed because the subject has been transformed by asking a question.

No longer limp and at rest, the subject has begun to exercise understanding; intelligence is now exercised, is trained on a question, is straining for an answer. The question has raised the level of my consciousness and I have passed through the gate opened up by the question into the intellectual stage of consciousness. If an answer is forthcoming, when I make a guess or a supposition or form a hypothesis, a new question spontaneously arises: 'Is that so? Is the answer correct or incorrect, probable or improbable?' This new question raises a whole new lot of considerations, by asking for confirmation or disconfirmation of the answer proposed at the preceding level. It raises the stakes, puts me onto a higher level of consciousness. By answering this new set of questions, I pass into the rational level of consciousness. The transition from this third level of consciousness to the fourth level is similarly effected by means of a question, this time a value question. Once more the stakes are raised. I am being asked not simply 'Is this so?' but 'Is this right? Is this good or bad? If it is good, how good is it?' Value questions require the subject not just to take a stand on a knowledge claim but to determine what it is she or he stands for. The answer says as much about the subject as it does about the object in question, which is why, at this fourth level, consciousness becomes self-conscious. The fourth level is preparatory to action, actual or potential, and encompasses evaluation, choice, decision, and action itself. It is a level characterized by deliberation as well as by freedom and, corresponding to that freedom, responsibility.

Those are the four levels of consciousness as described by Lonergan. The canal-lock analogy might help us to grasp how there is both continuity and discontinuity between the various levels or stages. For if the canal water is consciousness, we can see that the first level is passed beyond but is not lost as we move from the empirical to the intellectual level, that the second level is passed beyond but reintegrated as we move from the intellectual to the rational level, and that the third level is passed beyond but elevated as we move from the rational level to the level of deliberation. The canal-lock image might also help us grasp how the question controls the gate to each level and raises the level at each new stage. Questions are hugely important because they control our entry to each level, they determine the area of discourse we find ourselves in. In Lonergan's philosophy, an idea is the answer to the question posed at the intellectual level of consciousness, 'What is that?' For Bertrand Russell, an idea is something else altogether.

Bertrand Russell

There can be no doubt that Bertrand Russell presides over twentieth-century Anglo-American philosophy like a colossus. The colossus may be seriously flawed, it may have feet of clay, but a colossus Russell nevertheless is in respect of the influence his philosophy has exerted and continues to exert. Russell's influence is attributable to a variety of factors. Not only was he a famous philosopher, he was also for most of his long life a well-known figure in British, and to some extent American, public life, appearing on platforms, broadcasting on radio, and frequently in the news because of the notoriety of some of his well-publicized views on political, social, and ethical

– notably sexual – matters. He also suffered for his views, including a spell in jail in 1918, and with his halo of white hair and ardent, principled pacifism, he became something of a humanist saint, sometimes mentioned in the same breath as Buddha, Gandhi, and Christ. As a philosopher and academic he achieved fame while still very young through his early work on mathematical logic. This confirmed his reputation as a man of formidable intelligence whose system of logical notation, which he derived in part from others, continues to be used to this day. But Russell's influence also stems from the fact that, along with G.E. Moore, he overthrew the 'old guard' – the idealists who had led British philosophy from the nineteenth into the twentieth century – and initiated that revival of British empiricism that remained a central strand of English-language philosophy for most of the twentieth century.

Russell's development as a philosopher is somewhat tortuous. As Professor Broad remarked, '[A]s we all know, Mr Russell produces a different system of philosophy every few years.' Towards the end of his life, Russell responded to this charge of inconsistency by pointing to the fact that anyone who had kept abreast of physics since the beginning of the century would hold views at odds with the views widely accepted many years before. Certainly Russell presents difficulties to the historian: it is very difficult to pin him down on a large array of issues and claim that this is his position, for he frequently qualifies what he says and has a habit of changing his mind. It is all rather like Lloyd George's complaint about negotiating with De Valera – this, Lloyd George remarked, was like trying to pick up mercury with a fork! But my own complaint is not that Russell frequently changed his mind, but that he was unwilling to change his mind radically enough. He was rather like a First World War general, frustrated by the lack of progress, concerned about his position's vulnerability to attack, but unwilling or unable to make changes at a strategic level. He tinkers, and after 1920 he adopts a rather novel manoeuvre, but he never truly calls his basic approach into question.

A Summary of Russell's Philosophical Development

Before entering into a more detailed consideration of some of Russell's views, let me sketch lightly some of its major features.

Together with Moore, he undermines the hegemony of idealism in British philosophy and, in particular, attacks the notion that we cannot know the parts unless we know the whole; he favours a 'piecemeal' approach to knowledge, as in science.

Russell resurrects British empiricism and reshapes it for the twentieth century. He is anti-Hegelian and wishes to 'achieve maximum exposure to the external world.'[1] He accepts empiricism's notion that sensation is the conduit of knowledge and that ideas are images of sensations.

To some extent, however, he shifts the emphasis away from the eighteenth-century preoccupation with ideas and makes propositions the focus of attention. The business of philosophy, he says, is the analysis of propositions. Hence the 'analytic movement.' This is also part of Russell's contribution to the 'linguistic turn' in twentieth-century philosophy, though he is later to complain that, under Wittgenstein, this turn has gone too far.

Russell embraces the empiricist notion that the complex is built out of more simple entities. Atomic propositions are propositions referring to the simplest entities or what Russell calls 'atomic facts'; while molecular propositions do not refer to molecular facts, nevertheless molecular propositions must be truth functions of atomic propositions. This view is a combination of two influences: (1) empiricism and (2) the system of extensional logic devised by Whitehead and Russell, in which even the most elaborate formulae are truth functions of a few very simple forms in such a way that their truth or falsity is dependent on the truth or falsity of these simple forms.[2]

However, by claiming that words get their meaning from the objects they denote, Russell creates an identification of meaning and reference that is potentially embarrassing, since it is inclined to overpopulate the world with non-existent entities, such as 'golden mountains,' or with entities corresponding to nouns, such as 'no one,' 'someone,' 'everyone,' and so on. To overcome this difficulty, Russell devises the Theory of Definite Descriptions, whereby a description is substituted for most proper names. Most names are, he contends, simply disguised descriptions: so Julius Caesar is really a reference to the Roman leader who was killed on the Ides of March. Whereas logically proper names, to be true, must denote something that exists, this is not the case with descriptions that derive their meaning simply from their logical form.

Perhaps because of his work on the logical foundations of mathematics, Russell is never a pure or rigorous empiricist, embracing in his earlier period the belief that we have immediate knowledge not only of sense data but also ('probably') of self, ethical good and evil, and (strangely for an empiricist) universals. Without universals, he claims, it would be impossible to analyse anything.[3]

1 D.F. Pears, *Bertrand Russell and the British Tradition in Philosophy* (Collins Fontana, 1967), 198.
2 J.O. Urmson, *Philosophical Analysis: Its Development between the Two World Wars* (1956; Oxford University Press, 1969), 96–7.
3 B. Russell, 'Knowledge by Acquaintance,' in *Mysticism and Logic* (1918; Penguin, 1953), 200.

In the 1920s Russell assists empiricism in taking the 'behaviourist turn.' This seems to be an attempt to overcome the tensions between his own phenomenalism and the scientific account of the world. Behaviourism and pragmatism lay less stress on knowledge as a private possession and show it to be a matter of reacting to the environment, a part of man's biological adaptation in the struggle to survive and to 'cope.' Behaviourism also attempts to show that our knowledge of the meaning of words and much of our intellectual furniture are built up by means of association, the conditioned reflex, and the development of habits.

In this later period the logical strain in Russell's thinking is less dominant and the empiricist strain predominates: he jettisons (1) his belief in the self, (2) objective knowledge of right and wrong, as well as (3) any claim to have direct knowledge of universals.

Still, finding it impossible to claim to be unaware of awareness,[4] Russell is never a strict behaviourist, even recognizing the 'sudden illumination ... with which every serious student must be familiar'[5] (Lonergan's 'insight'), and indeed holding on to some aspects of introspection as providing grounds for his philosophical beliefs. However, some of the latter arguments (I shall argue) are of the kind that have given introspection a bad name.

Throughout both periods in his philosophical development, Russell retains his allegiance to science and to physics in particular; he never abandons his early pledge: 'It is, I maintain, from science, rather than from ethics and religion, that philosophy should draw its inspiration.'[6] In his later works he attempts some kind of rapprochement between mind and matter, psychology and physics.

Russell's earlier period is generally more admired than his later period – indeed, John Passmore speaks of Russell's followers walking past the works of the decades after 1920 'with averted eyes';[7] but the 'behaviourist turn' in Russell's thinking was to be extremely influential. Supported as it was by references to mainly American thinkers and philosophers, it foreshadowed the transfer of leadership in analytic philosophy from England to the United States.

This brief outline of Russell's philosophical development should provide a context within which more detailed discussion of some of his central positions and arguments can take place. Passmore has neatly summed up the course of Russell's philosophical journey as the passage from Descartes

4 B. Russell, *The Analysis of Mind* (1921; Unwin paperbacks, 1989), 115.
5 B. Russell, *Outline of Philosophy* (1927; Unwin paperbacks, 1979), 33.
6 B. Russell, 'On Scientific Method in Philosophy,' in *Mysticism and Logic*, 95–6.
7 John Passmore, *One Hundred Years of Philosophy* (Penguin, 1968), 214.

to Hume.[8] Certainly in Russell's earlier period there is an air of optimism and hope, a sense of setting out a program for future development, which is replaced by increasing pessimism and scepticism in the later works. For the purposes of this book, it has been necessary to select from Russell's Vesuvian outpouring of ideas and to focus in this chapter on those topics that are central to his reputation. For this reason I have selected three major topics or themes from Russell's oeuvre. The first two – his notion of logical atomism and his Theory of Descriptions – are from his earlier period, while the third deals with the 'behaviourist turn' that characterized his philosophy after 1920. All three have left a lasting mark on the history and practice of philosophy and should help critical realists to understand, from the inside so to speak, why certain ways of speaking and arguing are second nature for some members of the analytical tradition.

Logical Atomism

As Ayer has noted, Russell's starting point goes back to Descartes: 'We are to start with the elements which are the least susceptible to doubt and then see what can be constructed out of them, or inferred from them.'[9] Russell follows the old British empiricist tradition in claiming that what we can be most certain of are the data we make direct contact with through our senses. The basic starting point of logical atomism is that perception can never be in error, since 'whenever we perceive anything, what we perceive exists, at least so long as we are perceiving it.'[10] Russell never abandons his empiricist view that words are meaningless unless they are traceable back to the world via sensations. In the final analysis, I can be sure of what is under my nose at the present time, what I am presently making direct sensory contact with. For this reason he considers the demonstrative 'this' as the only true 'logically proper name' – that is, a name that means the entity that it denotes. Other proper names are derivative from 'this,' since only the act of present pointing is assured by the immediacy in experience of what is pointed at. Indeed, Russell's dependence on immediacy leads him to be unable to provide examples of simple entities in the world. To say, for example, 'this red,' is to introduce a universal ('red'), and Russell came to the understandable belief that a universal could not be the object of immediate experience. So he was reduced to the rather comical situation of giving as an example of a 'simple,' 'This ...' (pointing, as in a stage direction) or even, 'This that.'

8 Ibid., 239.
9 A.J. Ayer, *Russell* (Fontana, 1972), 36.
10 B. Russell, 'On the Nature of Truth and Falsehood,' in *Philosophical Essays*, (1910; Routledge, 1994), 156.

Sense data are the epistemological ultimates in Russell's system. What is more, Russell seeks to realize the ambition of Hume by showing how sense data not merely furnish the data for knowledge but act as the building blocks of the world we claim to know. Stating his version of Occam's razor, he says that, wherever possible, we should substitute constructions from known entities for inferences to unknown entities.[11] In Russell's vocabulary, 'inference' becomes a rather uncertain basis for any knowledge claim and sense data are posited as the basic building blocks out of which the empirical world is to be constructed. But Russell is also a logician and entertains the ambition along with his German fellow mathematician, Gottlob Frege, of formulating a logically perfect language, one capable of showing how propositions of all kinds can be translated into more basic propositions. Central to this ambition is the notion of 'truth function,' which Frege also shares – the notion that more complex propositions are truth functions of simpler propositions. In *Principia Mathematica*, Russell had argued that the whole of mathematics could be reduced to a relatively few axioms or principles of logic, and that ultimately all mathematical propositions are truth functions of these few logical propositions.

Russell's model of reality derives from two basic influences, the one empiricist and the other logicist. The first ensures that knowledge is properly 'doored' and 'windowed,' to borrow a phrase from Gilbert Ryle, that is, that it regards the world presented by our senses, the world 'out there now,' spread out in space and time. The second provides the structure of mathematical logic – as conceived by Russell – as a model on which to base the structure of the real world. The status and role of logic in Russell's philosophical thinking is not easy to identify with precision, but in his earlier phase logic holds out the promise of certainty in knowledge. Russell had undergone a Hobbesian conversion to mathematics when, introduced to Euclid's theorems by his brother Frank, he made the profound discovery that certainty in knowledge was attainable. The same certainty he discovered in logic, and he wished it might be possible to achieve similar lucidity and certainty in other forms of propositions such as those in use in politics or morality.[12] The early Wittgenstein also applied the structure of logic to mirror or picture the structure of the language through which we have access to reality, but since he sees no need to blend logic with the contents of sensory experience, Wittgenstein's use of logic is purer than Russell's. At one point he writes rather condescendingly to Russell, 'I cannot imagine your way of working from sense-data forward.' Wittgenstein felt no need to

11 B. Russell, 'The Relation of Sense-Data to Physics,' in *Mysticism and Logic*, 148.
12 Ray Monk, *Bertrand Russell: The Spirit of Solitude* (Vintage, 1997), 26, 44, 47. Biographical references to Russell are mainly from this book.

demonstrate that the notion of matter could be constructed from sense-data.[13] Coming from the empiricist tradition, Russell does feel this need, and from early on in his philosophical journey his ambition appears to be to combine the certainty that can be delivered by logical structure with the certainty that can be achieved through immediate sensory experience: mathematical logic would supply the structure of knowledge, its broad characteristics, while empirical experience would supply its content.

The combination of these two elements – empiricism and logicism – results in Russell's logical atomism, a theory that is at once about language and about reality. Take a word like red, Russell suggests. It is not capable of being analysed into something simpler than itself and for this reason is described as a simple symbol. Now propositions that attribute such a property as red to an object – for example, 'This is red' – state simple facts about the world, what Russell calls atomic facts; and for this reason such propositions are known as atomic propositions. An atomic proposition is true or false depending on its correspondence with the atomic fact: for every fact, two propositions are always possible, the one true and the other false. Not all propositions are atomic, of course. Some are molecular, such as those that link propositions together – 'This is red and that is green.' What makes such molecular propositions true or false is not their correspondence with some molecular facts – there are no such facts – but the truth or falsity of two distinct atomic propositions, 'This is red' and 'That is green.' In other words, molecular propositions are truth functions of atomic propositions; their truth depends on the truth of the atomic propositions of which they are composed, into which they can be analysed. In language, there exist only atomic and molecular propositions; in reality, there exist only atomic facts.

Logical atomism can thus be seen to be born of a marriage between old-fashioned empiricism and the new wizardry of logic, imported from the formidable *Principia Mathematica*. The logic is seen as coming to the rescue of empiricism, of getting rid of some of its well-known problems and foibles. For example, logic deals in propositions and so helps get rid of the old empiricist habit of speaking of sense data and ideas as isolated individual entities. A word or idea on its own is not a complete thought and cannot be considered true or false, but a proposition is a complete thought and comes under the rubric of truth or falsity: for this reason it is preferable to locate the language of sense data within propositions. Again, old-fashioned empiricism had thought it necessary to account for the meaning of every single word by means of a corresponding entity in the world. So Hume, for example, had attempted to explain the meaning of a conditional like 'if' by reference to feelings of hesitation that we sometimes

13 Ibid., 286.

experience. Russell makes it clear that words like 'if,' 'and,' 'but,' 'therefore,' and so on are formal, belonging to the logical form of propositions; and hence it is unnecessary for their meaning to be derived from something in the world.

Despite these undoubted improvements, the marriage between empiricism and the new logicism was not trouble free. One source of difficulty is that the epistemological ultimates of empiricism are particulars, the objects of smelling, touching, tasting, seeing, hearing, which are always particular in nature, whereas the ultimate axioms or principles of logic are general. Russell for a time was willing to accept that for general propositions to be true there must be corresponding general facts. Similarly, for a time he entertained the notion of negative facts in order to make sense of the possible truth of negative propositions.[14] But while Russell, unlike Wittgenstein and Moore, had scant respect for common sense, he did have what he called 'a vivid sense of reality,' and this sense, allied to the growing influence of empiricism on his thinking, began to wear down his logician's tolerance of such esoteric entities.

The Nature of Judgment

What is more, under the influence of Wittgenstein, it becomes clear to Russell that not all complex propositions are reducible to atomic propositions in the manner he envisaged. As we have seen, Russell held that the truth of a proposition depends on its correspondence with the fact that makes it true. A true proposition corresponds with the fact, a false proposition fails to correspond with the fact.[15] So the relationship between propositions and facts is dual, since about every fact two propositions are always possible, one true and the other false. By contrast, the relation between a name and that which it denotes is singular:[16] for example, the word 'red' gets its meaning from the encounter with a particular sense datum. 'Perceiving is a relation between the person perceiving and the thing perceived.'[17] For this reason perception can never be in error.

Now it may be possible (Russell continues) to argue that some judgments are based entirely on a single perception – such as the knife being to the left of the book – in which case they are true.[18] But other judgments where

14 G.J. Warnock, *English Philosophy since 1900* (Oxford University Press, 1969), 28–9.
15 B. Russell, 'On the Nature of Truth and Falsehood,' in *Philosophical Essays*, 156; Pears, *Bertrand Russell*, 203–4.
16 Pears, ibid.
17 B. Russell, 'On the Nature of Truth and Falsehood,' 150.
18 Ibid.

the relationship between the entities is not spatial cannot be reduced to perception in this way. For example, he argues, the judgment that A loves B requires a relationship of the person judging to A and to love and to B. But it cannot be a relationship to these three elements in any order or separately but only to love as proceeding from A to B. What Russell is saying here is that in judgment the various constituents of the judgment are put together in a very precise way. The relationship between A and B is posited as a whole, as a unit: it cannot be broken down into its constituents, it cannot be analysed further. Now this is a fairly major admission, for knowledge by acquaintance yields only knowledge of things separately or in spatial relationships. This amounts to an admission by Russell, and it is highly significant, that the person judging is doing something *additional* to recording perceptions of what is 'out there now,' that judgments amount to more than factual records of Humean gazing. As Russell himself expresses it at the end of his essay, 'On the Nature of Truth and Falsehood':

> We see that ... truth and falsehood are primarily properties of judgments, and therefore there would be no truth or falsehood if there were no minds. Nevertheless, the truth or falsehood of a given judgment does not depend on the person making it ..., since the 'corresponding' complex, upon which its truth or falsehood depends, does not contain the person judging as a constituent ... Thus the mixture of dependence upon mind and independence of mind, which we noticed as a characteristic of truth, is fully preserved by our theory.[19]

In this passage, Russell's reflections on the nature of judgment are beginning to take him away from pure empiricism towards a consideration of mind, of the subject, and of the unitary nature of judgment. Moreover, what Russell says about the mixture of dependence on mind and independence of mind, as a characteristic of truth, is clearly akin to Lonergan's account of knowledge, where knowledge is arrived at in cognitional judgment, the product of mind, but because the judgment is affirmed as true on the basis of 'fit' between the data and the suggested meaning, it can be detached from the subject who affirms it and stand on its own. Who knows what might have happened if Russell had pursued that line of inquiry? It might have led him towards a deeper consideration of understanding and knowing and of the role of the mind, and of the subject, in these activities. But Russell was not to pursue this line of inquiry. Nevertheless, consideration of the nature of judgment as well as the other difficulties he encoun-

19 Ibid., 158.

tered led Russell eventually to abandon logical atomism and to explore how behaviourism might account for the unity and pattern we discern in the world and in ourselves.

It was through conversations with Wittgenstein that Russell eventually came to the realization that his atomistic theory of judgment could not account for the unity of certain propositions. This realization came as a terrible blow to his philosophical self-confidence, causing him to put aside the ambitious book he was working on at the time (1913), and even to believe that he could never again do fundamental work in philosophy. His impulse to work was shattered.[20] Wittgenstein's criticisms stayed with him for a long time, and we find him as late as 1916 recording that 'Wittgenstein's criticism gave me a sense of failure.' In the light of this shattering upheaval in Russell's philosophical project, it is not surprising that a few years later his philosophical explorations took a different direction. More exactly, he was inclined to believe that he could attain his original objective by a different route – that he had found in behaviourism the mechanism that would allow him to reconcile phenomenalism with physicalism.

The Theory of Definite Descriptions

Before moving on to the behaviourist turn in Russell's philosophy, however, it is necessary to say something about the Theory of Definite Descriptions, since that is a feature of his earlier philosophy that remains powerful in analytic philosophy to this day. Logical atomism has been abandoned, but the position established by the theory of descriptions still remains in force. Besides, the Theory of Definite Descriptions brings out well the impulse towards objectivity that is common to both empiricism and Lonergan's critical realism. Empiricism, as we have seen, seeks to safeguard the objectivity of knowledge by insisting on the role played by the object in the establishment of meaning. So words in this theory derive their meaning from that which they are about, from the objects they denote. Lonergan is also keen to establish the objectivity of the meaning of words and of propositions, but, as we shall see, he does this by introducing the active involvement of the subject in a way alien to empiricism, yet without which empiricism (I shall argue) is doomed to fail in its efforts to achieve the objectivity it seeks to establish.

The ontology that Russell initially takes over from Moore and that he entertains in *Principia Mathematica* is that every word has a meaning corresponding to it and for every meaning there is a corresponding entity.[21]

---

20 Monk, *Bertrand Russell: The Spirit of Solitude,* 296–301.
21 Passmore, *One Hundred Years of Philosophy,* 226.

Under the influence of Meinong, Russell is prepared to accept the implications of this viewpoint by populating the philosophical world with entities corresponding to such terms as 'something,' 'no one,' and 'everything,' as well as non-existent entities such as 'the golden mountain' or 'the King of France.' However, his 'vivid sense of reality,' already referred to, gradually erodes his ability to tolerate such entities, and he devises a theory that shows that there is no need to retain them in order for words and propositions to be considered meaningful. This is the Theory of Definite Descriptions, for which Russell the philosopher is probably most celebrated. It is necessary to give a fairly detailed account of this theory, not merely because Russell's reputation is so closely bound up with it, but because it has created a way of talking philosophically, a mode of philosophical discourse, that followers of Lonergan find difficult to follow. Reciprocally, for exactly the same reason, Lonergan's way of talking about knowing and the meaning of words is unintelligible to analytic philosophers.

Russell's Theory of Definite Descriptions purports to show that names or noun phrases, which appear to denote entities and get their meaning from their reference, are in fact disguised descriptions. 'Common words, even proper names, are usually really descriptions. That is to say, the thought in the mind of a person using a proper name correctly can generally only be expressed explicitly if we replace the proper name by a description.'[22] Unlike names, descriptions are understood without the need for reference, without the need for denotation. This is the foundation of Russell's famous distinction between knowledge by description and knowledge by acquaintance, where the latter means direct sensory contact. Knowledge by description has no need for such direct sensory contact. Explaining how the translation from an apparent name to a description takes place, Russell considers the example of Sir Walter Scott, who wrote the novel *Waverley*. One reason why this example attracted Russell is because for some time the true identity of the author of *Waverley* was unknown: hence people identified the person who wrote the book, which was immensely popular in its day, simply as 'The author of *Waverley*.'

Russell claims that the statement 'Scott wrote *Waverley*,' where the proper name 'Scott' would appear to denote a particular individual and to make no sense unless it did so denote, in fact can be perfectly well translated into the statement 'One and only one man wrote *Waverley*, and that man was Scott.' In this version, the name 'Scott' has been replaced by the description 'One and only one man wrote *Waverley*' and, according to Russell, existence is being asserted in that proposition of that description. However, the meaning of the description is not dependent on the actual existence of

22 B. Russell, 'Knowledge by Acquaintance,' in *Mysticism and Logic*, 203.

the 'One and only one man' who 'wrote *Waverley*' because the meaning of such a sentence – unlike the meaning of a logically proper name – is distinct from its reference. It is the logical form of propositional sentences that gives them their meaning; whether or not the entities referred to in them exist is of no consequence to their meaning. Logic is prior to experience and for this reason the meaning of propositions can be grasped without reference to experience. The truth of the proposition is another matter, because the truth will depend on verifying or guaranteeing by experience the entities referred to.[23] So in the proposition 'One and only one man wrote *Waverley*,' the meaning of the statement is clear; existence is simply asserted and is not a requirement of meaning; the actual existence of the author of *Waverley* will depend on experience; the proposition could be wrong. As for the additional statement 'and that man was Scott,' the word 'was' is not an instance of the verb *to be* meaning *exists*, but rather of the verb *to be* signifying *identity*. The meaning of the demonstrative, 'that,' is its referential function; it has no meaning outside its referential use, its pointing to the putative entity named Scott. Existence is not being asserted of Scott, simply identity with the description preceding 'and that man.'

The point can be brought out even more forcefully by casting the statement 'Scott wrote *Waverley*' in the form of a propositional function, for unlike propositions, propositional functions cannot be true or false. So to recast the statement in the form of a propositional function is to underline its meaning as independent of the existence of any of its elements. Translated into a propositional function, the statement becomes 'X wrote *Waverley*, and for all values of X, X is C and C is Scott.' From this it is perfectly possible to work out that Scott wrote *Waverley*, but it is also clear that no claim of existence is being made on behalf of any of the propositional function's elements. For the propositional function to be translated into a proposition, which will for that reason be either true or false, and hence entail some notion of existence, the variables or argument places – the Xs and Cs, and so on – are replaced by nouns or proper names. The usefulness of this procedure is more apparent when dealing with non-existent entities such as 'the golden mountain.' For example, for the statement 'The golden mountain does not exist' to be considered meaningful does not require us to entertain the notion that a non-existent entity (the golden mountain) exists. This is so because the statement can be recast in the form of a propositional function: 'There is no entity C such that "X is golden and mountainous" is true when X is C, but not otherwise.'

Explanation of Russell's Theory of Descriptions is apt to be rather mind-boggling both because of its technical nature and because critical realists, since they have never equated meaning with reference in the empiricist way, cannot help wondering what all the fuss is about. Propositional functions can certainly play a useful role in logic – a critical realist might concede – because segmenting propositions, breaking them into their component parts, can often overcome confusions over meaning. For example, to say that 'The president of the United States is a woman called Clinton' is false (at least at the time of writing), but it cannot be assumed from its falsity that the president of the United States is not called Clinton. This is because the statement comprises several segments or parts, as becomes clear if we were to say, 'One and only one person is the president of the United States and that person is a woman and that person is called Clinton'; such segmentation allows us to pinpoint exactly where the falsity lies. But to grasp why the Theory of Descriptions has been greeted as a great philosophical triumph it is necessary to see how it allowed Russell and his followers to escape from a real philosophical difficulty by providing a device for separating sense and reference. In his *History of Western Philosophy*, Russell concludes his account of the theory by saying in his modest way, 'This clears up two millennia of muddle-headedness about "existence," beginning with Plato's *Theaetetus*.'[24] The theory has also been seen as epoch-making because it suggests that the logical structure of a sentence might be quite different from its surface structure or grammatical structure.[25] This view was to prove influential in subsequent philosophy, not least in the early work of Wittgenstein, who later reacted strongly against it.

For critical realists, Russell's Theory of Descriptions is perhaps most important because it introduces the notion that existence is the property of propositions. The notions of 'existent' and 'non-existent' derive from the notions of 'true' and 'false,' and these apply only to propositions.[26] Now critical realists would have no argument with the notion that existence and non-existence are known through the truth or falsity of propositions; they would not, however, draw from this the conclusion that existence is a property of propositions. They would instead claim that existence quite clearly is a property of the entities affirmed in propositions. The claim that existence is a property of propositions reinforces the view that philosophy is primarily a linguistic activity and ushers in a mode of discourse, a way of speaking of objects and their existence, that critical realists find strange. According to descriptivism, existence is something added to a concept

24 B. Russell, *History of Western Philosophy* (1946; Unwin University Books, 1961), 785.

25 Anthony O'Hear, *What Philosophy Is* (Penguin 1985), 170.

26 B. Russell, 'The Relation of Sense Data to Physics,' in *Mysticism and Logic*, 203.

when the concept is seen to 'have application' in experience. The concept is said to be 'satisfied,' to 'apply,' to be 'instantiated,' or to 'touch down' in sensory experience.

From this notion Quine draws his formulation 'To be is to be the value of a variable.'[27] For a concept to be satisfied, certain conditions have to be met: if these conditions are met, the concept is said to be satisfied; if they are not met, the concept is not satisfied. The attribution of existence depends on satisfaction by experiential encounter. Epistemology moves away from accounts of how we come to know something and becomes preoccupied instead with theories of truth and truth-conditions. We can see, then, how Russell's Theory of Descriptions is the father of a very potent form of conceptualism, which takes some extreme forms, such as the denial of the distinction between synthetic and analytic propositions in the hands of Quine. In turn, Rorty uses this denial to repudiate the notion that knowledge and truth are about how the inquiring subject relates to an object and to attempt to replace it with his notion of 'epistemological behaviourism.' (See chapter 7.) These developments should convince critical realists of the importance of Russell's theory in introducing a decisive turning point in the history of philosophy.

Yet if critical realists might learn from the theory of descriptions why analysts speak as they do, members of the analytical tradition might be interested in the critical realists' lack of enthusiasm for Russell's theory. Critical realists have found the Theory of Descriptions rather odd because it goes to rather amazing lengths to establish a distinction they believe can be established with much greater economy.[28] Russell's theory was called the Theory of *Definite* Descriptions because it purported to show how a general or universal descriptor, such as man or author, could pick out a unique individual, Scott. Some critics of the theory, including several within the ranks of analytic philosophy itself, have diagnosed the weakness of Russell's theory to lie in the inability of a description to pick out an individual entity, the object we bump up against with out senses. Personally, I wonder if some of the persuasive power of Russell's argument lies in the examples he chooses to illustrate his theory: Sir Walter Scott, Napoleon, the King of France, Julius Caesar, Bismarck – these are all unique historical personages, even when, like the King of France, they do not exist. Some of them are already well established in the public mind

---

27 W.V. Quine, *From a Logical Point of View* (Harper and Row, 1963), 15.
28 See Andrew Beards, 'On Knowing and Naming,' *Method: Journal of Lonergan Studies* 8 (October 1990). I am indebted to this article in this part of my argument, though I should point out that the presentation, with any attendant failings, is my own.

along with certain specific descriptive tags, such as 'assassinated on the Ides of March' or 'crossed the Rubicon' in the case of Julius Caesar. Brief references to the Ides of March or crossing the Rubicon, used by Russell as examples, conjure up for most of us the reference to the individual Julius Caesar. But more mundane persons do not enjoy such uniqueness, and descriptivism may be less persuasive when we attempt to apply it to the man or woman in the street.

For example, like any individual, I may be known under a variety of descriptions. I could correctly be identified as 'the author of articles on Lonergan's philosophy' or 'the father of Fiona and Matthew' or 'a supporter of Glasgow Celtic Football Club.' The question is how any one of these descriptions, or all of them together, could serve to pick me out as an existing individual. If we make a distinction between meaning and reference, and that is the intended outcome of the theory, how is rigorous identification or designation obtained by means of meaning alone? Quite possibly, another individual could be the author of articles on Lonergan's philosophy, the father of a Fiona and a Matthew and a Glasgow Celtic supporter. In other words, designation is not rigorously entailed in description. A blunter way of putting this objection is to ask, if we make a distinction between meaning and reference, can we then turn round and say that reference is somehow achieved by meaning alone?

If the ability of descriptions to act as 'rigid designators' of existing individuals remains a moot point, even among analytic philosophers,[29] a prior question arises concerning the legitimacy of Russell's distinction between meaning and reference, between description and naming. Names do seem intended to pick out individuals; reference seems to be an indispensable part of their function. But it is difficult to see how names alone, stripped of all descriptive content or association, can achieve their role of designating particular individuals with particular personal histories. There are, after all, many individuals with the same name. Secure or 'rigid' identification, it would appear, is achieved by combining descriptive content with reference. To refer simply to 'John Smith' is not to designate anyone in particular, but to speak of 'John Smith, the Scottish leader of the British Labour Party in opposition in the 1990s, who died suddenly of a heart attack and was succeeded by Tony Blair' – that combination of naming and description does designate a particular person without ambiguity.

Designating a particular individual by combining naming with description would seem to correspond with the reality of human practice. The use of a bare noun or name to identify a particular entity is relatively rare and not particularly informative: we do not usually say, 'It is a ship,' but rather

29 O'Hear, *What Philosophy Is*, 160f.

'It is a battleship'; rather than say, 'It is a boat,' we say, 'It is a fishing boat'; it is less precise to say, 'He is an inspector' than to say, 'He is a school inspector.' Descriptive content cannot be easily detached from naming and reference, since the description helps to narrow down the range of possible references by eliminating whole classes of ships or boats or inspectors. Description, in other words, has an important referential function. But Russell's distinction does not allow reference and meaning to be combined in this way.[30]

By maintaining a strict distinction between meaning and denotation, Russell deprives denotation of any meaning other than its use for the purpose of referring; strictly speaking, denotation can only truly be performed by demonstratives like 'this' or 'that' whose meaning or sense is reduced to their referential use.[31] It is for this reason that demonstratives are the only true logically proper names, other proper names being derivative from them. Meaning stands apart from existence because existence adds nothing to descriptions other than that they are satisfied or instantiated. Satisfaction takes the form of applying the concept to a particular; the particular instantiates the general concept: this explains why the demonstrative 'this' is presented by descriptivism as if it occurred at the end of inquiry, at the point of identification.

The reason why this long exposition strikes critical realists as a rather tortuous way of resolving a problem – or attempting to resolve it – is that the problem does not arise in critical realism. Critical realism contends that we live in the here and now and that we first ask questions about particulars: 'What is that?' 'How often does this occur?' 'Why does this happen?' Questions are asked about particulars: 'thisness' is built in from the start. The word 'this' occurs more typically at the beginning than at the end of inquiry, while we are still in ignorance, since at this point we have no other way of indicating what we are referring to. (Russell was right: 'this' has no descriptive content because the data identified by 'this' or 'these' are not yet meaningful.) In the stream of individual data we ask, 'What is this?' If inquiry is successful, then despite the spatial and temporal multiplicity of the data there is grasped an intelligible unity, a single whole, an identity that unites what in space is here and there and what in time is then and

30 I accept that in stating the position in this way I am cutting through the complex reasoning provided by Russell on this topic – see his paper 'On Denoting' in *Logic and Knowledge*, ed. R.C. Marsh (George Allen and Unwin, 1956) – but Russell's exact position is notoriously hard to pin down, and the ultimate point of my argument in this section is to contrast two distinct ways of thinking about being or existence.

31 B. Russell, 'Knowledge by Acquaintance,' in *Mysticism and Logic*, 212, 214–16; *Human Knowledge* (1948; Routledge, 1992), 100–1.

now.[32] Only when we have grasped the idea in the particular data can we exploit its potential for generalization and form a concept. At the end of the process we do not normally say 'this,' but rather fill in the initial 'this' by saying, 'It is an X.' The judgment that it is an X is not a mindless reference or pointing to the representations of sense, but the full act of meaning that takes place when first insight has been confirmed as correct: being and meaning are coextensive, not mutually exclusive. Reference, in Lonergan's analysis, takes place at two points: first of all at the point of questioning, when we ask, 'What is this?' Second, at the point of judgment, when we provide an answer to the question and say, 'It' (meaning 'this') 'is an X.' By the time 'It' is identified or referred to at the point of judgment, it is full of meaning. Reference and meaning go together.

Existence is not the application of a concept to a set of particulars; rather the particulars are what have been given to me from the outset, at the empirical level of consciousness; meaning takes place at the second level, and is provided by the subject who is making the inquiry; and judgment, which takes place at the third level of consciousness, is the full term or end point of meaning. Rather than a mindless act of application, judgment is full of meaning, since it confirms that understanding is correct: the affirmation that the meaning is true at one and the same time affirms that the entity exists. The coherence and correspondence theories of truth come together in Lonergan's epistemology: in judgment, meaning is affirmed as true and reference made together, at once.

We can now see that the model of knowledge by description that Russell provides is almost an exact inversion of the model of knowledge provided by Lonergan. With Russell most knowledge is knowledge by description and begins with a general concept; with Lonergan it begins with a question and the question is about particulars. With Russell knowledge moves from the general to the particular; with Lonergan it moves from the particular to the general and then back to the particular. Russell's theory of definite descriptions is an attempt to get over the problems deriving from the assumption that names get their meaning from that which they are about. Now the reason why Lonergan is able to maintain that meaning and reference are one and the same and yet does not incur the problems we saw Russell incurring when he maintained something similar – the apparent existence of non-existent entities like 'golden mountains' and the like – is that Lonergan does not envisage meaning as transferring directly from sense data to words. For Lonergan, the data are not the source of meaning; meaning is supplied by the subject who inquires into the data. The intervention of the subject breaks the vicious circle of object-meaning/meaning-

32 B. Lonergan, *Collection* (Darton, Longman & Todd, 1968), 161.

object, and for this reason there are never any grounds for claiming that because something is meaningful it must exist, in some form or other: Meinong presents no temptation to Lonergan. Lonergan can nevertheless affirm that words get their meaning from what they are about – thereby safeguarding one of empiricism's most cherished doctrines – because to claim that meaning is true is to claim that the meaning supplied by the inquirer fits the data. The data have their purchase on meaning at the point of verification, because meaning is proposed as the meaning of these data. Lonergan's theory of cognition escapes the charge of subjectivism, which empiricism is also concerned to avoid, because for the meaning to be considered true it has to fulfil the conditions that show that it truly fits the data. These conditions are imposed by the need, the exigence, to fit the data; as such, they establish a standard quite independent of the subject; and they thereby establish knowing as objective.

The Theory of Definite Descriptions illustrates an intriguing characteristic of Russell's general approach to philosophy. One of Russell's problems as a philosopher is his fertile inventiveness. Whenever Russell encounters a problem in philosophy, rather than revise his position he is more inclined to invent theories or distinctions or axioms to overcome the difficulty. We have seen this in his theory of meaning and the Theory of Definite Descriptions. It occurs repeatedly over his philosophical career. For example, when he encounters the major problem that has become known as 'Russell's Paradox,' we find him importing the Theory of Types into his logical system in order to overcome the problems associated with his notion of class. (See the next chapter.) This tendency to come up with new axioms or theories whenever his position comes under attack looks out of place in a philosopher who began by considering inference an insecure basis for the findings of philosophy. Russell's prolific inventiveness might be considered a weakness, since it shores up his somewhat aristocratic confidence that whatever problems might surround his initial hunches or guesses, ingenuity or mental agility will always devise a way through, and the initial hunches themselves need not be subjected to radical scrutiny.

Behaviourism, Introspection, and Psychologism

It would be neither possible nor desirable to offer a complete account of Russell's philosophy in the second part of his career, but some mention must be made of his work *The Analysis of Mind*, not only because it marks an important milestone in the history of twentieth-century English-language philosophy, but also because it gives rise to, defends, and exemplifies a notion of introspection that has brought introspection into disrepute. This poor reputation of introspection is thoroughly deserved in the case of

Russell; but it has told heavily against other philosophers who have made use of introspection, such as Lonergan, although Lonergan's notion of introspection bears little comparison with Russell's.[33]

Published in 1921, *The Analysis of Mind* marks the behaviourist turn in Russell's philosophy, and might be regarded as the forerunner of Gilbert Ryle's similarly named *The Concept of Mind*, notwithstanding the heavy Wittgensteinian influence in Ryle's book. But I believe Russell's work most vividly foreshadows Richard Rorty's *Philosophy and the Mirror of Nature*, and so it anticipates the transfer of leadership in analytic philosophy from England to the United States. The innovative influences in Russell's book are mainly American: William James, John Dewey, John B Watson – the father of psychological behaviourism – and others. Indeed, Watson read the manuscript and made 'many valuable suggestions.'[34] Russell's ambition in the book is not so much to promote behaviourism as such, as to promote a certain rapprochement between psychology and physics, between mind and matter. He hopes to have found an answer to the question that dogged him all his philosophical life – and to which he never did find a satisfactory answer – namely, what is the relation between the data of sense and the scientific account of reality?

In his earlier period, Russell had asked whether the data of sense were mental or physical and had answered that they were physical.[35] The question then arose of how the data of sense (particular patches of colour, particular sounds, particular tastes, and so forth) can be shown to relate to the basic entities of science such as molecules, atoms, electrons, and corpuscles. As Russell noted, these entities have no colour, no taste, and no smell.[36] How, then, can the data of sense account for physics? Russell raised the question, but in his earlier period he could find no answer. In *The Analysis of Mind*, he hopes he may have found the answer. He is attracted by William James's attack on consciousness, which is in reality an attack on the duality of consciousness and matter, and by the American realists' notion that there is some 'neutral stuff' anterior to both mind and matter from which both are composed.[37] Russell hopes such a stuff may be found in his basic datum, namely sensation, for sensations – what is heard and seen –

33 For an insight into Lonergan's notion of introspection, see *Understanding and Being*, vol. 5 of the Collected Works (University of Toronto Press, 1990), 238–9.
34 Russell, *The Analysis of Mind*, 6.
35 B. Russell, 'The Existence of Matter,' in *The Problems of Philosophy* (1910; Oxford University Press, 1967), 9–10; 'The Ultimate Constituents of Matter,' in *Mysticism and Logic*, 122, 144.
36 'The Ultimate Constituents of Matter,' 139–40.
37 *The Analysis of Mind*, 25.

belong equally to psychology and physics. By analysing mind in terms of sensation, Russell is hopeful of moving some way towards the solution of how sense-data can explain the world of matter. It would be fair to say, however, that what has endured from Russell's book has not been any solution to this problem but the behaviouristic turn he gave philosophy. The end has not been achieved, but the means have endured.

The end has been sought, however, by several philosophers in the analytical tradition. Not only Russell, but also Ayer and, to some extent, Quine have attempted the experiment of translating language about physical objects into language about sense-data, of reconciling phenomenalism with physicalism. In this sense, Ayer and Quine are the inheritors of a long-standing ambition entertained by Russell, who as early as 1912 wrote to Ottoline Morrell that he believed he had the makings of a really 'big book' requiring 'a combination of physics, psychology and mathematical logic.' At the time, the project of combining these three strands of thinking was conceived as a long-term project that might take ten years to complete. As it was, Russell's earlier period is dominated by his attempt to combine the strands of physics and mathematical logic; in his later period he attempts to combine physics and psychology. Although the projects of his earlier period and of his later period appear to be quite separate and different, in fact they were originally conceived as part of a single larger scheme or enterprise in which all three strands came together. In view of this, Russell's turning to psychology in his later period is less surprising than at first may appear.

From Lonergan's standpoint, *The Analysis of Mind* marks Russell's decisive turning away from the desirability of exploring the role of the subject in knowing that was opened up briefly by his focus on propositions and his analysis of judgment, where it became clear that judgment was more than Humean gazing at the world out there, and more than the mere passive reception of sensory stimuli and the resulting ideas or copies. Part of Russell's motivation in focusing on the proposition was that propositions liberated his theory of knowledge from the tyranny of the moment, imposed on any theory that reduces knowing to perceiving.[38] Propositions seem to show how beliefs can endure beyond the moment of perception. Now Lonergan would be quite happy with this, seeing the act of understanding as moving the subject beyond the 'now' of perception through the grasp of intelligible unities free of the accidental features of time and place. Unlike the fleetingness of sensory perception, the product of understanding endures, as do the judgments based on understanding, which are expressed in propositional form. Russell's philosophy, however, does not

38 Pears, *Bertrand Russell*, 195f.

take such a Lonerganian turn. Instead, Russell seeks to explain the enduring quality of propositions by the creation of habits, of conditioned reflexes, of expectation-beliefs, and the like. Behaviourism explains the durability of beliefs, thus overcoming the tyranny of the immediate and the momentary that bedevils perceptionism.

Rather than an exploration of the subject, *The Analysis of Mind* gives us the opposite. Russell dispenses with the self or the 'I' of propositions. The act of thinking that I am supposed to perform, as when I say, 'I think so-and-so,' cannot be observed and is not logically deducible from what can be observed.[39] Hence, Russell discards both the act and the 'I' that is supposed to be the subject of the act. In *Outline of Philosophy*, published in 1927, where Russell provides further support for the behaviourist position expounded in *Analysis*, he uses the Humean argument against the self, claiming that what is grasped in introspection is simply a succession of images and accompanying feelings.[40] On behaviourist grounds, terms like 'mind' and 'thought' are also nothing more than inferences and, as such, cannot be considered parts of the real.[41] And consciousness, while not discarded completely, is reduced to 'an unimportant outcome of linguistic habit.'[42] Having disposed of the subject in this fashion, Russell has set the stage for that elimination of the subject for which analytic philosophy is notorious. At one point Russell says that grammatical forms like 'I think' or 'You think' are misleading, and it would be better to say, 'It thinks in me' or 'There is a thought in me,' rather like 'It rains here.'[43]

At the outset of *The Analysis of Mind* Russell expressed the wish of creating a rapprochement between psychology and physics, mind and matter. Behaviourism may well have seemed like a way round the tension he undoubtedly experienced between his own phenomenalism and the orderly world ruled by scientific laws, which is predictable, and explainable in terms of cause and effect. Behaviourism clings to the Humean 'cement' of associationism, while at the same time it champions the scientific canon that only that which is capable of being observed can have any claim to be considered real. Russell clearly trusts behaviourism to show that the world of matter and of mind are made out of the same basic stuff that involves sensations, which are common to both matter and mind.[44] But no such neutral stuff emerges from his investigations. Far from assisting the scientific explanation of the world, behaviourism only supports the phenom-

39 *The Analysis of Mind*, 18.
40 *Outline of Philosophy*, 10.
41 *The Analysis of Mind*, 28–9.
42 Ibid., 40.
43 Ibid., 18.
44 Ibid., 121.

enalism of empiricism and the belief that the world is an orderly, predictable place. Behaviourism is not an explanation of the *world* in terms of
cause and effect or measurable correlations, but a theory of the *mind* that
purports to explain how the mind comes to believe that the world is
ordered and characterized by cause and effect. Behaviourism is essentially
compensatory. While it subscribes to the notion that all relations in the
material universe are contingent and accidental – 'one damn thing after
another' in space and in time – it also claims to show us why, through the
development of certain habits and associations, we tend to *think* of the
world as ordered and as consisting of relations that are in some way
significant. As for explaining the mind itself, associationism is the enemy of
logic, because it creates links that are purely contingent, and it has no way
of explaining relations of logical necessity or of rational compulsion. So in
respect both of how the world of matter works, as revealed by science, and
of how the mind operates, as revealed in logic, philosophical behaviourism
leaves much to be desired.

It is typical of Russell, however, that he refuses to go all the way with
behaviourism. This is what makes him so infuriatingly difficult to summarize. He rejects the notion that there is no awareness of awareness[45] and
takes Watson to task for his denial of images – Russell rightly argues that
Watson's denial is based on the dogma that introspection is not possible.[46]
On the contrary, Russell wishes to uphold the possibility of introspection
and to hold on to his basic empiricist belief that mind is built up of
sensations and the images they produce in us: 'I propose to argue that
thoughts, beliefs, desires, pleasures, pains and emotions are all built up out
of sensations and images alone.'[47] Note that while introspection is retained,
its scope is severely limited to the images and feelings that accompany
sensation. Great mathematician and logician though he is, nowhere in
Russell do we find any sign of introspective awareness of the force of logical
inference, or of logical necessity, the rational exigence, the grasp of the
unconditioned, the 'thud' of the logical 'must.' Nor do we find in Russell
any inkling of the dynamic, active character of thinking and problem
solving, of how we use the known to attack the unknown, of how we bring
with us our previously acquired learning and understanding to tackle the
problem at hand, of how we bring meaning to the task of making sense of
the data. There is none of that in Russell as he attempts to limit the scope of
introspection to the inner side of sensation.

Not surprisingly, given the rather rudimentary tools he allows himself,

45 Ibid., 115.
46 Ibid., 152.
47 Ibid., 121.

some of Russell's arguments in *The Analysis of Mind* are weak and some rather pathetic. By means of association he feebly accounts for the meaning of words by virtue of the ideas they call up.[48] He pathetically attempts to explain memory by the fading of images and by 'a feeling of pastness' that certain images carry with them.[49] Not only is the latter argument totally question-begging, it offends against some of the criticisms that Russell had levelled against introspection earlier in the book.[50]

Russell's and Lonergan's Uses and Notions of Introspection

In this section, I submit that introspection is in such bad philosophical odour not only because of the kind of criticisms that philosophers like Russell subject it to (pointing out that psychoanalysis has shown it to be fallible and that those who rely on it are easily led),[51] but also because of the palpable falsity of their arguments based on introspection. For example, it is difficult to agree with Russell that the meaning of words derives from the sensory associations – the images – they conjure up in the hearer. As Wittgenstein points out, there is no reason to believe that what I associate with my sensations or images will be the same as what you associate with yours: the sensations or images I associate with the word 'red,' for example, are private to me and hence there is no way of knowing, in such a theory of meaning, that what I mean by 'red' is the same as what you mean by 'red.' The very privacy of sensation and of the images sensation creates works against the argument that word meaning (or communication) could possibly be founded there. Russell's account of memory on the basis that some images carry with them a feeling of pastness is the type of argument that provides ammunition for those who wish to attack introspection as a source of reliable information.

So how does Lonergan's advocacy of introspection stand up to the criticisms that have been levelled against introspection as a reliable source of knowledge? Any convincing answer to this important question must be capable of showing that Lonergan's use of introspection is quite different from Russell's and other empiricists' use of introspection. What makes introspection vulnerable to attack is the link between introspection and privacy, and the instability introduced into meaning when it is considered to be a result of mere association. A convincing answer needs to be able to show that Lonergan's use of introspection is

---

48 Ibid., 191.
49 Ibid., 162–3.
50 Ibid., 122–3.
51 Ibid., 122.

not vulnerable on these grounds. This, I believe, can be argued success-fully in a series of steps.

First and foremost, introspection will be vulnerable to the same criticisms as the model of knowledge in which it stands. Consider. The knockdown argument against the empiricist model of knowing is that it is impossible to line up the proposed ideas on the one side, and the realities they are supposed to represent on the other side, and see how they compare. In the same way, it is impossible to hear someone's account of what they privately entertain or are privately aware of and claim that the account truly corre-sponds to the reality purportedly being reported. Accounts based on intro-spection understood as a kind of internal looking or perception suffer from exactly the same deficiency as accounts based on what Russell terms 'exter-nal perception': it is never possible for a third party to gain a vantage point from which the accuracy of the claimed representation or correspondence might be verified. In both cases, a 'superlook' capable of looking both at the looking and the looked at or at the reporting and the reported, would be needed, but such a superlook is not available. In other words, the introspection that is in such bad philosophical odour is the empiricist understanding of introspection, based on the notion that knowing is like perception. This is ironic, since the most common criticisms of introspec-tion come from within the empiricist-analytical tradition. I will argue that introspective knowledge based on the awareness that accompanies con-scious operations is free of the weaknesses of empiricist psychology. The irony attending the common criticism of introspection from within the empiricist-analytical camp is compounded by the historical fact that philo-sophical behaviourism is the child of the psychologism Hume depends on to explain the permanence of objects or causal relationships. Philosophical behaviourism would not have emerged within the history of Western phi-losophy had empiricism, with its methods of introspective analysis, not purported to have found in associationism the 'cement' holding the uni-verse together.

Second, it is important to grasp the limited role played by introspection in Lonergan's philosophy. It has no normative or constitutive function, and this distinguishes it from the role it plays in empiricism and behaviourism. It does not establish the meaning of terms or determine the truth of propositions. For this reason it cannot be considered foundational in any sense. It provides no logical or cognitional grounds for believing, for example, in the permanence of external objects or in a relationship of causality and the like. Its role is restricted to providing access to the process of cognition. Because this process, and the operations that make up the process, is conscious and not unconscious, it is experienced by us and, as experienced, it can become the object of understanding and judgment. In other words, Lonergan's use of introspection is not the *addition* of another layer or floor of mental operations on which the truth of other propositions rests, but rather a heightening of consciousness by means of which the subject focuses on her own subjective experience in the very same act by which she focuses on the object she is investigating. In order to uncover the pattern of cognition we do something that is not very common: as we work out a problem or conduct an investigation, we take note of the subjective operations we go through in order to achieve an accurate descriptive account of cognition; we can do that because these operations are conscious.

Third, the data we gain access to by performing operations that are conscious is the experiential awareness that accompanies sensory contact, the experiential awareness that accompanies understanding, and the experiential awareness that accompanies verification of our understanding. Now it may be that some philosophers would deny such awareness. In that case they should cease to talk about sensory contact, understanding, or verification, because if they lack all experiential awareness of these phenomena they cannot possibly know what they mean. If no form of introspective knowledge (understood in a non-empiricist sense) is possible, philosophers would have to stop talking about argument, proof, demonstration, evidence, thinking, reasoning, inference, logic, premises, conclusions, judgment, etc., etc. None of these terms would make the slightest sense to us if all we were capable of investigating was the world of matter, if our awareness were confined to sensory awareness, turned exclusively outwards to the material world 'out there.' These terms are not about sensibly observed matters of fact, and they are unintelligible outside the field of conscious intentional activity.

Fourth, Lonergan's defence of introspection is based on a model of knowing quite different from empiricism, so that introspection avoids the criticisms that can be ranged against empiricist introspection. If we are aware when we make sensory contact, if we are aware when we move from ignorance to understanding, if we are aware when we confirm that our understanding is true, then such awareness in each case can act as the conscious basis for *understanding* sensation-understanding-judgment and for achieving *judgments* about sensation-understanding-judgment. Critical realism does not claim that introspection is privileged in any way, or that it yields immediate and indubitable knowledge any more than external perception yields indubitable knowledge. Introspective knowledge is composed of experiencing, understanding, and judgment in just the same way as knowledge of the external world. And introspective knowledge is as capable of being expressed in propositions as knowledge based on external sensory experience. It is subject to exactly the same intersubjective checks and need for verification.

Let me put this part of the argument in a slightly different form. The privacy attending my awareness of awareness is real, but it is no less and no greater than the privacy attending my awareness of the objects of the senses, at the purely sensory level – the privacy attending my claim to see a boat or a plane, for example. Neither internal awareness nor external awareness is more or less private – both are equally private to the subject. In the same way, understanding of internal awareness is just as capable of being shared and communicated as understanding of external experience (experience of the data of the senses) – both are intelligible interpretations of the private acts of experiencing the data. And my judgments concerning the correctness or incorrectness of my understanding of internal experience are just as capable of being publicly demonstrated or verified as my judgments concerning the correctness of my understanding of the objects of the senses.

Like verification in natural science this verification takes place in an intersubjective context. It can be achieved by sharing with others the fruits of one's understanding of the processes of cognition and asking if they too experience similar processes when they come to know something. Verification in this form is equivalent to intersubjective agreement that such direct experience takes place. Verification can also take the form of studying how a third party goes about seeking verification of a hypothesis, as we saw in the example of the accident investigator in the first chapter; such 'third party' studies carry a lot of conviction because they are patently free of any special pleading that might be thought to accompany my accounts of my own mental operations. They enable us to focus on the various 'moves' made by the investigator on the basis of the available evidence and to grasp why some hypotheses and not others are considered to have merit.

Finally, verification can take the negative form of showing how those who claim not to perform the conscious and intentional operations inherent in generalized empirical method are constrained to appeal to the operations themselves as proof of their position. So someone denying that generalized empirical method is the basic method of inquiry would have to appeal to new data in support of their position, or to a new interpretation of the data, or to new methods of verification to support their interpretation. In other words, would-be revisers of generalized empirical method would have to appeal to the method in their efforts to revise it. As such they would be involved in a performative contradiction, a contradiction between what they were saying and what they were, in fact, doing. This form of verification is in fact the falsification of all attempts to deny the validity of generalized empirical method. As a universal method of falsification its powers of verification are very great, equivalent in logical force to the principle of non-contradiction.

Fifth, Lonergan's analysis of cognitional process is of a different order from the empiricist use of introspection – the psychologism favoured by Hume, Russell, and others, with all its difficulties. The point of Lonergan's exploration of intentional mental acts is to lay bare what is normative in human knowledge so that it becomes possible to move from a descriptive cognitional theory to a prescriptive epistemology, an epistemology that sets forth the norms and conditions for validating any kind of knowledge claim. In other words, it is not introspective analysis that is foundational but the cognitional process and the rational norms inherent in such a process, which introspective analysis is used to uncover.

In summary, Lonergan's notion of introspection does not derive from empiricist psychology that rests on the association of ideas and is open to the objections raised against psychological privacy. It relates to and upholds the durability of meaning and the permanence of truth not by appeal to associationism but by acknowledging the role of understanding and judgment. At the same time, as a method whose first step is rooted in the particularity and temporality of experience – the fact that experience is of this and that as well as of here and now – Lonergan's cognitional process does not possess the invariance of a logical system. Logical invariance is static since outputs are simply determined by inputs. Logic is employed usefully in systematizing what is known, and in working out its presuppositions and its implications, but it is not a vehicle of discovery, innovation, and change. The method of cognitional process, however, is historical and evolutionary, capable of moving and changing as new data are encountered or uncovered. It combines invariance of structure with the possibility of new data or new evidence, of new interpretations or readings of the data, of new judgments and findings, and hence it is able to explain the ongoing development and changes in human knowledge in a way that logical process on its own cannot do.

Bertrand Russell's philosophical history charts a movement – paradoxical and quixotic in its way – from a program of logicism to a program of behaviourism. The shift is paradoxical because logicism and behaviourism are philosophically at extreme odds with each other. It is significant that other philosophers who shared Russell's early reliance on logic, such as Frege and the early Wittgenstein, both repudiated psychologism and associationism. They refused to contaminate their use of logic with anything remotely resembling the privacy and arbitrariness of psychologism, because in their different ways they found in logic the qualities of invariance, impersonality, and normativity so conspicuously absent in psychologism. Russell never overcame his empiricist presuppositions; unlike Frege and Wittgenstein he sought certainty not in the impersonal laws of logic but in the immediacy of sensory perception. For a while he entertained the hope that mathematical logic might supply the pattern for the structure or the general characteristics of reality while empirical knowledge would supply the particular content, but since his empiricism and his logicism proved incompatible bedfellows, in the end this ambition foundered and we find him going over to philosophical behaviourism which, in so far as rules and norms for the explanation of meaning and the relations between terms are concerned, is located at the opposite end of the philosophical spectrum from his earlier logicism. While this was not Russell's final resting place, it is a significant development in the history of Anglo-American philosophy, since behaviourism is in many ways native to the United States, and its employment by a philosopher of Russell's stature signalled to American behaviourists, naturalists, and pragmatists – already in possession of the field, so to speak – the opportunity to gain philosophical ascendancy in the English-speaking world.

6

Descartes under Fire:
Lonergan and Wittgenstein

To move from Russell to Wittgenstein is to move from clutter to clarity. While the content of Wittgenstein's *Tractatus Logico-Philosophicus*[1] is not always transparently clear, it is immediately obvious that immense pains have been taken over its form. The argument advances by means of a series of propositions set out in a studied order aimed at helping the reader to come to a methodical understanding of the position being advocated. Each major proposition is numbered and is supported by several subsidiary propositions whose numbers indicate how they relate to the major proposition. The whole work is carefully shaped, with a beginning, a middle, and an end. Altogether it is a work of great purity and discipline, rather like a carefully wrought musical composition. And just as in music the focus is exclusively on the aural and the visual world, for example, is deliberately excluded, so in the *Tractatus* the world of matter, the physical universe, is excluded and the focus is kept relentlessly on logic and the logical structure of language. No examples drawn from the physical world are ever provided.

Although it was not always appreciated by some of the earlier commentators, there is no trace of empiricism in the *Tractatus*, no dependence on sensation as the conduit of the real, no place for associationism and the development of habits, conditioned reflexes, and the like. All that apparatus which Russell and many of his followers have imported into philosophy is conspicuous by its absence. Wittgenstein is no empiricist. He is very much his own man, but in so far as he does resemble any other philosopher, it is

---

1 *Tractatus Logico-Philosophicus* (1922), trans. D.F. Pears and B.F. McGuinness (Routledge, 1974). Cited in the text as TR.

Kant, concerned as he is with the limits of language, with the limits of what can be said, in both his earlier and his later works.

Sir Isaiah Berlin compared the fox and the hedgehog. The fox knows many things but the hedgehog knows only one thing, albeit it is one very big thing. If Russell is a fox then Wittgenstein is a hedgehog. Russell knows a great many things, his philosophical trail zig-zags hither and thither; at times he camouflages weak argument with vigorous assertion or goes over old territory with unexpected variations, and he is capable of holding onto contradictory positions without apparently adverting to the contradiction. Reading Russell is like overhearing a long, elaborate story told by a leading member of the club, a born raconteur who is not at all shy about putting the world to rights and, especially in his *History of Western Philosophy*, about dwelling on his own central role in the story. Wittgenstein, by contrast, is incapable of living with contradiction. Once he has convinced himself that his position is untenable, then it becomes imperative to change his position. Abrupt and abrasive, he hammers away at the problem that is preoccupying him, often apparently interrupting his lectures to interject in his strong Austrian accent comments like 'This is hellishly hard' or 'By God, this is tough.' The opposite of clubby, his tone is challenging, dogmatic, oracular. His relationship with Russell underwent a complete U-turn, starting off an ardent disciple, then for some time becoming himself the master, and finally ending with dislike and distrust and prolonged alienation.[2]

The estrangement was not merely personal but at its heart professional. Wittgenstein shared Russell's love of logic but disliked his ability to ignore logic when it suited him. Not very long before he died, at the age of sixty-one, in 1951, Wittgenstein said that Russell's books should be divided into two colours, one for his works of logic, which should be required reading for every philosopher; the other for his more popular philosophical writings, which should be burned! He also disliked Russell's polemic against religion and Christianity in particular, and as he grew older – though he was never old – he himself professed increasing fear of science and what it was doing to our lives, and a deepening interest in religion.

Tractatus Logico-Philosophicus

We can best understand what Wittgenstein is striving to achieve in the *Tractatus* – and later on in *Philosophical Investigations*,[3] for that matter – if we

---

2 See Ray Monk's excellent biography, *Ludwig Wittgenstein: The Duty of Genius* (Vintage, 1991).

3 *Philosophical Investigations*, trans. G.E.M. Anscombe (Basil Blackwell, 1953). Cited in the text as PI.

contrast his position at certain points with Russell's. For Russell, objects are concrete existents; but for Wittgenstein, 'Objects contain the possibility of all situations' (TR 2.014). Objects are defined as the possibilities present in states of affairs, as possible occurrences in states of affairs. It is through names correlated with objects that propositions make contact with reality – but not with actual existents, only with possible states of affairs. 'The propositions of logic describe the scaffolding of the world, or rather they represent it. They have no "subject matter." They presuppose that names have meaning and elementary propositions sense; and that is their connexion with the world' (TR 6.124). Meaning determines no facts in the world, but it determines the limits of the world, what is possible. Because Russell believes that meaning is conferred on words directly by the objects the words denote, he is tied to an identification of meaning and truth, the full consequences of which he has to take rather complicated steps to avoid. Wittgenstein never posits such an identification of meaning and truth. For when he talks about objects he is talking only about logical possibilities, and throughout the *Tractatus* he talks only about the logical preconditions that must obtain for language to picture reality. It is rather like the rules of chess – the rules do not make the actual moves; for that to happen real chess players are needed. But the rules do create the possibilities and impose the limits within which the game can be played.

For Russell, to know the meaning of the word is to know something about the world, because the meaning must always be objects that one is directly acquainted with. The objects are concrete existents, they can be observed. Wittgenstein, by contrast, denies that philosophers deal in facts. His position in the *Tractatus* is that a proposition, to be meaningful, must be either true or false: either 'p' or 'not-p.' He believes that names have reference but no sense; and that propositions have sense but no reference. Propositions convey a sense that is either confirmed or not confirmed by reality. To say that is simply to show that logical propositions are tautological; but tautologies are useful because they show the limits of what it is possible to say in this world, they reveal the essential structure of reality. We can begin to see, then, how the *Tractatus* is first and foremost a work of logic, in which logic is understood as providing the rules that determine both the possibilities and the limits of what can legitimately be said.

The essential skeleton of the *Tractatus* is as follows. First, on the side of language. A name or 'simple symbol' does not describe but designates or denotes that of which it is the name. 'A name means an object. The object is its meaning' (TR 3.203). An elementary proposition is 'a nexus, a concatenation, of names' (TR 4.22): it has a precise meaning. 'A proposition has one and only one complete analysis' (TR 3.25). The ultimate constituents of language must be elementary propositions and names. Hence, all meaningful language must ultimately be reducible to elementary propositions, which in turn consist of names in immediate combination (TR 4.221).

Second, on the side of reality. Reality must, in the last analysis, consist of 'simple objects': objects are 'simple' in the sense that the only way we can use language to refer to them is by naming them. So it is by analysis of language, and of names in particular, that Wittgenstein draws the conclusion that objects constitute 'the substance of the world' (TR 2.021), rather as Aristotle derived the notion of 'substance' from grammar. An atomic fact is a combination of objects (TR 2.01) and 'the world divides into facts' (TR 1.2). Facts are either atomic facts or molecular facts, the latter being capable of being analysed into the former. The world consists of facts or states of affairs, which in turn consist of objects (TR 2 and 2.01). And objects, as we have seen, are possibilities in states of affairs, capable of different combinations or configurations (TR 2.014 and 2.0121).

A clear isomorphism between language and reality can by now be discerned: name – object; elementary proposition – atomic fact or state of affairs; molecular proposition – molecular fact, and so on. But there is nothing here of real sounds conjuring up images, which in turn convey the meaning of the objects we associate with them, and so forth. For Russell, language is meaningful because it mirrors reality; for Wittgenstein, the world is meaningful because it mirrors language. For Russell, logic increasingly becomes the servant of empiricism; for Wittgenstein, logic is master, it determines what is and what is not possible. In many ways Wittgenstein's position is less fraught with difficulties than Russell's. For while Russell might claim that language mirrors reality, in fact he is no more free of language than is Wittgenstein, and has the embarrassment of having to explain how certain words or propositions with which he is inclined to agree can be said to mirror the world out there: I am thinking of words such as universals, or propositions that are counterfactual. In fact, we find Russell trying to square the world to suit these forms of language despite his avowed empiricism, though his empiricism does tend to create complications. The result is a not inconsiderable muddle. By contrast, Wittgenstein is clear and consistent.

In the *Tractatus*, the way in which a proposition pictures reality is by being correlated by a law of projection with the state of affairs that it represents (TR 4.0141). What this means is that a proposition is a sentence understood as referring to reality. It is so understood when the elements of the proposition are related by laws, or rules, of projection with the elements in reality to which they refer. Propositions picture reality (TR 4.01), but not in the sense of providing a pictorial representation of reality; rather in the sense that '[p]ictorial form is the possibility that things are related to one another in the same way as the elements of the picture' (TR 2.151). They picture reality in the same way that written notes picture a piece of music or the phonetic alphabet pictures our speech (TR 4.011). A proposition is not meaningless if it is false – the proposition is an experiment and as such is meaningful. Whether it is true or untrue is only discovered by comparing it with reality. There is, then, in the *Tractatus* a clear distinction made between sense and reference, again avoiding some of the confusion we find in the early Russell.

This is just about the minimum of what can be said about the *Tractatus* if we are to understand what it is about and catch something of its flavour. In this chapter I wish to show how it leads into the *Philosophical Investigations* and how the position on logic taken in the *Tractatus* and the position of the later Wittgenstein relate to Lonergan's position. It is worth pausing at this point to see the *Tractatus* as part of a trend in philosophy that has serious implications for Lonergan's philosophy. First, as can be seen, the *Tractatus* is not a theory of knowledge nor an account of how we come to know, but a system of semantics, a theory about how words mean. As Wittgenstein remarks, 'Psychology is no more closely related to philosophy than any other natural science. Theory of knowledge is the philosophy of psychology. Does not my study of sign-language correspond to the study of thought processes, which philosophers used to consider so essential to the philosophy of logic? Only in most cases they got entangled in unessential psychological investigations' (TR 4.1121). We have here a foretaste of Wittgenstein's critical remarks about thought processes in the *Investigations*, which I shall consider in a later section. While it is certainly true that Russell and others have made use of psychology in their investigations into knowing, there has developed a strong belief in some quarters that psychological approaches to knowledge are passé, outdated, an unfortunate hangover from the seventeenth and eighteenth centuries. The figure of Wittgenstein (as well as of Frege) stands behind that belief. The question that must be asked here is whether this applies to all psychology – *to the study of intentional acts, for example* – or merely to the philosophical use of empiricist psychology.

Second, the role of the subject in philosophy is considerably diminished in the *Tractatus*, not in the manner of empiricism or behaviourism with the claim that the subject, the 'I,' cannot be observed, but rather in the manner of Kant, with the claim that '[t]he subject does not belong to the world; rather, it is a limit of the world' (TR 5.632). Wittgenstein is a good deal less rash than empiricists tend to be; he does not deny the subject or the soul or the self or the right of psychology to study such an entity (TR 5.641), but he does exclude such a subject from philosophy. The only fact that brings the self into philosophy 'is the fact that "the world is my world"' (TR 5.641). The 'I' of philosophy is in fact compared to the 'eye' of vision, and the comment added that the eye of vision is not itself within the visual field and there is 'nothing in the visual field [that] allows you to infer that it is seen by an eye' (TR 5.633). So the subject or ego is literally marginalized, becoming in effect the limit to what can be known.

Wittgenstein in the *Tractatus* sees language and the world as two impersonal systems, the one picturing or mirroring the other by means of impersonal laws of projection. It is an impersonal mirror reflection to which logic holds the key: '*The limits of my language* mean the limits of my world. Logic pervades the world: the limits of the world are also its limits' (TR 5.6 and 5.61). But while language is seen as a sign system governed by an impersonal logic, logic also holds a deep reassurance for Wittgenstein, because it provides the clue to meaning and to the rules that govern meaning. Wittgenstein shows a very real hunger for rules – for norms – in both his major works. Referring to logic in the *Tractatus*, he says, 'Men have always had a presentiment that there must be a realm in which the answers to questions are symmetrically combined – a priori – to form a self-contained system. A realm subject to law: Simplex sigillum veri' (TR 5.4541). I cannot read those words – 'presentiment,' 'realm,' 'a priori,' 'a realm subject to law,' and finally 'simplex sigillum veri' – without sensing how much Wittgenstein himself has invested in them. They resonate with relief, a sigh of reassurance emanates from the Latin tag: 'The simple seal of the true, of the real.' Logic might appear impersonal, but Wittgenstein has much of his humanity tied up in it precisely because it is impersonally subject to *law*.

All of this – the exclusion of psychology from philosophy, the exclusion of the self or ego from philosophy, the impersonality of the logical system – is at one with the famous ending of the *Tractatus*. Wittgenstein takes what some have regarded as the heroically self-destructive course of saying at the end of the *Tractatus* that everything he has said is nonsense. The reason is that only empirical propositions say anything about the real world. But, as we have seen, the propositions of philosophy are not empirical, they are not informative of the real world. It follows that they say nothing. The best that Wittgenstein can claim for them is that they are elucidatory: they are like a ladder that should be thrown away once one has climbed up it and passed beyond (TR 6.54). The book finishes with the rather cryptic comment, 'What we cannot speak about we must pass over in silence' (TR 7). But in coming to this conclusion, Wittgenstein is simply being consistent with the position he has adopted throughout. It is not simply that, being non-empirical, philosophical propositions are not informative of reality. Because a psychological approach has been prohibited and because the subject has been excluded from any active role in philosophy, it is not possible to take an overview of how logic hooks onto the world. Logic, so to speak, is on its own. And that is the way Wittgenstein sees it. 'Logic must look after itself,' he says (TR 5.473). Again, he says that logic cannot reflect on itself, but manifests its laws from within itself (so to speak): 'Clearly the laws of logic cannot in their turn be subject to the laws of logic' (TR 6.123); and again, 'Propositions can represent the whole of reality, but they cannot represent what they must have in common with reality in order to be able to represent it – logical form' (TR 4.12). There is no vantage point beyond logic, he is saying, that allows one to survey logic and the validity of its operations. We do not rule logic but, to put the same point another way, we are ruled by logic (TR 6.124). To use a more Lonerganian way of speaking, we might say that for the early Wittgenstein logic is transcendental.

Thus, Wittgenstein's claim that what he has said hitherto is nonsense follows not merely from the nature of logic and its inability to tell us about the real world – a point frequently made – but follows also – a point less frequently made – from his view of logic, whereby no higher vantage point than logic can be achieved. If that is the case, then Wittgenstein's claim that he cannot say but he can show – a dictum he believed went to the heart of his philosophical position in both his earlier and his later work – becomes clear, for exactly the same claim is made on behalf of logic (TR 4.022, 4.1212, 6.122, 6.1221). Logic cannot claim on behalf of itself but it can – and does – show.

Logic

The foregoing exposition of Wittgenstein's position in the *Tractatus* should leave us in no doubt concerning the high esteem in which the early Wittgenstein held logic and the importance of logical form for understanding the hidden form of language and the reality that language gives us access to. We can also see how logic plays the role reserved in *Philosophical Investigations* for forms of life – it is at once the seat and the source of the norms to which language and life are subject. It is the centre of the rule of law, so to speak; its structure determines what can legitimately be said, and hence imposes limits on the knowledge I can claim of the world. Lonergan does not see logic playing quite such a central role in his philosophy. For Lonergan puts logic within method and sees it playing an indispensable role within the movement from ignorance to answer; but logic by itself is only a component in knowing and by no means the whole of knowing. Lonergan does not deny the logician his own rightful territory, the study of the forms of inference, of the relationships between words and sentences, and the like, but when he considers the structure of knowledge he maintains that logic is simply a component and not the whole works. Logic does have its own transcendence for Lonergan, as it does for Wittgenstein: the principle of contradiction, for example, is not something we can gainsay;

we do not determine it, so to speak, but it determines us and what we can legitimately say. Nevertheless, logic is not all that is transcendental; the whole of method, each of the operations of cognition and evaluation and also the links between the operations, have the same transcendental quality of determining the legitimacy and validity of our rational investigations.

Yet if Lonergan and Wittgenstein differ in their respective claims for logic, there is an intriguing area of mutual agreement, which they share at the expense of Russell, that turns out to be of considerable significance in understanding what each is up to. Wittgenstein's interlocutors in the *Tractatus* are Russell and Frege and Whitehead, fellow logicians, but especially Russell. At certain points Wittgenstein chooses to pick a bone with one of them, and most commonly it is with Russell. This happens when he calls in question Russell's theory of types (TR 6.123). Now Russell introduced his theory of types in response to a famous paradox, which has become known as Russell's Paradox. Noting that some classes have themselves as members and others do not, Russell adverts to 'the class of all classes that are not members of themselves.' Does this class have itself as a member? If it does, then it ceases to belong to the class of all classes that are not members of themselves. If it does not have itself as a member, then it clearly does belong to the class of all classes that do not have themselves as a member. Either way, the proposition is involved in a contradiction. Russell rightly sees the problem as arising from the relation of the whole to its parts, and the theory of types is designed to break up what he considers to be pseudo-totalities such as 'all propositions' into sets of propositions, each of which can be treated as a totality in its own right.[4] Here I do not wish to explain further Russell's theory of types, accounts of which can be had from several sources, but to draw attention to Wittgenstein's response, which indicates a disagreement with Russell and an agreement with Lonergan of some considerable significance.

The passages in which Wittgenstein registers his disagreement with the theory of types deserve to be quoted at length:

> 6.031   The theory of classes is completely superfluous in mathematics.
> This is connected with the fact that the generality required in mathematics is *not accidental* generality.
> 6.1   The propositions of logic are tautologies.
> 6.11   Therefore the propositions of logic say nothing ...
> 6.111   All theories that make a proposition of logic appear to have content are false ...

4 John Passmore, *A Hundred Years of Philosophy* (Penguin, 1968), 201f. For Lonergan's comments on Russell's Theory of Types, see note 12 below.

6.113   It is the peculiar mark of logical propositions that one can recognize that they are true from the symbol alone, and this fact contains in itself the whole philosophy of logic ...

6.1222   This throws light on the question why logical propositions cannot be confirmed by experience any more than they can be refuted by it ...

6.1224   It also becomes clear now why logic was called the theory of forms and of inference.

6.123   Clearly the laws of logic cannot in their turn be subject to laws of logic.

(There is not, as Russell thought, a special law of contradiction for each 'type'; one law is enough, since it is not applied to itself.)

6.1231   The mark of a logical proposition is *not* general validity. To be general means no more than to be accidentally valid for all things. An ungeneralized proposition can be tautological just as well as a generalized one.

6.1232   The general validity of logic might be called essential, in contrast with the accidental general validity of such propositions as 'All men are mortal' ...

What Wittgenstein is attacking here is, at heart, Russell's conception of logical entailment. When he speaks of classes and members of classes, Russell sees logical entailment as being essentially the entailment of 'some' or 'one' in 'all.' Classes consist of members. It is this notion of entailment that creates Russell's Paradox and, in turn, spurs Russell on to introduce his theory of types. Wittgenstein sees no need for the theory of types because his own conception of logical entailment is fundamentally different from that of a class and its members, of 'all-some.' Rather, logical entailment for Wittgenstein follows from the fact that '[t]he propositions of logic are tautologies' (TR 6.1). The tautologous character of logical propositions is sufficient to account for the nature of their entailment – that is why he sees the general validity of propositions like 'All men are mortal' as merely accidental. To speak of the entailment of 'some' in 'all' is to confuse logical propositions with empirical propositions such as 'All roses are either yellow or red' (TR 6.111). To utter such a proposition is to make a claim about the empirical world, and Wittgenstein is totally opposed to theories that appear to make the propositions of logic share the contingency of fact in this way (ibid.). Logical form, Wittgenstein is urging, has no requirement of 'all-some' entailment, it is independent of the accident of fact. In the same way, it has no need for more than one law of contradiction – the motivation to create more than one arises from the complications induced by the 'all-some' formulation and simply does not arise once we have grasped the true nature of tautologous implication.

In an early essay, 'The Form of Inference,'[5] published in 1943, Lonergan reduces the various forms of syllogism found in scholastic philosophy to one basic form of inference, which he calls 'the simple hypothetical argument,'[6] which takes the form 'If A, then B. But A. Therefore B.' Lonergan describes the process of thought involved in the simple hypothetical argument as 'connotational,' meaning formal,[7] since the conclusion follows from the form of the argument and not from what he calls 'denotational coincidence,'[8] the phrase he uses to indicate the way in which 'some' is implied in 'all.' He says, 'The same point may be put differently by asking the logician, If when you say that all organisms are mortal you do not mean to speak of "all organisms" but of the nature of "organism," then why on earth do you say "all organisms"? To that query I have never heard a sensible answer and on the present hypothesis of connotational interpretation there is no answer possible.'[9] Against the view that logical implication is demonstrated by the implication of 'some' or 'one' in 'all,' a form of implication that he considers to depend on the contingent fact that the terms employed denote objects in the world, Lonergan posits a form of implication that arises from the connotational relations of the terms. These relations are of a condition – 'If A' – and a conditioned – 'then B.' The condition is the antecedent, the conditioned the consequent. It is the fulfilment of the condition, stated in the minor premise, that licences the conclusion to be drawn by force of logical necessity. Such a conclusion follows by virtue of the form of argument alone and in no way depends on the world being the way it is, empirically speaking.

Now what is striking about the respective comments of Wittgenstein and Lonergan is that both regard the explanation of logical entailment by means of the implication of 'some' in 'all' as misleading and false for exactly the same reason, namely, that such an explanation is dependent on accidental features of the world, on what Lonergan calls 'denotational coincidence.' Both are at pains to explain implication in a manner that is totally independent of factual content. There is that amount of agreement between the two. The disagreement between them – their differing ways of explaining the nature of implication – is highly revealing. Wittgenstein, as we have seen, explains implication entirely by means of tautology. It is, in turn, the structural properties of tautology, the way in which propositions yield a tautology when connected in a certain way, that reveals the general

5 'The Form of Inference' in *Collection, Papers by Bernard Lonergan,* ed. F.E. Crowe (Darton, Longman & Todd, 1967).
6 Ibid., 3.
7 Ibid., 3.
8 Ibid., 9 and 14.
9 Ibid., 10.

structure of reality: 'It is clear that something about the world must be indicated by the fact that certain combinations of symbols – whose essence involves the possession of a determinate character – are tautologies. This contains the decisive point' (TR 6.124). The early Wittgenstein's view of the structure of language and of the world is uniquely dependent on the structure of tautology, its 'yes-no' character. If the tautologous character of language and of reality is called in question, then so must be the role of logic in Wittgenstein's thought. This, as we shall see in a moment, is what happened and helped to determine the move from the *Tractatus*'s view of language to that of the *Investigations*. Why Lonergan was not tempted to follow a similar path is explained to some extent by the different way in which he treats the notion of inference or implication.

Lonergan is attracted to the simple hypothetical argument taking the form 'If A, then B; but A; therefore B' on account of its 'indefinite flexibility': 'A and B each stands for one or two or any number of propositions; the propositions may be categorical, disjunctive or hypothetical ... No less apparent is the radical simplicity of this type (of argument). Every inference is the implication of a conclusion in a premise or in premises: the conclusion is B; the premise or premises are A; the implication is, if A, then B.'[10] It should be clear that this way of accounting for implication is perfectly compatible with tautological implication. Indeed, Lonergan's 'simple hypothetical argument' might be understood as a way of setting out tautological entailment in conditional format: *if A, then B* indicates that wherever there is an A, there must be a B. But such a conditional form of tautology is not confined to the field of logic, and that is where it differs from pure logical entailment. It can be applied or married quite easily to empirical propositions, while ensuring that the logically necessary conclusion does not depend on the contingency of fact. Thus: 'If it is raining, then the streets will get wet. But it is raining. Therefore, the streets will get wet.' Clearly, Lonergan has found a form of inference that is compatible both with tautological implication and with cognitional implication, where the validity of the latter no more depends on the factual content than the validity of the former. If the factual content is wrong, that is another matter; *the form of inference* remains the same in both types of proposition.

Like Wittgenstein, Lonergan denies the validity of the 'all-some' formulation as an explanation of logical implication, but unlike Wittgenstein he does so without staking his all on logic or logical tautology. He is, in fact, after something different from Wittgenstein, as his questions at the start of his article on the form of inference make clear: 'Is the human mind a Noah's ark of irreducible inferential forms? Is there no general form of all

10 Ibid., 3.

inference, no highest common factor, that reveals the nature of the mind no matter how diverse the materials on which it operates? Is everything subject to measure and order and law except the mind which through measurement and comparison seeks to order everything with laws?'[11] Once he has concluded his exercise in reduction, Lonergan draws out the lesson that can be learned: '[W]e have taken as our empirical basis not particular instances of inference but generally recognized types, and from them as starting-point we have worked to the ultimate unity of the simple hypothetical argument. Thus, our conclusion has to do with the nature of the human mind. We have not sought the reduction of one inferential type to another because we thought one more valid or more obviously valid than the other. On the contrary we assumed all to be valid, and our concern with reduction has been a concern with the one law or form of all inference ... We... have aimed at taking a first step in working out an empirical theory of human understanding and knowledge.'[12]

If Lonergan posits an isomorphism not between logic and reality but

---

11 Ibid., 2.

12 Ibid., 15. Lonergan's position might be clarified further by two separate comments he made on Russell's Theory of Types. In the first quotation he is seeking to illustrate the need for 'normative objectivity' at the second level of cognition, the level of understanding. He says, 'The enemies or adversaries of Lord Russell say that his postulate that regards the hierarchy of classes can be expressed as follows: there is no valid proposition that regards all classes. They say Lord Russell's postulate is a proposition, and it regards all classes. Therefore, Lord Russell postulates the invalidity of his postulate. It is incoherent, self-refuting. That is an exclusion of objectivity, not because someone experienced or did not experience something, but because it is against normative objectivity.' See Lonergan's *Philosophical and Theological Papers 1958–1964*, Collected Works vol. 10, 228. The second comment refers to the attempts of Russell and Whitehead in *Principia Mathematica* to base mathematics on a few logical axioms. The following is a transcript of Lonergan's spoken reply to a question: 'Now the ideal of Russell and Whitehead was to base mathematics on logic ... Now the logic they conceived was a purely extensional logic. It is 'all men' and 'all mortals' that they think of: concrete multiplicities, and relations between classes. The logic is developed along those lines; it is the extensional and not the connotational side of logic ... The idea of Russell and Whitehead was to base it [mathematics] on logic. But they were not able to do that. They had to bring in further axioms. They had to bring in an axiom of infinity and another axiom that has to do with the theory of types. Now it is very difficult to formulate the theory of types; it holds that propositions that regard all types are not valid – that is the general idea of it. And, as you can see, that is a proposition that regards all types; so it is not valid.' See Lonergan's *Understanding and Being*, Collected Works vol. 5, 255f. The section from which this second quotation is taken consists of a wide-ranging discussion of the relation between mathematics and logic.

between knowing (the method or process of cognition) and reality, his reasoning is not dissimilar to that of the early Wittgenstein: it is the normativities he finds in method that justify this conclusion, just as it was the rule-governed nature of logic, its submission to the impersonal rule of law, that induced the early Wittgenstein to attempt the experiment of considering the structure of logic to be the key to the structure of language and, hence, to the structure of the reality we can know. And Lonergan's study of the method of cognition is remarkably similar in intent to Wittgenstein's study of the structure of logic. Wittgenstein's protracted reflections on the central characteristic of tautology reveal that logical coherence and its opposite, the logical incoherence of contradiction (TR 6.1202), lend to reality its basic 'yes-no' characteristic because they determine what can and what cannot be legitimately claimed. In refusing to posit an isomorphism between logic and reality, Lonergan agrees with the strictures passed by the later Wittgenstein on the early Wittgenstein: logic is too narrow and rigid to explain the complexity of language and of reality. But in positing an isomorphism between investigational method and reality, Lonergan sides with the early Wittgenstein against the later Wittgenstein. The early Wittgenstein's experiment might have failed, but that is because the basis for the isomorphism he posited was too narrow. In his inquiry into cognitional and evaluative method, Lonergan discovers a broader isomorphism than that allowed by logic alone: as experienced by our senses, the world is sensible; as understood, the world is intelligible; as known, the world is rational; as valued, the world is valuable. The structure of method, we might say, allows for a much more wide-ranging and variegated view of language and of reality than does the structure of logic.

It is also clear that Lonergan is in disagreement with the early Wittgenstein's elimination of the subject, the 'I,' as being of any philosophical importance other than as showing the limit of what can be known, a point not disconnected with the foregoing. Lonergan would claim that we can know much more about the subject than that it is the limit of what can be known. In the example used by Wittgenstein, where he claims that there is nothing in the visual field to show that it is seen by an eye, a Lonerganian rejoinder might be that while this may be true of the eye, it is not true of the 'I.' Such is the bipolar structure of consciousness that I am always present to myself as a precondition for anything else being present to me. Wittgenstein, in fact, is somewhat disingenuous, for although he speaks of *the visual field,'* with the impersonality of the definite article, any visual field is, in fact, someone's visual field, is always *her* or *his, my* or *our* visual field. One can, however, see why Wittgenstein wishes to eliminate the subject from any position of philosophical importance: it is because he considers the subject to be a potential 'loose cannon'; if meaning were made dependent on the subject, then meaning would appear to become merely subjective. Meaning is tied to subjectivity in the empiricist psychology that Wittgenstein, like Frege, wished vehemently to stay free of. Much better to marginalize the subject and make meaning entirely dependent on the impersonal laws of logic – that way the rule of law, and with it the objectivity of knowledge, can be maintained. While Wittgenstein was to change his centre of normativity and law from logic to forms of life, and much was to hang on this change, the impersonality of this centre was to remain an abiding feature of his later philosophy.

One might be allowed to speculate, however, that it was the narrowness of the logical basis for the isomorphism he claimed between language and reality that led to the early Wittgenstein's virtual elimination of the subject. Logic appears to provide little handle on the subject and on subjectivity. Indeed, the norms of logic have all the appearance of impersonality and seem to stand over against the subject, determining what she can legitimately talk about. And that appears to be the view of the early Wittgenstein. But if coherence is wider than mere logical coherence, if logical coherence is taken up and meshed with cognitional and volitional coherence, and if moreover the authenticity of the subject is tied up with abiding by such coherence when it is recognized, then it is just possible that subjectivity and objectivity are capable of being reconciled in a way that logic on its own would find hard to contemplate.

From the *Tractatus* to *Philosophical Investigations*

Wittgenstein said that in both his earlier and his later works the main thread of continuity was that he was attempting to show rather than to say. I wish now to develop that point and in so doing to draw out the reasons that moved Wittgenstein from his position in the *Tractatus* to that in *Investigations*. It is hard to separate Wittgenstein's life from his philosophy; the reasons that led him to change his position have become part of the argument, part of the philosophical climate of our times.

In the *Tractatus* Wittgenstein says that every proposition is a truth function of elementary propositions. What he has in mind is the notion of 'logical space,' which allows a certain number of relations to exist between two elementary propositions. If we call the propositions 'p' and 'q,' then a range of combinations between them is possible: for example, 'p and q,' 'not-p but q,' 'p but not-q,' 'either p or q,' 'neither p nor q,' 'if p, then q,' and so forth. These combinations represent the range of possibilities open to molecular propositions consisting of two elementary propositions. But the meaning of propositions admits only a Yes-No space, for depending on the actual state of affairs they are either true or false. Wittgenstein began to feel that this Yes–No antithesis was too narrow, that a series of alternatives in language was required. The system he had set up in the *Tractatus* had required atomic or elementary propositions to be independent of each other. In the post-*Tractatus* period he begins to move to a more holistic position under the influence of his examination of statements about degrees of difference. When one speaks about shades or degrees of colour, for example, it is not enough to posit only two possibilities, such as that something is either red or not red: something might be a particular shade of red. To speak of shades or degrees of red implies knowledge of the other shades of red. Furthermore, to say that something is red is to claim that it is not green or blue or any other colour; and here we can only substitute other colours for 'red,' not other adjectives like 'hard' or 'soft.'

It is when Wittgenstein accepts that the same object cannot be red and green all over, and yet denies (with argument) that this exclusion is synthetic and a priori, that he hits on the notion of syntax – or 'logical grammar.'[13] (Here it is worth noting in passing that Lonergan would be less worried than Wittgenstein with the question whether the assertion 'An object cannot be red and green all over' is analytic or synthetic. The reason lies in his 'If ... then' formulation: 'If the object is red all over, then it cannot be green all over.' Here the conditional 'If' does justice to the contingency of fact – as it happens, the object is red all over. But while facts may be contingent and things might have been otherwise, it remains that the facts are as they are; hence they are also of necessity not as they are not. This necessity is a factual necessity that follows from the contingent facts being as they are. So: 'If I am sitting down, then I am not standing up'; this is the same as saying, 'If I am sitting down, then I am not not sitting down.' Similarly, 'If the object is red all over, then it is not green all over' means 'If the object is red all over, then it is not not red all over.' Facts may be contingent but, given that they are so, they are as a matter of necessity not not so. Wittgenstein's problem stems in part from the way in which he isolates or insulates logic from the world of empirical fact: 'Just as the only necessity that exists is *logical* necessity, so too the only impossibility that exists is *logical* impossibility' (TR 6.375). Lonergan distinguishes between logical necessity and factual necessity, but his philosophy allows for a transference from logic to the empirical world, in the sense that the binary structure of logic, its 'yes-no' character, is translated into the judgment that something is in fact the case or is in fact not the case. The technical name he gives to this is sublation. The operations at the level of judgment 'sublate' the logical norms present at the level of understanding, even when the judgment in question is an empirical one. Wittgenstein has

13 Anthony Kenny, *Wittgenstein* (Penguin, 1973), 111–12.

nothing equivalent to sublation, and he cannot straddle the divide between logical necessity and empirical necessity. He wishes logical propositions to be neatly tautologous and their tautologous character to be perspicuously revealed in the proposition. Given a 'border line' case where this does not happen, there results some considerable hesitation and confusion.)

Wittgenstein's notion of syntax is more complex, has greater explanatory power, than the notion that molecular propositions are truth-functions of elementary propositions. Syntax provides a greater range of possibilities than the language of propositions. The notion of antithesis remains, and remains important, but the range of antitheses is greatly expanded. It is no longer a matter of Yes-No but of shades of difference; gradations and refinements of meaning are now possible in a way that the tautologies and contradictions of logic did not allow. We are entering the era of so-called 'informal logic': the differences between words are no longer as clear cut as they appeared at the time of the *Tractatus*. In place of 'either-or' Wittgenstein proposes the notion of 'family resemblances,' the notion that the meanings of words often overlap, being in some ways the same but in other ways different (PI 67, 108). Propositional language is not jettisoned but super-seded, being embraced within the notion of syntax, just as Russellian notation is seen as only one of several possible notations that merely bring out what is already in syntax.[14] Logic is still essentially linguistic, but the kind of logic revealed by a study of ordinary language in use is quite different, and much more wide ranging, than the logic presumed in the *Tractatus* to be the hidden essence of language.

We can see, therefore, how there is continuity and discontinuity between the *Tractatus* and the position Wittgenstein comes to adopt in the *Philosophical Investigations*. The notion of syntax or grammar is inherent in the notion of language game, to which Wittgenstein makes frequent reference in the *Investigations* (PI 23, for example), and indicates the rules according to which the language game is played, the rules that make the language game intelligible. A young child who knows how to use the word 'red' in appropriate circumstances can be said to know the language game of colour, to know the 'rules' that lie behind the use of colour vocabulary. This is what Wittgenstein is referring to in the *Investigations* when he says that 'when we speak of someone's having given a name to pain, what is presupposed is the existence of the grammar of the word 'pain'; it shows the post where the new word is stationed' (PI 257). It is no longer a matter of knowing how words refer to things in the world but of knowing how to use words: 'The meaning of a word is its use in language' (PI 43). Language is a tool kit and words are tools whose use we learn by taking part in 'forms

14 Ibid., 113.

of life' (PI 23). Again we can see continuity in the role of philosophy and of the philosopher between the *Tractatus* and the *Investigations*. In both, the role of the philosopher is not to say things about the world; that remains the role of the scientist. Rather the task of philosophy is elucidatory. In the *Tractatus* it was to help people climb the ladder of logic before discarding it. In the *Investigations* it is to help rid people of misconceptions about language and assist their understanding that language is a set of tools used in a variety of life situations. In both works, philosophy is engaged in showing rather than in saying: not in helping people to acquire a lot of new factual knowledge, but in helping them to acquire a new way of seeing things, or a new way of doing things. And in both, the philosophical impulse is restorative, conservative, therapeutic. Compare these two statements, the one from the *Tractatus* and the other from *Investigations*: 'In fact, all the propositions of our everyday language, just as they stand, are in perfect logical order' (TR 5.5563) and 'What *we* do is to bring words back from their metaphysical to their everyday use' (PI 116).

Philosophical Investigations

There is, of course, considerable discontinuity between the *Tractatus* and the *Investigations*. For a start, the later Wittgenstein repudiates the 'logician's must' on which the whole program of the *Tractatus* is founded – the notion that there must be a hidden essence of language and that the key to how language mirrors the world must be found in logic (PI 91–109). In the *Investigations* Wittgenstein, as part of the new notion of 'logical grammar' or syntax, adopts a much more empirical approach to language in all its abundant variety. Where the logician tended to restrict his attention to language as propositional, as making indicative statements about the world or as having the properties of indicative statements, thereby privileging factual language and raising the problem of how other types of statements – such as aesthetic or moral statements – can be considered to have meaning, language is now seen as serving a multiplicity of functions: giving orders, describing, speculating, forming and testing a hypothesis, asking, translating, praying, and so forth (PI 23). This was to prove a liberating breakthrough within the analytic tradition. Philosophers began to look at forms of language other than the propositional, to break free of the straitjacket of propositional language that the analytical tradition had imposed with almost military rigour and rigidity. While much useful work has been done in collecting and analysing and classifying forms of language other than factual propositions, however, analytical philosophers have not always been clear about what to do with their findings. Analytic philosophers still, I feel, evince a certain blankness about how to account for the *significance* of the different forms of language they classify. While pure or rigorous positivism has been left behind, it has been succeeded by a form of linguistic positivism: these language games are played (PI 654), but as for their meaning (their significance for me and others), well ... Here, I will suggest, is an area where Lonergan's framework of transcendental method might be of some assistance.

The major criticism of his former position made by the later Wittgenstein relates to the fact that his former position presumes that a private language is possible. In the *Investigations*, the notion of a private language is shown to be untenable. A strictly private language would be incapable of furnishing any criterion of right or wrong. 'One would like to say: whatever is going to seem right to me is right. And that only means that here we can't talk about "right"' (PI 258). Names, which are considered to lie at the heart of the notion of language put forward in the *Tractatus*, are said to acquire their meaning from the objects they denote or point to. But a private ceremony of pointing is empty because it is subject to no rules. It is not possible to know if others have the same or a quite different experience of the object pointed to. 'I could not apply any rules to a *private* transition from what is seen to words. Here the rules really would hang in the air, for the institution of their use is lacking' (PI 380).

The Role of Understanding

At several points in *Philosophical Investigations* Wittgenstein comes close to a Lonerganian formulation of the question of how words are charged with meaning.

> There is a gulf between an order and its execution. It has to be filled by understanding.
> Only in the act of understanding is it meant that we are to do THIS. The order – why that is nothing but sounds, inkmarks.   (PI 431)

This observation is immediately followed by questions.

> Every sign *by itself* seems dead. What gives it life? – in use it is alive. Is life breathed into it there? – Or is the *use* its life?   (PI 432)

Here we have a dilemma that Wittgenstein confronts at several places in *Investigations*. What confers meaning and life on words and signs? Is it understanding – an inner mental process – or is it the (public) use of words in social contexts? In PI 433 he considers how someone may make further signs in order to make the meaning clear, 'as if the signs were precariously trying to produce understanding in us. – But if we now understand them, by what token do we understand? ... [T]he gesture – we would like to say – *tries* to portray but cannot do it.' At this point the reader might well expect Wittgenstein to declare that it is understanding that fills the gap between hearing the order and executing it, between receiving the signs and acting on them. But Wittgenstein immediately undercuts any such expectation.

> Here it is easy to get into that dead-end in philosophy, where one believes that the difficulty of the task consists in our having to describe phenomena that are hard to get hold of ... We find ordinary language too crude, and it looks as if we are having to do, not with the phenomena of everyday, but with ones that 'easily elude us, and, in their coming to be and passing away, produce those others as an average effect' (Augustine).   (PI 436)

We can detect in this treatment of understanding something of the tone and vocabulary of Wittgenstein's earlier attack on the logician's quest for the hidden essence of language. Always we are tempted to reach beyond everyday language and find the source of meaning in some esoteric source, in some occult entity or happening. The purpose of *Philosophical Investigations* is to disabuse us of notions of this kind and provide us with a simpler, more straightforward set of philosophical tools, to be found in language and in how it is used in forms of life.

In another passage Wittgenstein again toys with the idea that understanding is the key to linguistic meaning. He asks the question:

> When are we said to *tell* anything? ... I should like to say: ... we are so much accustomed to communication through language, in conversation, that it looks as if the whole point of communication lay in this: someone else grasps the sense of my words – which is something mental: he as it were takes it into his own mind. If he does something further with it as well, that is no part of the immediate purpose of language ... As for what this queer phenomenon of knowledge is – there is time enough for that. Mental processes just are queer. (It is as if one said: 'The clock tells us the time. *What* time is, is not yet settled. And as for what one tells the time for – that doesn't come in here').   (PI 363)

Again we note the pejorative reference to mental processes as 'queer' – Wittgenstein clearly entertains the conviction that those who have recourse to mental processes as an explanation of meaning simply do not know or understand what they are talking about; he sees it as a knee-jerk reaction devoid of any true explanatory force. The other point to grasp is that the champions of understanding, as Wittgenstein presents them, are only interested in talking about *meaning in the head,* overlooking what language is used *for* – 'that is no part of the immediate purpose of language.' The later Wittgenstein is dead set against the notion that meaning exists in some mental limbo, cut off from language and the business of living. Language is something we *use* in our interactions with the world and other people.

Running through the *Investigations* like an obsession is a consideration of the role played by understanding, thinking, intending – what are normally understood as mental processes. If we wish to know why Wittgenstein, while rejecting the accusation that he is a behaviourist (PI 307–8), nevertheless insists that attention to mental processes is something the philosopher should avoid, a further indication is given in a passage in the second part of *Philosophical Investigations,* when he asks:

> How should we counter someone who told us that with him understanding was an inner process? – How should we counter him if he said that with him knowing how to play chess was an inner process? – We should say that when we want to know if he can play chess we aren't interested in anything that goes on inside him. – And if he replies that this is in fact just what we are interested in, that is, we are interested in whether he can play chess – then we shall have to draw his attention to the criteria which would demonstrate his capacity, and on the other hand to the criteria for the 'inner states.'
>
> Even if someone had a particular capacity only when, and only as long as, he had a particular feeling, the feeling would not be the capacity. (PI, part 2, vi)

It would appear, then, that Wittgenstein downgrades the philosophical or epistemological importance of inner processes because they are esoteric, hidden, and elusive – those who refer to them have only a vague notion of what they are referring to; but, more importantly, because they yield *no criteria* of right and wrong by which the validity of the particular claim being made – such as, 'I can play chess' – might be tested. Appeal to inner processes is no proof or acceptable evidence that anything holds.

Wittgenstein's argument against understanding – considered as a mental process – as the source of linguistic meaning can be seen to be identical with his argument against the possibility of a private language. To his thinking, both are founded on the illusion that they model or represent the world when in fact such representation by a private act is impossible. According to his former position, 'These concepts: proposition, language, thought, world, stand in line one behind the other, each equivalent to each' (PI 96). There is little to choose between inner processes and language's hidden essence. Several times understanding is presented as a kind of inner picturing (PI 139) or inner pointing (PI 258, 362); Wittgenstein's understanding of understanding, understood as something 'mental,' exactly mirrors his understanding of a private language. And just as his thinking on language was corrected by the notion of 'grammar,' so his thinking on understanding requires the wider context of public action and behaviour to become philosophically respectable.

In a telling metaphor that occurs several times in the *Investigations* Wittgenstein says that 'a wheel that can be turned though nothing else moves with it, is not part of the mechanism' (PI 271). That is the mistake made by those who appeal to private ostensive definition as the source of a word's meaning: they forget the public conventions and circumstances on which any meaningful use of words depends. In the same way, thinking and understanding are meshed with all sorts of other kinds of behaviour, and it is only in so far as these so-called 'inner processes' are tied to what is publicly observable or audible that they have any value. 'When I think in language, there aren't "meanings" going through my mind in addition to the verbal expression: the language is itself the vehicle of thought' (PI 329). Mental processes are not what we mean by thinking and understanding, which are inseparable from linguistic expression. 'Say a sentence and think it; say it with understanding. – And now do not say it, and just do what you accompanied it with when you said it with understanding: (Sing this tune with expression. And now don't sing it but repeat its expression ...)' (PI 332). Thinking and understanding considered as mental processes that do not share the properties of outer expression are as mysterious as musical expression that is not articulated in notes. It is for this reason that Wittgenstein writes: 'Thinking is not an incorporeal process which lends life and sense to speaking, and which it would be possible to detach from speaking, rather as the Devil took the shadow of Schlemiel from the ground' (PI 339).

What are we to make of insight, the flash of illumination, when we suddenly understand and catch on? Surely that is incontestably a mental phenomenon? Wittgenstein answers:

> The question is badly framed. If it is a question about the meaning of the expression 'sudden illumination,' the answer is not to point to a process that we give this name to ... [U]nderstanding is (not) a specific identifiable experience.   (PI 321 and 322)

What sudden insight denotes is not a process in the mind but 'Now I know how to go on' (PI 323). Just as a word's meaning is its *use*, so we might say that understanding or insight amounts to knowing how to go on – for example, how to apply the formula. Understanding is externalized, becoming something that informs behaviour, that is nested into behaviour.

> Try not to think of understanding as a 'mental process' at all ... In the sense in which there are processes (including mental processes) which are characteristic of understanding, understanding is not a mental process.
> (A pain's growing more and less; the hearing of a tune or a sentence: these are mental processes.)   (PI 154)

Wittgenstein is not interested in the particular experience or sensation that accompanies suddenly knowing how to go on, but he is interested in knowing *the particular circumstances* that justify me in saying I can go on (ibid.). In this way, inner or mental processes are equated with feelings or sensations or psychological states that Wittgenstein wishes to distinguish from thinking, intending, understanding, and knowing. The former are fleeting, capricious, they follow no rule. By contrast, understanding and thinking are part of the machinery of social living, which is rule-governed.

Wittgenstein sets great store by the rules and regularities of human behaviour that allow us to make sense of life and interpret new experiences. 'The common behaviour of mankind is the system of reference by means of which we interpret an unknown language' (PI 206). When it comes to following a rule established by custom or repeated use, there is no need for us to precede our behaviour with some private parade of mental images or acts of interpretation – we just act in conformity with the rule, that is all. Pole observes that all of Wittgenstein's 'illustrations point to behaviour, to the public use of words, as the sole source of meaningfulness; all his arguments are directed to the elimination of psychological factors as inessential.'[15] Wittgenstein considers understanding, intending, and so forth to be important, but only in so far as they are meshed with the language we use and the way we behave. The reason is that only in the public realm can we find norms and standards, by reference to which we can speak of 'right' and 'wrong.' Both the privacy of a private language and the privacy of sensation are bereft of the rules that enable us to say of a move in a language game that it is correct or incorrect.[16] The conception of the mind that Wittgenstein is attacking is of some isolated, disembodied entity standing behind the body and looking out at the world. He is opposed to what

15 D. Pole, *The Later Philosophy of Wittgenstein* (London, 1958), 89.
16 The virtual equivalence of these two forms of privacy is crucial to much of my argument.

Fergus Kerr has called the notion of the self as an isolated centre of consciousness, to the 'mentalist-individualist' conception of the human subject, which is closely associated with the tradition of 'epistemological solitude.' Against these notions Wittgenstein provides the antidote of 'forms of life' – the one given in his philosophy (PI, pt 2, 226). Forms of life are Wittgenstein's only a priori, which have to be accepted, and which cannot be explored or explained further because they are the foundation of every kind of exploration or explanation.[17] And underpinning the notion of forms of life is Wittgenstein's insistence on our bodiliness. It is the body's basic needs, appetites, and instincts – our need for food, drink, and shelter, for example – and the communal economies and institutions these give rise to that provide the common core of the wide variety of forms of life within which individuals operate and order their lives. It is for the same reason that Wittgenstein writes, 'The human body is the best picture of the human soul' (PI, pt 2, 178). Feelings should not be interpreted as lying behind someone's physical expression but are *revealed by* their physical expression.[18]

Reacting to the Tradition

The more we read the later Wittgenstein, the more we see that he is not just modifying his former views but is offering a whole new vision for philosophy and a wholly new method of philosophizing. He is not only engaged in correcting what he perceives to be his own former error, implied in the notion of the possibility of a private language, but is in reaction against a whole tradition that has dominated Western philosophy since Descartes; he takes a stand against notions of language, meaning, understanding, and knowing and of the human person that this tradition has propagated and sustained. This is brought out more clearly in the last text Wittgenstein wrote before he died, *On Certainty*,[19] where his interlocutors are Moore and Descartes. Moore is the bluff champion of common-sense certainty, who

---

17 Fergus Kerr, *Theology after Wittgenstein* (Oxford, 1986), 69.
18 Ibid., 93. Lonergan's view is similar: 'Human communication is not the work of a soul hidden in some unlocated recess of a body and emitting signals in some Morse code ... The bodily presence of another is the presence of the incarnate spirit of the other; and that incarnate spirit reveals itself to me by every shift of the eyes, countenance, color, lips, voice ... Such revelation is not an object to be apprehended. Rather it works immediately upon my subjectivity, to make me share the other's seriousness or vivacity.' See 'Dimensions of Meaning,' in *Collection*, 264.
19 *On Certainty*, trans. D. Paul and G.E.M. Anscombe (Basil Blackwell, 1979). Cited in the text as OC.

believes that by and large philosophers spend their time attempting to solve problems they have created themselves (a view shared by Wittgenstein), and who feels it incumbent on the philosophers who call the certainties of common sense in question to show that their arguments are easier to accept than the certainties of common sense.[20] Against Moore stands the philosophy of Descartes, whose approach to philosophy is to doubt everything that can be doubted and then to see how far reason on its own can reclaim the certainties lost through doubt. A great deal of *On Certainty* is devoted to showing up the artificiality and impossibility of the Cartesian project, while at the same time going far beyond Moore in explaining why this is so.

Wittgenstein points out that our most fundamental beliefs and concepts, and the language in which they are expressed, are not the product of ratiocination (OC 475); they are part and parcel of the way of life into which we are born and as such they are groundless. 'Giving grounds, however, justifying the evidence, comes to an end; – but the end is not certain propositions' striking us immediately as true, i.e. it is not a kind of *seeing* on our part; it is our *acting*, which lies at the bottom of the language-game' (OC 204). Wittgenstein considers as illusory the metaphysical search for first principles or transcendental truths whose role is to be the grounds for the rest of our intellectual beliefs or convictions. Rather than it being the case that we prove or justify our most fundamental beliefs and from these derive or with these build the rest of our knowledge, he contends that the beliefs we are able to justify presuppose others that are groundless. A project such as Russell's Logical Atomism would now be considered to be hopelessly misleading. 'At the foundation of well-founded belief lies belief that is not founded' (OC 253). Rather than the bottom-up metaphor of foundations and what rests on them, Wittgenstein favours the image of a nest or network of linked propositions that hold each other in place. 'When we first begin to *believe* anything, what we believe is not a single proposition, it is a whole system of propositions. (Light dawns gradually over the whole.)' (OC 141). There are no primordial beliefs or privileged beliefs, but the elements of our language game are mutually supportive and interdependent: 'It is not single axioms that strike me as obvious, it is a system in which consequences and premises give one another *mutual* support' (OC 142). All of this is of a piece with the claim in the *Investigations* that the only given, the one a priori, are 'forms of life.' The phrase is notoriously vague, but that is inescapable since the position Wittgenstein wishes to overcome is one associated with clear and identifiable foundational concepts or beliefs, and the position he wishes to uphold is holistic, a world picture of mutually

20 Passmore, *A Hundred Years of Philosophy*, 201f.

supporting elements that we inherit and acquire when first we acquire language and begin to live our lives. The world picture itself is what is presupposed by reason and is not subject to reason: 'If the true is what is grounded, then the ground is not the true, nor yet the false' (OC 205).

On Certainty serves to bring out more sharply how the later Wittgenstein saw his philosophy as a correction of and therapy for the Cartesian and Enlightenment program of finding a set of beliefs, justified by reason, that serve as the foundations on which the whole edifice of knowledge rests. Against this view of philosophy and of the role of reason with which it is associated, Wittgenstein reinstates the ordinariness of life and language and the subordinate and practical role that reason plays in it. He is aware that this can sound like pragmatism (and certainly pragmatists have found support in the later Wittgenstein), but is clearly uneasy with such an association: 'Here I am being thwarted by a kind of *Weltanschauung*' (OC 422). Rather than endorsing pragmatist criteria of correctness or incorrectness, Wittgenstein in *On Certainty* is simply reinforcing and extending the position developed in the *Investigations,* drawing out the intersubjectivity of meaning and stressing the priority of the communal to the individual, in order to rid philosophy of the notion of reason as disembodied consciousness standing over against life and imperiously passing judgment upon it. Meaning is not something in the head, detached from the business of living. At the same time, he signals a move away from his preoccupation in the *Tractatus* with individual propositions by making the focus of attention a whole language game. It is because of the holistic character of human discourse, because we share a set of concepts that are mutually supportive and interdependent that the sceptic's doubt looks odd and out of place: 'Doubt gradually loses its sense. This language-game just *is* like that' (OC 56). Far from it being the case that it is incumbent on reason to reclaim by argument what doubt has called in question, doubt itself presupposes the notion of a language game and could not be entertained except in the context of a language game. Cartesian doubt, for example, presupposes the meaningfulness of the language in which it is expressed (OC 144). In fact, doubt presupposes certainty because doubt is only possible where testing is possible and testing presupposes something that is not doubted or tested (OC 125, 163): 'Now am I to say that the experiment which perhaps I make in order to test the truth of a proposition presupposes the truth of the proposition that the apparatus I believe I see is really there (and the like)?' Justification and explanation have to come to an end sometime. 'My life consists in my being content to accept many things' (OC 344).

Wittgenstein begins the *Philosophical Investigations* with a quotation from St Augustine, a quotation he apparently chose with great care and forethought.

> When they [my elders] named some object, and accordingly moved
> towards something, I saw this and I grasped that the thing was called
> by the sound they uttered when they meant to point it out. Their
> intention was shown by their bodily movements, as it were the natu-
> ral language of all peoples: the expression of the face, the play of
> the eyes, the movement of other parts of the body, and the tone
> of voice which expresses our state of mind in seeking, having, reject-
> ing, or avoiding something. Thus, as I heard words repeatedly used
> in their proper places in various sentences, I gradually learnt to
> understand what objects they signified; and after I had trained my
> mouth to form these signs, I used them to express my own desires.
> (Augustine, *Confessions* 1.8; quoted by Wittgenstein, PI 1)

This quotation is used by Wittgenstein as a way of exemplifying the mistaken ideas he is going to attack in the work to follow, namely, that we learn
words by pointing and by means of private association. But the quotation
also contains the seeds of some of the ideas he is going to advocate in the
work that follows, namely, that we learn language in a variety of human
contexts, that we are trained in its use, and that language is part of behaviour
– 'the expression of the face, the play of the eyes, the movement of other
parts of the body, and the tone of voice' (PI 1). In other words, the passage
has an intriguing ambiguity that appears to have appealed to Wittgenstein,
as it points backwards to the error he had been guilty of in the *Tractatus*,
thinking that language was primarily private and only derivatively public,
but also points forward to a new view of language that will overcome his
former error: language as inherently behavioural, as – in a word – embod-
ied. Wittgenstein saw the *Investigations* as growing out of the *Tractatus*, and
at one time he expressed the wish that both books should be published
together, within the same covers. Given this understanding of the link
between the two works, the quotation from Augustine begins to take on a
new and quite powerful significance as a link between them. It is a hinge
statement or, if you like, a Janus statement. The Roman god Janus was
portrayed as having two faces, one pointing backwards, the other forward,
and the faces of Janus adorned the doorway, looking in but also looking
out.

The quotation from Augustine is a Janus statement, standing at the
doorway of *Philosophical Investigations*. It looks backwards and inwards at the
Tractatus and the old notion, the old error, of language and knowledge as
primarily 'private' matters that only later become public, and it looks
forwards and outwards to the *Investigations* and the new notion of language
and knowledge being first and foremost public phenomena, social creations, before being learned and used by the individual. And it would be

true to say that just about every major philosopher in the English-language tradition has followed Wittgenstein through that door. Philosophy has moved out of doors, away from the notion of knowledge as something that is privately acquired by the individual on his own before being shared with others.

The shift effected by Wittgenstein from logic as the seat and source of the rules, conferring meaning on language, to forms of life as the one and only given has had important implications for philosophy. For according to his earlier position, the norms with which we are required to conform are imposed, as it were, by the nature of logic itself. The only conventionalism allowed in the *Tractatus* relates to accidental features of logical symbolism, the form of notation we prefer, and so forth. The actual ground plan is fixed by reality itself, which manifests the tautological, the yes-no character, of logical propositions. Conventionalism becomes a much more central and powerful force in Wittgenstein's later philosophy, for here forms of life fix the boundaries of what can legitimately be said, and forms of life are human creations, social artefacts (PI 241). Forms of life determine the wider notion of syntax or grammar that the later Wittgenstein swaps for his earlier notion of logic. Both the *Tractatus* and the *Investigations* are concerned with the limits of what can meaningfully be said, but in the former the limits are imposed by logical possibility; in the latter there is no concern to impose limits in any similarly systematic way. Grammar or syntax is a much broader notion, tied to the conventions of particular societies.

There are no certain first principles, no privileged primordial beliefs that confer certainty and security on the rest of our beliefs. Rather our beliefs occur in a network of presuppositions and consequences and have their place in the language game, at the bottom of which is action and not ratiocination (OC 204). Meaningless language in the *Investigations* is language 'gone on holiday,' language that is disengaged from its use in the business of living and that, as a consequence, is 'running idle': 'a wheel that can be turned though nothing else moves with it, is not part of the mechanism' (PI 271).

A Lonerganian Response to Wittgenstein

In comparing Lonergan's position with that of the later Wittgenstein what strikes me most forcibly, in the first instance, is the extent of their agreement in opposition to major aspects of the Western tradition. This is surprising and also very real. Both are opposed to the notion of the self as the 'res cogitans' standing over against the 'res extensa' and passing judgment upon it; they are opposed to the notion of the self as disembodied consciousness hidden behind the body and to the accompanying 'mentalist-individualist' notion of epistemology; both repudiate the Robinson Crusoe model of knowledge as the product of the individual on his own, constructing the edifice of true and certain knowledge on the basis of what reason can achieve by and for itself.

This agreement is perhaps best seen first of all in their response to Descartes's proposal of universal doubt. We have already seen Wittgenstein's response to this in *On Certainty*. Lonergan is no less robust in considering this approach to be incoherent and disastrous for philosophy. In nine paragraphs of *Insight*[21] he develops nine critical points vis-à-vis Descartes's precept, Doubt everything that can be doubted. Such a program of universal doubt, he argues, will eliminate all concrete judgments of fact – for while these may on occasion be invulnerable they are never indubitable – as well as both empirical science and common sense, since neither succeeds in reaching the indubitable. Moreover, in arguments that recall some of Wittgenstein's, Lonergan goes on to say that the meaning of all judgments becomes obscure and unsettled, that not even the criterion of indubitability is indubitable, and that every assignable reason for practising universal doubt is eliminated by a coherent exercise of the doubt. He also points to the presuppositions and prejudices that tend to survive the injunction: 'For doubting affects, not the underlying texture and fabric of the mind, but only the explicit judgments that issue from it ... [O]ne cannot abolish at a stroke the past development of one's mentality, one's accumulation of insights, one's prepossessions and prejudices, one's habitual orientation in life.'[22] Rather than endorse Descartes's proposal, Lonergan sees more sense in Newman's remark that it would be better to believe everything than to doubt everything. 'For universal doubt leaves one with no basis for advance, while universal belief may contain some truth that in time may gradually drive out the errors.'[23] Lonergan's considered view is that philosophy should be left to apply its own method in respect of itself; it should not be expected to usurp the methods or underwrite the conclusions of science or of common sense: '[I]t is only a mistaken argument from analogy that expects of them [philosophers] a validation of scientific or common-sense views.'[24]

The major object in the Western philosophical tradition of Wittgenstein's attack is the notion that language is primarily private and only derivatively public; his objection to this is that a private language could not be rule-

21 *Insight: A Study of Human Understanding* (Longmans, Green & Co., 1957) 408–10.
22 Ibid., 410–11.
23 *Method in Theology* (Darton, Longman & Todd, 1972), 223.
24 *Insight*, 411.

governed and hence would be bereft of the criteria required for a proposition to be considered correct or incorrect. The central object of Lonergan's attack in the tradition is the supposition that knowing is like looking. His argument against this is not unlike Wittgenstein's attack on private language, since Lonergan contends that this model of knowing leads to an incapacity to verify any proposition. For verification in such a model of knowing would require checking that what is claimed to be so truly corresponds with what in fact is so; and this would require, in turn, something like a superlook, capable of looking at both the claim and the objects looked at. In short, such a model of knowing is mired in the privacy of sensation and incapable of furnishing criteria or procedures for the verification of its knowledge claims. Problems over verification, Lonergan believes, have led philosophers in the tradition to have recourse to 'occult' entities or habits to shore up beliefs that are otherwise untenable.

In place of the Enlightenment and post-Enlightenment attempts to privilege certain beliefs or truths as foundational for the rest of knowledge, an attempt that has clear links with the Cartesian project of universal doubt, Lonergan's approach is to say that knowing is already going on – in mathematics, science, history, common sense, and so on – and to suggest that we carry out an empirical investigation of what is going on in these areas of knowledge. It is not philosophy's task to provide foundations for the knowledge claims made in mathematics or science or history or any other discipline. There is something Wittgensteinian in Lonergan's appeal to the existing methods of investigation to be found in mathematics, science, and common-sense knowing. Where Wittgenstein wished to bring words back to their everyday use (PI 116) or claimed, in the *Tractatus*, that all the propositions of everyday language were in perfect logical order as they stood (TR 5.5563), Lonergan might be understood as claiming that the methods of investigation in mathematics, science, and common sense are in perfectly good working order: the philosopher should attend to these methods and find their common core, the metamethod of intellectual operations that underpins them. As Wittgenstein avowed, philosophers should attend to what is already going on. Wittgenstein moved from the logician's quest for the hidden essence of language, the claim that this is how language 'must' be, to a more empirical and broader investigation of how language is in fact used. Lonergan is also resistant to any a priori fixing of what must be the case for knowledge to be valid.

Lonergan is also opposed to conceptualism and the notion that meaning resides primarily in the head and only occasionally is applied to the concrete world around us. As we saw in the last chapter, his epistemology takes off from the here and now of experience; for him, concepts are grounded in an understanding of the concrete data of experience. Knowledge is not a matter of consulting concepts resident in some inner space called the mind and asking if they 'apply' to the world of here and now. Concepts are abstract entities formed on the basis of an understanding of the concrete and particular data of sense. Far from endorsing the Cartesian notion of the 'ghost in the machine,' the notion of the isolated disembodied mind – the *res cogitans* – looking out at the world 'out there' in space and time, Lonergan conceives of knowledge as rooted in sensory experience. According to him, the cognitive subject is a body hooked through the senses to the strip of space-time he or she occupies; we are umbilically tied to the world of sensory experience, and there is no way we can break loose and become detached. Without our bodies we could not know anything. What is more, the individual ego, 'I,' or person is socially rooted and unintelligible outside the context of the relationships in which she or he is situated.

> From the 'we' of the parents comes the symbiosis of mother and child. From the 'we' of the parents and the symbiosis of mother and child comes the 'we' of the family. Within the 'we' of the family emerges the 'I' of the child. In other words the person is not the primordial fact. What is primordial is the community.[25]

Finally, the social and historical dimensions of understanding and knowing are evident in the importance Lonergan attaches to belief. Almost all of us, and some more than others, move on occasion from ignorance to answer, by our own efforts, so to speak: we come to knowledge on the basis of evidence or proof that we truly understand. But such occasions of 'immanently generated' knowledge are the exception. More common is knowledge based on belief, on 'taking someone's word for it'; and even immanently generated knowledge is meshed with commonly held presuppositions. So much for the cognitive subject as a solitary inquirer in the Robinson Crusoe mould.

Indeed, just as one might contrast the early with the later Wittgenstein, so one might contrast, in a way that is roughly parallel but less dramatic, the early with the later Lonergan. This can be seen in the later Lonergan's abandonment of faculty psychology – talking of 'intellect' and 'will' doing things – and his stronger focus on the existential subject. It is evident in the emphasis the later Lonergan lays on living over theory, his concern with the priority of community to the individual, and his later comments on the social formation of the individual. In this process of formation language has a vital role to play: 'So it is that conscious intentionality develops in and is moulded by its mother tongue ... Not only does language mould develop-

25 *Philosophy of God, and Theology* (Darton, Longman & Todd, 1973), 59.

ing consciousness but also it structures the world about the subject' –
spatially, temporally, and existentially.[26] The intentionality that is manifested in the different questions we ask – questions for intelligence,
questions leading to judgment, and questions prompting evaluation and
action – does not exist in a social or historical vacuum, but is part and
parcel of the business of living.

The development and change in Lonergan's thinking, which took place
gradually over many years, correspond with a shift from a rather cerebral
intellectualism to the concreteness of method. As he explains it himself:
'Basically the issue is a transition from the abstract logic of classicism to the
concreteness of method. On the former view what is basic is proof. On the
latter view what is basic is conversion. Proof appeals to an abstraction
named right reason. Conversion transforms the concrete individual to
make him capable of grasping not merely conclusions but principles as
well.'[27] While the shift from *Insight* to *Method* is less extreme than the shift
from *Tractatus* to *Investigations*, there is an interesting parallel between the
two philosophers, since in each the later thinking is to some extent more
gritty, more sociologically aware, and manifests a reduced emphasis on
impersonal or disembodied logic or – in the case of Lonergan – on mind
working on problems at a purely intellectual level. In Lonergan, the new
emphasis is found in two notions: (1) 'the world mediated by meaning' – 'a
world known not by the sense experience of an individual but by the
external and internal experience of a cultural community, and by the
continuously checked and re-checked judgements of the community';[28]
and (2) the related notion of 'horizon,' which is both the condition and the
limitation of the individual's further learning and development.[29]

Wittgenstein's comments in the *Investigations* undermine the Enlightenment notion of disembodied consciousness confronting the world and
attempting to understand it by some form of picturing or pointing. Such a
conception of the self and of reality gives rise to all sorts of dislocations –
between thought and language, mind and body, self and others, meaning
and behaviour – that Wittgenstein exposes brilliantly. It is, I hope, by now
clear that Lonergan supports none of these dislocations and repudiates
them with the same force as Wittgenstein. Both philosophers are united in
rejecting these aspects of the tradition and to that extent both are in
reaction to the Enlightenment tradition. Kenny has said that Wittgenstein

26 *Method*, 71. My attention to these features of Lonergan's thought has been
      prompted by Joseph A. Komonchak's comments in his *Foundations in
      Ecclesiology* (Boston College, 1995), 29–35.
27 Ibid., 338.
28 Ibid., 238.
29 Ibid., 237.

has undermined the assumptions of post-Cartesian philosophy and that if 'Wittgenstein was right, philosophy has been on a wrong tack since Descartes.'[30] Lonergan goes even further in his diagnosis of the durability and influence of the ocular myth and the confrontational view of knowing it has supported. 'Five hundred years separate Hegel from Scotus ... [T]hat notable interval of time was largely devoted to working out in a variety of manners the possibilities of the assumption that knowing consists in taking a look.'[31]

If united on negative grounds – in opposition to a huge error that has blighted Western philosophy for so long – it nevertheless remains the case that Wittgenstein and Lonergan are in disagreement over what is foundational in knowing; and upon that central disagreement hang others. Wittgenstein proposes forms of life as foundational; Lonergan proposes method – the method by which we come to know and evaluate. Lonergan considers knowing to consist of three steps, on the side of the subject: experience, understanding, and judgment. We must now consider whether he is vulnerable to criticisms that we have seen Wittgenstein make against understanding as a source or basis of meaning.

The notion of understanding that Wittgenstein censures is of understanding as a kind of inner picturing or inner pointing (PI 6, 139, 258, 362). On this understanding of understanding, the supposed relationship between understanding and the world is the same as that between a name and its object, and since Wittgenstein rejects the latter he naturally rejects the former. Now Lonergan also repudiates the notion of understanding as standing over against the world 'out there' and attempting to represent it by means of picturing or pointing. Such a model of understanding, he believes, stems from the ocular myth that knowing is like looking, and is based on the assimilation of knowing to sensation. And because the relation between sensation and the object of sensation is confrontational, a theory of knowledge modelled on sensation will inevitably be confrontational. In Lonergan's account, however, sensation is not knowing but only a first stage in knowing. Building on sensation is understanding, and understanding is nothing like sensation. Understanding is not, therefore, some kind of mental copy or picture or pointing at reality 'out there.' Rather, understanding is the insight that yields an answer to the questions for intelligence – what? why? how often? and so on. Understanding on this account is a preverbal act that builds on the data of sense to produce intelligibles that unify the data and in this way provide an answer to the question being asked. Understanding yields unities and relations that de-

30 Anthony Kenny, *Aquinas* (Oxford University Press, 1980), 28.
31 *Insight*, 362.

scribe, interpret, or explain the data of sense, depending on the require-
ments of the investigation at hand and the questions that direct that
investigation. It is quite different from picturing or pointing. Images and
pictures do not reveal reality, but remain to be interpreted or understood;
they can perform a heuristic function to assist understanding to take place
– for example, images such as sketches or geometrical diagrams or statistical pie charts – but they are not themselves understanding or a substitute
for understanding.

Moreover, once understanding is achieved, the inquirer moves from the
privacy of sensation, on which Wittgenstein has a good deal to say, to the
sphere of the intelligible, and the intelligible in principle is capable of
being communicated. The sensible as sensible is particular, private, and
incommunicable; the sensible as intelligible is generalized, communicable,
and, even when private, potentially public. It becomes actually public with
outer speech. Because he refuses to assimilate knowledge to sensation,
Lonergan is free of the entrapment in the unfathomable privacy of sensation that such assimilation entails. There is no thought, therefore, of
language being infused or injected with meaning by some purely private act
of naming or the like. You cannot share my senses and feel what I feel nor
can you share my eyes and see exactly what I see; but I can tell you that I feel
pain and I can say that I see something blue. 'Feeling pain' and 'seeing
blue' are both intelligibles that describe the data of sense as I experience
them. Without doubt I have learned to use these terms, been trained, if you
like, by observing how they are used in public discourse. But that is not the
end of the matter; I have also had to learn how to use them by understanding the meaning of the terms. As any teacher would tell you, if understanding were absent it would soon become obvious that I did not know how to
use the relevant terms appropriately. Without understanding, the use of
words is blind. Understanding cannot be dispensed with simply because the
empiricist understanding of understanding as some kind of inner picturing
or pointing is misguided.

'Feeling pain,' a favourite Wittgensteinian example, and 'seeing blue'
are examples of intelligibles that describe the data: they relate things to our
senses. Explanation, by contrast, works by relating things to each other. So I
understand that the angles of a triangle are equal to one hundred and
eighty degrees by showing how they equal the angles that make up a
straight line: explanation consists in relating the two sets of angles, those of
the triangle and those of the straight line, to each other and, in this case,
showing that the angles of the one set are individually, and then collectively, equal to the angles of the other set. Or, to take another example, the
engineers seeking to understand the cause of an aircraft crash will interview
the witnesses and heed the descriptions they give of what they saw: blue

flashes, loud bangs, billowing smoke, and so forth. But in providing an *explanation* the engineers will not simply repeat the descriptions of eye witnesses – what they saw and heard – but will seek to relate events to each other in a perspective that yields a causal sequence that brought about the crash. Description is understanding that relates things to us and our senses; explanation is understanding that relates things to each other.

Wittgenstein's example of the chess player who claims to understand how to play chess, on the basis of some 'inner process,' is revealing. Of course, only the person who openly and publicly demonstrates how to play the game in accordance with the rules knows how to play chess. But if one of the two players consistently moved one of the pieces incorrectly, moving bishops as if they were knights, for example, or showed no inkling of how to achieve checkmate, we would feel that he had something to *learn*. Proof of true learning would take the form of his demonstrating that he knew how to move the various pieces correctly and had a grasp of what constituted endgame, but on seeing the improved performance we would infer that the player in question had come to a new *understanding*: it would not be a matter simply of observing that the player now knew, mechanically, how to move the pieces in accordance with the rules, but that he had *changed his mind in some important respect*. While overt behaviour is undoubtedly the sign that a person knows how to play chess, inappropriate behaviour will *not be truly corrected* merely by ape-like *copying* of how to move the pieces and will always be accompanied by a *change of understanding*. Those who claim that understanding and knowing are simply instances of 'following a rule,' in Wittgenstein's sense of that phrase, forget that to follow a rule intelligently – and that is what Wittgenstein means by the phrase – is to understand the rule, to be able to interpret the rule and to apply it in a range of appropriate circumstances. Following a rule and understanding are not synonymous: one can follow a rule blindly, a situation that usually leads to blunders and disasters. In other words, understanding is frequently slipped quietly and unobtrusively into philosophical discourse, presumed to be operative whenever rules and concepts are being discussed, but for some reason understanding itself is considered unworthy of investigation.

What is more, by bypassing understanding and other mental operations, ruling that they are of little philosophical importance, Wittgenstein lays himself open to the condemnation that Gellner has heaped on linguistic philosophy generally, as 'the systematic indulgence in the generalized form of the Naturalistic Fallacy, the inference from the *actual* to the *valid*.'[32] This is a criticism aimed at the abandonment of old-fashioned theory of knowledge, concerned as it traditionally has been with notions of truth and

32 Ernest Gellner, *Words and Things* (Oxford Univesity Press, 1959), 203.

verifiability, and at the attempt to reduce philosophy to semantics, to establishing how words mean. Wittgensteinian linguistic philosophy considers it the task of philosophy to elucidate and not to justify. But is not the philosopher entitled to question not only the internal consistency of a particular language-game but the very validity or desirability of a language-game, of a whole species of thinking?[33] I may, for example, be quite conversant with the 'astrological realm of discourse' to the point of being able to adjudicate on what constitutes a correct and what an incorrect 'move' in the astrological language-game, but still find the whole business of astrology misguided and mistaken and the beliefs and predictions of astrologers without foundation in reality. By overlooking understanding and the further, related question of whether understanding is correct – by abandoning the theory of knowledge, in other words – linguistic analysis leaves untouched the question of the ontological status of the terms and concepts involved. By virtue of the limitations it imposes on philosophy, it does not contain the wherewithal to promote us from the conceptual to the ontological level of knowledge.

The four levels of human consciousness revealed in and through transcendental method have the capability of transforming the study of language in which groups of philosophers within the analytical tradition are engaged. We have seen how Wittgenstein liberated the analytical tradition from its obsession with propositional language that has the properties of declarative statements of fact. By drawing attention to the multifarious uses of language, Wittgenstein set in motion the study and classification of non-declarative uses of language, such as performative utterances that do not simply tell us about the physical world but appear to create new relationships, to place us in new commitments, to *do things*. The work of J.L. Austin has been seminal in this field, and John Searle's study of speech acts is another example of this extension and broadening of the philosophical investigation of language in use. Now the fourth level of human consciousness is commensurate with human personality and is centred on action, on human doing, and the conscious intentional operations we perform when action is being considered or contemplated. The fourth level is the level at which for the most part we live our lives, the level at which values play an important role. A detailed and accurate study of the four levels of consciousness would, I believe, provide philosophers in the analytical school interested in the study of language with a framework for their investigations. This would help them to explain how even in speech – when, for example, I say 'I do' at a marriage service – I can be seen to be doing something and not merely saying it. Language is isomorphic with all four

33 Ibid., chapter 1.

levels of consciousness. Meaning is not just something that takes place *in the head*; it has to do with living in all its abundant variety. The four levels of consciousness provide an explanation of why Wittgenstein is right to complain about the confinement of meaning to thinking, to something that goes on in the privacy of the head. The four levels are a ladder reaching from the privacy of experience to publicly observable action: as such, they could provide the empirical study of language with a fruitful, unifying explanatory framework.

Intentionality

At several points in his writings, Wittgenstein appears to dwell on the strange dynamism of the human mind:

> A wish seems already to know what will or would satisfy it; a proposition, a thought, what makes it true – even when that thing is not there at all! Whence this *determining* of what is not yet there? This despotic demand? ('The hardness of the logical must.')   (PI 437)

Observations like this recall Lonergan's contention that human beings are consciously oriented to the truth. It is this orientation, this dynamic drive or thrust that causes us to raise questions and seek to answer them. It is this same drive or intentionality that lies behind our impatience with half-answers and unsatisfactory solutions. Not only do we know things, but we know when we know, when our answers are supported by relevant evidence, when the process of inquiry has been satisfied because all relevant questions have been answered. Our intellectual dynamism guides our inquiry, it knows when inquiry is incomplete and recognizes when completion has been achieved. It recognizes that the hypothesis proposed at the second level of consciousness is provisional, that it is a conditioned whose conditions await fulfilment; but it also recognizes if and when those conditions have been fulfilled, when the imperious demands of the 'logical must' have been satisfied. This is not an automatic response, but remains always a matter of judgment; it is not a matter of feeling merely – though intellectual investigation has its emotional highs and lows, as Wittgenstein was well aware – but a matter of 'the native spontaneities and inevitabilities of our consciousness which assembles its own constituent parts and unites them in a rounded whole in a manner we cannot set aside without, as it were, amputating our own moral personality, our own reasonableness, our own intelligence, our own sensitivity.'[34] Lonergan's analysis of intentionality is a

34 Lonergan, *Method in Theology,* 18.

careful and measured exploration of the conscious spontaneities inherent in human intellectual inquiry, spontaneities that Wittgenstein recognizes and alludes to but that he ultimately shies away from, captivated as he is by the idea that the mind is an erroneously conceived inner space where immaterial ideas reside and immaterial thoughts are thought. Since such an inner space can yield no rules governing the correct use of language, Wittgenstein is right to dismiss it. But what he appears to overlook is that this idea of the mind is the correlative of the ocular model of knowing, which conceives the mind as an inner or spiritual space housing the ideas which themselves correlate with the objects of ocular vision housed in outer physical space. The notion of the mind against which Wittgenstein rightly protests is a product of the error that knowing is like looking.

In the place of this notion of the mind one can posit the concrete human subject as the source of numerous *intentional acts*, acts that are about something or that intend to bring something about. To speak of acts as intentional is to say that there is a certain direction to them, that they are pointed or aimed in a particular way, that they have behind them a specific purpose or intention. To ask questions is intentional, not in the everyday sense of that term, but in the sense that questions have the purpose of achieving answers and that different kinds of questions have the purpose of achieving different kinds of answers. To attempt to answer questions is also intentional, since this too is an activity aimed or directed at bringing something about. Questioning and answering questions are the opposite to drifting along. Now intentional activities are also spontaneous activities: we do not normally decide to ask the questions What is that? or Is that so? Such questions are not usually the object of preliminary debate and deliberation. We say that they occur *naturally*. To say that something occurs spontaneously is not the same as saying that it occurs automatically, since 'automatically' suggests that something is caused to occur in the manner of some mechanical effect following on some mechanical cause – the bulb lights up when I flick the switch or the car engine roars when the ignition key is turned. Rather, to say that something occurs spontaneously is to say that it follows from the nature of the organism being considered: it is of the nature of this organism to behave or react in this way when such and such occurs. Spontaneity need not be the enemy of freedom and may be, as it is in humans, the precondition for free action. For to ask rational questions, to seek the evidence or proof of something, is to act freely. It is to show that one is free to follow the evidence wherever it may lead, that one is free to consider a range of possibilities before selecting the one that is best supported by evidence and logic. To act like that is, for a human being, to act freely but it is also to act spontaneously. Rationality is the seat of freedom, for to reason and to act for a reason is to be free.

Now what Lonergan is saying is that reasoning and acting for a reason are spontaneous activities for human beings; they are irresistible, following from our nature as human subjects. What is more, such spontaneous activities are also structured, they follow a definite pattern. This pattern is not something we determine from without or by our own volition; it occurs spontaneously and is self-assembling, self-constituting, one stage or part summoning forth the next, as it heads for completion; it is a basic intentionality aimed at achieving the truth and what is right. It is a conscious process and as such one that we can reflect on and analyse. At the fourth level of consciousness, intentionality becomes self-conscious and here we find people using the word explicitly, saying 'I intend (to keep my promise),' 'You intentionally (set out to insult him),' and so forth. At the fourth level of consciousness we take possession of our intentionality and become consciously responsible for it: we can say either 'I intended it' or 'I meant it.' The four stages of conscious intentionality stretch from sensory experience to action, but always they have to do with meaning: with its discovery (through inquiry) or with its creation (through planning and action). Such is the native dynamism of our intelligence that we are meant for, or ordered for, the discovery and creation of meaning. While the analysis of intentionality may legitimately be termed a psychological activity, it is totally different in its outcomes from empiricist psychology. Empiricist psychology gives birth to *associationism* and all its attendant problems for epistemology. By contrast, *intentionality analysis* uncovers the norms by which the legitimate discovery and creation of meaning are governed.

Wittgenstein appears to have had inklings of what human intentionality is, of its self-directing nature and its spontaneity; but he never fully developed his thought on these matters, and his insights remain at the level of inklings.

From Classical to Historical Consciousness

In his writings, Lonergan distinguishes between what he terms respectively 'classicism' and 'historical consciousness.' Classicism is a conservative, traditional outlook that holds to a normative definition of culture as a unique and permanent achievement of universal validity into which 'outsiders' – the young or barbarians – have to be inducted if they are to escape the charge of being uncultured. Clearly, this is the notion of culture entertained in ancient Greece and Rome and, most notably, in Europe of the eighteenth century, but it is a notion that survives to this day. Against the classicist notion of culture stands the empirical notion of culture as the set of meanings and values that happen to inform a particular way of life.[35] Rather than culture being considered unique, the empirical approach finds that there are many cultures; rather than culture being a permanent achievement, the empirical approach finds that cultures shift and change over time. Cultures are the product of human history, of that endless flow of invention, decision, and action that makes up the human story. The empirical notion of culture makes us aware of change and development, and stands behind what Lonergan terms 'historical mindedness' and 'historical consciousness.'

Michael H. McCarthy has taken Lonergan's distinction between classical and historical consciousness and allied it to the distinction Lonergan also makes between the Aristotelian and the modern ideas of science in order to fashion a broad-brush distinction that enables us to reconceive and reclassify movements within the history of philosophy. The classical ideal is seen to lie behind the Aristotelian notion of science as 'true, certain knowledge of things through their causes.' By this definition, what is discovered in science is true, invariant, permanent, and closed to revision. By contrast, the modern notion of science is of provisional knowledge based on a dynamic, open-ended method of inquiry that yields cumulative and progressive results. Rather than knowledge, modern science speaks of opinion – the best scientific opinion of the day; it is not fixed or permanent, but radically open to change and development. The radical overthrow of scientific opinion in the modern era is not a cause for despondency but for celebration, since it is in this way that science advances. Modern historical consciousness has redefined what is meant by science, and this redefinition of science has contributed in turn to a reconception of culture. The modern understanding of science lies at the heart of the empirical notion of culture, and has given rise to modern historical consciousness. According to historical consciousness, science is an ongoing normative process of inquiry resulting in a continuing succession of theoretical systems.[36]

Movements within the history of philosophy can be seen to be informed by one or the other of these forms of consciousness – the classical or the historical. McCarthy sees philosophy from Aristotle to Kant as informed by the classical ideal.[37] It is present in Descartes's attempt to form 'a unified

35 Ibid., xi.
36 M.H. McCarthy, *The Crisis of Philosophy* (State University of New York Press, 1990), 9. Analytical philosophers keen to understand Lonergan better and Lonergan scholars seeking a deeper understanding of the various movements in the history of philosophy, including recent developments in American philosophy, should find this book invaluable.
37 Ibid., 6.

axiomatic system founded on intuitively evident truths'[38] and in Kant's appeal to an ahistorical, transcendental realm of forms and categories to explain how empirical science is possible. Classical consciousness pervades the Enlightenment attempts to find in philosophy or by means of philosophy the secure foundations on which the certainty of scientific or mathematical knowledge could be grounded. The same classical ideal lies behind Frege's ambition to ground mathematical knowledge in logic, in Russell's quest for incorrigible elementary propositions, and in the early Wittgenstein's proposals that language and reality mirror the invariant rules of logic. Although McCarthy finds Hume to be an exception to the rule, since Hume's sceptical conclusions are tantamount to a denial that the project of finding secure foundations is feasible,[39] I would contend that at the outset of his philosophical inquiries Hume also shares the classical ambition, hoping to find firm ground in the science of man: 'In pretending therefore to explain the principles of human nature, we in effect propose a compleat system of the sciences, built on a foundation almost entirely new, and the only one upon which they can stand with any security.'[40] Hume's original impulse is classicist; but the conclusions of his inquiry run counter to his initial ambitions.

By contrast, the later Wittgenstein's approach to culture and philosophy appears thoroughly empirical and historical. There is no one fixed form of life underlying all others; rather forms of life as we find them are many and varied. The approach taken to the use of language within a form of life is empirical and conventionalist; language is a tool and the appropriate use of language is not determined by some invariant substratum – the later Wittgenstein has given up the quest for the 'logical must.' Rather than search, in classicist fashion, for language's hidden essence, we should accept that habitual usage determines the meanings of words and serves as the arbiter of correctness when meaning is contested. The thesis pursued in *On Certainty* is that knowledge is groundless and the search for secure foundations illusory. A similar 'historical' approach is taken by Sellars, Quine, and Rorty. It is in fact by reviewing and deconstructing the philosophical tradition, as we shall see in the next chapter, that Rorty attempts to establish his position that the epistemological enterprise itself is part of the illusory search for foundations and that philosophy should abandon the age-old endeavour of establishing a true theory of knowledge. Abandoning the quest for some 'Archimedian point outside the series of actual and

38 Ibid., 2.
39 Ibid., 8.
40 David Hume, *A Treatise of Human Nature* (1739; Selby-Bigge ed., Clarendon Press, 1888), xvi.

possible beliefs,' Rorty recognizes no determining 'conceptual scheme' other than the collection of views that make up modern culture – the criteria or norms that justify a proposition are internal to the culture that produces it.

So far, on the basis of McCarthy's use of classical and historical consciousness to distinguish philosophical movements, history and modernity would seem to be on the side of Wittgenstein and Rorty, and Lonergan's pursuit of the theory of knowledge would seem to cling to an outdated classicism. However, from the point of view of historical consciousness, the later Wittgensteinian project suffers from a single fatal flaw. For historical consciousness is consciousness attuned to the expectation of change and development over time: as we have seen, the distinguishing feature of the modern understanding of scientific knowledge is that such knowledge is provisional; the only permanent feature of the theoretical knowledge of science is that it is permanently open to development and revision. By contrast, the mechanism proposed by Wittgenstein for determining the meaning of words is thoroughly conservative and quite lacking in any explanatory value concerning how linguistic change occurs. The whole thrust of Wittgenstein's argument in *Philosophical Investigations* and *On Certainty* presumes that the network of word meanings in any language-game is settled and established so that the meaning of any term or word or sentence in that game can be determined by reference to established practice. It is a technique designed to uphold and maintain the linguistic status quo and, as such, quite out of step with what today we would understand as scientific. While there are undoubtedly many factors that contribute to linguistic change, one prominent factor is conceptual or intellectual change. Once we had no vocabulary for describing and explaining microbes, genes, and atomic particles, but today we do and, with further scientific advancement, new terms and new vocabularies will be generated. Language changes *pari passu* with changes and developments in understanding, and the meaning of words is empty without originating acts of understanding. Cultural change or revolution implies a change in the conceptual schemes of men and women. Only an epistemology or a method of inquiry that *can account for* conceptual change could be considered compatible with the modern understanding of science.

It is such a method of inquiry that Lonergan proposes to be foundational in philosophy. The method of inquiry he proposes embraces the invariance required in foundations with the pattern of sensitive, intellectual, and rational operations that generate the changed understandings and the changed knowledge claims – and hence the changed vocabulary – required for scientific and intellectual advancement. As McCarthy notes, the search for foundations in philosophy should not be abandoned, but should be reconceived as the need for cognitive integration.[41]

Lonergan has brilliantly shifted the search for foundations away from a search for static entities such as privileged representations, incorrigible propositions, logical invariants, and the like – a quest truly at odds with the methodology of modern science and hence doomed to failure – to a search for method. The one constant in modern scientific investigation is the scientific method of gathering the data, forming hypotheses to explain the data, and testing and verifying the hypotheses; it is this constant threefold method that produces and accounts for scientific change and advancement. Only a general, empirical method that can account for intellectual change and development in a broadly similar fashion can validly claim to be on the side of historical consciousness. Compared with such a method, the techniques advocated by the later Wittgenstein must be rated as positively anti-historical because mired in the stasis of habit and custom.

41 McCarthy, *The Crisis of Philosophy*, chapter 7.

7

Town Criers of Inwardness: Lonergan and Rorty

It is not surprising that the philosophy of Richard Rorty, as articulated in his much-acclaimed and widely influential work *Philosophy and the Mirror of Nature*,[1] has attracted fairly extensive comment from followers of Bernard Lonergan.[2] For in season and out of season Lonergan attacks the notion that understanding is like looking, that knowledge is some kind of copy or representation of reality 'out there,' and that the mind is analogous to an inner or spiritual eye that does the looking. Rorty and Lonergan agree that the major Western epistemological tradition has for too long been dominated by what Rorty calls the 'ocular metaphor' and that this metaphor is, to quote Rorty again, 'the original sin of epistemology.'[3] There is much that unites the two philosophers, particularly in their critiques of the dominant epistemological tradition. Yet there is much that separates them. This chapter attempts to examine, by means of historical investigation, the roots of the agreement and disagreement between Rorty and Lonergan. I wish to explore and assess their respective readings of the tradition. Rorty is on record as saying that one's approach to philosophy is 'motivated almost

---

1 *Philosophy and the Mirror of Nature* (Basil Blackwell, 1980). Cited henceforth as PMN.
2 See, in particular, Hugo Meynell, 'Reversing Rorty,' *METHOD: Journal of Lonergan Studies* 3/1 (Spring 1985); Garrett Barden, 'Insights and Mirrors' and Hugo Meynell, 'Reply to Garrett Barden,' *METHOD* 4/2 (Fall 1986); and Hugo Meynell, 'Post-Analytic Philosophy: Its Causes and Its Cure,' *METHOD* 10/2 (Fall 1992). See also Andrew Beards, 'On Knowing and Naming,' *METHOD* 8/2 (Fall 1990) and Michael H. McCarthy, '"The Critique of Realism,' *METHOD* 10/2 (Fall 1992).
3 PMN 60 note 32.

entirely by a perception of one's relation to the history of philosophy.'[4] *Philosophy and the Mirror of Nature* is at once a deconstruction of the tradition and a construction of a form of pragmatism that embodies his program for philosophy. It is fascinating to see how far Lonergan's reading of the tradition agrees with Rorty's and how far, in fact, it reveals that Rorty departs radically from the dominant tradition he so acutely deconstructs.

Rorty's Thesis

The argument adduced by Rorty, though intricate in its details and extensive in its range of reference, is in broad outline fairly straightforward: 'It is pictures rather than propositions, metaphors rather than statements, which determine most of our philosophical convictions.'[5] Philosophy in the West has been held captive by a metaphor depicting the human mind as a kind of mirror or inner eye. Rooted in Platonic thought, this metaphor extends through the medieval debate about universals, continues through the Cartesian and post-Cartesian period, and, notwithstanding the linguistic turn taken by their philosophies, is inherent in Frege, Russell, and Ayer.[6] The metaphor of the mirror or eye, however, has given rise to representationism and all its attendant difficulties. 'Without the notion of the mind as mirror, the notion of knowledge as accuracy of representation would not have suggested itself.'[7] The inescapable difficulties surrounding representationism lead Rorty to conclude that the eye metaphor is finished, played out, bankrupt, and to take the step, first decisively taken by Wittgenstein, from the arena of the mind into the world of society and public discourse.

The epistemological enterprise should be abandoned, Rorty urges, and the theory of knowledge should be handed over to the physiological psychologists capable of dealing with the neurological 'wiring' by which we interact with objects.[8] Instead of concerning itself with questions about the mind, consciousness, the epistemological subject, and so forth, philosophy becomes for Rorty a hermeneutics for which societal approval is the tribunal of correctness. He opposes the move inwards; he approves the move outwards to society and behaviour, to societal techniques and criteria for settling arguments and advancing learning.

4 R. Rorty, *Consequences of Pragmatism* (University of Minnesota Press, 1982), 41.
5 PMN 12.
6 PMN 8, 112.
7 PMN 12.
8 PMN 239–42.

How the Ocular Metaphor Arose

Rorty speculates that the historical origin of the metaphor of the mind as a mirror or spiritual eye is linked to the notion of universals. If only our race had confined itself to statements about particulars, then the 'Mind's Eye' metaphor might never have arisen.[9] In a passage that captures the tone as well as much of the substance of his argument, Rorty indicates the connection between spiritual seeing and belief in the existence of the soul:

> Philosophy undertook to examine the difference between knowing that there are parallel mountain ranges to the west and knowing that infinitely extended parallel lines never meet, the difference between knowing that Socrates was good and knowing what goodness was. So the question arose: What are the analogies between knowing about mountains and knowing about lines, between knowing Socrates and knowing the Good? When this question was answered in terms of the distinction between the eye of the body and the Eye of the Mind, *nous* – thought, intellect, insight – was identified as what separates man from beasts. There was, we moderns might say with the ingratitude of hindsight, no particular reason why this ocular metaphor seized the imagination of the founders of Western thought. But it did, and contemporary philosophers are still working out its consequences ... Given this model and with it the Mind's Eye, what must the mind be? Presumably something as different from the body as parallelness is from visible mountain ridges. Something like that was ready to hand, for poetry and religion suggested that something humanoid leaves the body at death and goes off on its own. Parallelness can be thought of as the very breath of parallels – the shadow remaining when the mountains are no more. The more wispy the mind, the more fit to catch sight of such invisible entities as parallelness ...

> Philosophers have often wished that Aristotle had never fallen in with Plato's talk of universals and his spectator theory of knowledge – But once again there is no point in trying to pin the blame on Aristotle and his interpreters. The metaphor of knowing general truths by internalizing universals, just as the eye of the body knows particulars by internalizing their individual colors and shapes, was, once suggested, sufficiently powerful to become the intellectual's substitute for the peasant's belief in life among the shades.[10]

 9 PMN 38.
10 PMN 38–41.

It is worth pausing at this point to reflect on Rorty's style and what emerges as a guiding principle in his argumentation. Rorty's writing is highly readable despite being buttressed by a formidable array of references. It has self-deprecating humor ('with the ingratitude of hindsight') and there is frequent use of the pronoun *we* – an assumed consensus runs throughout the book. Above all there is the striking phrase *we moderns*. The subtext of much of the book is that modernity is to be preferred to tradition, that modernity confers legitimacy. The theme of chronological supersession, that simply by virtue of the passage of time new and better viewpoints emerge and old viewpoints are superseded, is both an explicit theme, and, perhaps more significantly, part of an insistent undercurrent of belief and assumption informing the book.

Explicitly, Rorty invokes the support of Thomas Kuhn for a certain irrationality in fundamental paradigm shifts. 'So bad arguments for brilliant hunches must necessarily precede the normalization of a new vocabulary which incorporates the hunch. Given that new vocabulary, better arguments become possible, although these will always be found question-begging by the revolution's victims.'[11] This, of course, makes Rorty a difficult opponent to argue with, for even if the arguments ranged against him are overwhelming, he can always shrug them off and claim that history is on his side. Rorty's book gains greatly in persuasive force through his identification with modernity and his careful choice of images. In the passage quoted it is instructive to note how his modernity is the robust companion of belief in things like mountains, a carefully chosen image conveying all that is palpable, obvious, and substantial. By contrast, the view being criticized (if that is the word) shares the lightness, frothiness, and general insubstantiality of 'breath,' 'shadow,' 'wispy,' 'invisible,' leading up to 'immaterial.'[12]

It is to highlight this informing principle of 'chronological supersession' that I have chosen the phrase 'town criers of inwardness' as the title of this chapter. This is the phrase by which Rorty describes those philosophers who attempt 'to bully the Antipodeans' – a fictitious population dwelling on the other side of our galaxy who do not know they have minds and whose existence is discovered in the middle of the twenty-first(!) century – 'across an invisible line and into the Realm of the Spirit.'[13] As suggesting an attitude to a group of philosophers whose views are at variance with his own, 'town criers of inwardness' is, in terms of rhetoric, quite brilliant. It conveys a mixture of pity and resignation – hostile aggression is not part of

11 PMN 58 note 28.
12 PMN 40.
13 PMN 73.

Rorty's armoury – about certain hopeless cases who cling to the outmoded and useless habits of a bygone age. I have no wish to detract from the quality of Rorty's more strictly philosophical argument, but the point that *Philosophy and the Mirror of Nature* is as much an exercise in persuasive rhetoric as it is a work of philosophical argumentation should not be overlooked. Put more positively, to overlook this point is to do less than justice to Rorty's book.

From Descartes to Kant (1)

With the notion of the mind as mirror or eye firmly installed by the end of the medieval period, Descartes enters the running and draws up a new boundary between the mind and the physical universe. In particular, he includes sensations as well as thoughts and beliefs among 'ideas' – the contents of the mind – and this gives rise to a strict form of mind-body dualism.[14] According to Descartes, we know the contents of the mind, ideas, with greater certainty than we know the physical universe, which these ideas are said to represent. From this arises the problem of 'the veil of ideas,' the notion that the idea is intermediary between the knower and reality. Scepticism arises as a problem not just about attaining certainty (Pyrrhorian scepticism) but about our ability to know the external world at all.[15] The idea of the 'theory of knowledge,' Rorty claims, grew up around the latter problem – the problem of knowing whether our inner representations are accurate. 'The Cartesian mind simultaneously made possible veil-of-ideas skepticism and a discipline devoted to circumventing such skepticism.'[16]

Locke's singular contribution to the rise of epistemology was to confuse explanation with justification.[17] By this Rorty means that Locke offered a quasi-mechanical explanation of how we achieve knowledge as if such an account would 'help us know what we are entitled to believe.'[18] Against attempts to ground our knowledge claims on mechanistic explanations of the operations of the mind, Rorty places the notion that justification is achieved by reasons and that knowledge is 'justified true belief.'[19] 'We,' Rorty claims, think of knowledge as a relation between a person and a proposition rather than between a person and objects.[20] Not so Locke, who

14 PMN 36.
15 PMN 139.
16 PMN 140.
17 PMN 139.
18 PMN 143.
19 PMN 143.
20 PMN 142.

thought of knowledge as 'knowledge of,' whereas today 'we' think of knowledge as 'knowledge that.' Rorty wishes to break the notion that knowledge is dependent on some kind of link between a person and a body or bodies 'out there,' and to replace this 'Platonic' notion of knowledge as 'confrontation' with the notion of knowledge as 'conversation.'

Kant not only moved epistemology forward – Rorty claims that Kant virtually invented the history of modern philosophy[21] – he also moved halfway towards Rorty's position that knowledge is 'knowledge that' rather than 'knowledge of.'[22] Kant, however, confused 'predication (saying something about an object) and synthesis (putting representations together in inner space).'[23] Instead of arriving at a Rortyan position, modelling knowledge on predication or conversation, Kant retained Locke's ambition of trying to explain knowledge by means of some kind of causal machinery.[24] Through his distinction between intuitions and concepts Kant invented the theory of knowledge as it has come down to us in the twentieth century. The weakness in Kant's account is to assume that there is a 'given' manifold that is unified somehow by the synthesizing activities of the understanding. If intuitions cannot be brought to consciousness except by means of a second, conceptual, synthesis, how can we possibly know that manifold is given and the unity made? Rorty uses this not uncommon objection to Kant's a priori mental structures to attack the very notion of a distinction between intuition and concept, between what is said to be given and what is said to be constituted in knowledge[25] – distinctions he believes to be fundamental to the epistemological enterprise. This destructive criticism leads to a critique of epistemology as a search for the foundations of knowledge; the Kantian development is considered to be merely an extension of that search, inasmuch as it takes us beyond the search for privileged representations to 'search for the rules which the mind had set up for itself.'[26]

Rorty offers the following succinct summary of the course taken by the history of epistemology under the sway of the metaphor of the mind-as-mirror:

> Perhaps it helps to think of the original dominating metaphor as being that of having our beliefs determined by being brought face-

---

21 PMN 148.
22 PMN 147.
23 PMN 148.
24 PMN 161.
25 PMN 154.
26 PMN 160.

to-face with the object of belief. The next stage is ... to think of knowledge as an assemblage of representations. Then comes the idea that the way to have accurate representations is to find, within the Mirror, a special privileged class of representations so compelling that their accuracy cannot be doubted. These privileged foundations will be the foundations of knowledge, and the discipline which directs us towards them – the theory of knowledge – will be the foundation of culture ...

Philosophy-as-epistemology will be the search for the immutable structures within which knowledge, life, and culture must be contained – structures set by the privileged representations which it studies. The neo-Kantian consensus thus appears as the end-product of an original wish to substitute *confrontation* for *conversation* as the determinant of belief.[27]

The Analytical Tradition

Following his critique of Kant, Rorty completes his task of dismantling the traditional machinery of epistemology by attacking the last vestiges of Kantian epistemology in the analytical tradition of the twentieth century. That tradition continued to believe 'that philosophy stood to empirical science as the study of structure to the study of content.'[28] The analytical tradition continued to posit some kind of isomorphism between language and the world as an extralinguistic reality.[29] To undermine any such isomorphism Rorty makes use of Sellars's attack on 'the myth of the given' and Quine's attack on the 'analytic-synthetic' distinction.[30] Both are essentially attacks on the notion of privileged classes of propositions that command assent either by expressing the 'given' or by being 'analytically or conceptually true.' Rorty thinks the criticisms offered by Sellars and Quine complete the destruction both of the traditional understanding of knowledge in terms of two poles (the one subjective and the other objective, the one referring to the mind and the other to the empirically given) and of the truth of propositions as determined by the relation between these two poles. Such a view of truth (he believes) continues to be parasitic on the mind as mirror of nature and generates the search for a bridge between mind and nature. Rorty wishes to replace this confrontational view of

27 PMN 163.
28 PMN 169.
29 See McCarthy, 'The Critique of Realism,' 108.
30 PMN 170ff.

knowing with the notion of philosophy as conversation. In the former, justification is atomized and reductive; in the latter, justification is by means of propositions and is holistic.[31]

In *Consequences of Pragmatism* Rorty sums up the impact of Sellars's and Quine's criticisms for a pragmatic understanding of knowledge:

> Now that these criticisms have taken hold the time may have come to try to recapture Dewey's 'naturalized' version of Hegel's histori-cism. In this historicist vision, the arts, the sciences, the sense of right and wrong, and the institutions of society are not attempts to embody or formulate truth or goodness or beauty. They are at-tempts to solve problems – to modify our beliefs and desires and activities in ways that will bring us greater happiness than we now have. I want to suggest that this shift in perspective is the natural consequence of dropping the receptivity/spontaneity and intuition/concept distinctions, and more generally of dropping the notion of 'representation.'[32]

Rorty hopes this view will help us to 'finally move beyond realism and idealism.'[33]

The Way Forward

There is nothing outside the philosophical conversation that bestows cred-ibility or validity upon it. There is no 'Archimedian point outside the series of actual and possible beliefs,'[34] no 'neutral matrix,' no 'foundations of knowledge.' The only 'conceptual scheme' Rorty will allow is 'the collection of views which make up our present-day culture'[35] – that is, the criteria or norms that justify a proposition are internal to the culture that produces it. The conversational model of doing philosophy Rorty advocates is behaviouristic in the sense that conversation is a form of social practice.[36] He is willing to take this model to pretty extreme conclusions. Even the certainty with which we assent to the Pythagorean Theorem, for example, is explained by 'victory in argument,' by the fact that nobody can find an effective objection to the premises on which our inference rests, rather

31 PMN 170.
32 *Consequences of Pragmatism*, 16.
33 Ibid., 17.
34 PMN 296–7.
35 PMN 276.
36 PMN 178.

than 'by the relation of reason to triangularity.'[37] Truth is 'warranted assertibility,'[38] knowledge is 'the social justification of belief.'[39]

The hermeneutics Rorty proposes in his final chapter as the new enterprise for philosophy is presented as a rather low-grade activity that will allow us to cope with reality rather than to know it.[40] Modesty among philosophers is the keynote of these closing pages. Philosophers should abandon attempts at unifying the disciplines and putting everyone to rights, and the term *cognition* should be reserved for the predictive sciences. For Rorty 'edifying philosophies,' rather than 'systematic philosophies,' take us out of ourselves by making us new beings, capable of redefining ourselves. Choice, options, freedom are the emphases here. Rorty sides with Sartre, saying that to expect truth to claim us is to avoid the burden of choosing; man only knows himself or anything else under 'optional descriptions.'[41] So *Philosophy and the Mirror of Nature* moves from epistemological or cognitional issues to ones that have more of a moral or existential air to them. We are invited to explore new ways of making ourselves and new ways of defining philosophy.

Lonergan's History of Philosophy

I wish to juxtapose Rorty's reading of the tradition, outlined above, with Lonergan's to throw light on the roots of the agreement and disagreement between the two. Paradoxically, while Rorty presents himself as a defender of the Enlightenment there is one area where, surprisingly, it is Lonergan who is the true heir to the Enlightenment program. Rorty rejects the Enlightenment quest for a general framework of inquiry; Lonergan's lifework was devoted to discovering one, and to exploring its possibilities. Unlike the framework of inquiry sought in the eighteenth century, however, Lonergan's 'method' shows no trace of the occult: his claims rest on the deliveries of consciousness. Rorty, it is clear, would not allow conclusions based on such a 'foundation' – consciousness is, in fact, a major casualty of his thesis.

I cannot pretend that what follows is, strictly speaking, Bernard Lonergan's history of philosophy. I have found Lonergan's broad-brush treatment in *Insight* and *Method in Theology*, where the history of philosophy forms a somewhat sketchily drawn background to other matters, useful in making

37 PMN 157.
38 PMN 308.
39 PMN 170.
40 PMN 356.
41 PMN 379.

the comparison with Rorty. This treatment, though exceedingly spare at times, points up what Lonergan sees as the turning points in the history of philosophy, the core ideas; and my own treatment is guided by these 'markers' along the route taken by the Western tradition. In that sense, what follows is Lonergan's account of the history of philosophy. Inevitably, I shall go over some of the territory already traversed by Rorty, which is necessary, not only for shifts in emphasis to be noted, but to clarify Lonergan's basically different approach and radically differing reading of the tradition.

Galileo

Lonergan's account accords Galileo unusual prominence in the history of philosophy. It is as if he sees in Galileo's distinction between primary and secondary qualities a fault line running through the philosophical understanding of knowledge in the modern period. Many of the epistemic puzzles and problems of Cartesian and post-Cartesian philosophy are linked with Galileo's fateful distinction. In the tale of modern philosophy, Galileo opens Pandora's box.

It was perfectly understandable for Galileo to distinguish between primary and secondary qualities. Although the secondary qualities perceived by sense, such as colour, heat, and smell seem to common sense to be the most palpable and felt, and hence the 'most real' of realities, Galileo spent a good deal of his time in robust disagreement with those champions of common sense, the Aristotelian scientists of his day. He defied the views of common sense, which with its customary self-assurance claims to *know* that objects remain at rest unless moved by some external force, and so forth; and he defended the Platonic notion that mathematics holds the key to the true understanding of the universe. He expresses his view in a well-known passage in *The Assayer:*

> Philosophy is written in that great book which ever lies before our eyes – I mean the Universe – but we cannot understand it if we do not first learn the language and grasp the symbols in which it is written. The book is written in the mathematical language, and the symbols are triangles, circles and other geometrical figures, without whose help it is impossible to comprehend a single word of it; without which one wanders in vain through a dark labyrinth.[42]

42 Galileo Galilei, *The Assayer (Il Saggiatore)* (1623).

With Galileo's new science, the colourful, varied world of sense percep-tion yields to the bloodless, hidden world of number, the mathematical dimensions of matter in motion. Such is the mathematical structure of reality that the qualities of green and red, hard and soft, loud and quiet, and the like all arise in our senses only as a result of the 'shapes, number, sizes and slow and rapid movements' of 'external bodies' – they are second-ary qualities. The primary qualities of the universe are quantitative; the universe's true nature is revealed by the primary qualities that are capable of measurement and numerical calculation. Scientific experiment is not just the exercise of the senses, so much lauded by the Aristotelians, but the putting of questions to nature in the language of mathematics. It is the a priori mathematical structure of the universe that makes scientific experimentation fruitful and lays the foundation for the new science of motion – the 'new knowledge,' the *scienza nuova.*

The story of Galileo and his distinction between primary and secondary qualities is important to the story of modern philosophy, as Lonergan conceives it, in a number of ways. First and foremost, it introduces the subject. Where Aristotelian science had dealt in objective categories and relations, continuous with metaphysics, Galileo speaks of the subject. The subject confronts the universe 'out there,' which she has to get hold of somehow. The wedge driven by Descartes between subject and object has already been insinuated by Galileo. What is the relation between subjectiv-ity and objectivity? Does the subject operate by means of a priori reasoning or a posteriori experimentation? Is it to be a rationalist or empiricist account of knowledge? Or possibly a synthesis of the two? One of the most dramatic outcomes of Galileo's distinction, which Lonergan points out is philosophical and does not follow from his scientific findings,[43] is the pitting of sense and intellect one against the other, and the oscillations that occur as now one and now the other is upheld as the conveyor of the real.

At a more basic level, by introducing the subject in the way he did, Galileo supplied it with an extremely wobbly basis. The subject is not just acted upon, but in a certain sense is activated and actualized by Galileo's primary qualities. That which is 'subjective' is secondary, because it is brought into being by the activity of matter in motion. By according primordial status to what lies 'out there' Galileo invites the assumption that true objectivity consists in reaching out and grasping the mathematical properties of matter in motion that are already out there. But what if the object of our attention is not 'out there' but 'in here'? And what if it is not

43 B. Lonergan, *Insight: A Study of Human Understanding* (Longmans, Green & Co., 1957), 85, 130; Collected Works of Bernard Lonergan, vol. 3 (University of Toronto Press, 1992), 107, 152–3.

amenable to measurement and mathematical manipulation? In that case, its status as an entity with any claim to objective validity is open to question. The Galilean distinction implies the possibility of legislating the subject out of existence.

Thus Galileo, the Renaissance scientist, sets the agenda for modern philosophy. But if Galileo opens Pandora's box, Descartes gives its contents a definitive shape and character. Subsequent philosophers were to dispute many of Descartes's findings, but his basic division of the universe into two broad and opposing substances – *res cogitans* and *res extensa* – brought Galileo's distinction into the mainstream of European philosophy, and continues to exert enormous influence on philosophy to this day.

From Descartes to Kant (2)

A mathematician and scientist familiar with Galileo's writings, Descartes finds in the certainty yielded by mathematical method a weapon with which to combat the pervasive scepticism of his age. His genius seized upon the fact of doubt itself and made it the starting point of his philosophy. However, as Lonergan notes, the injunction to doubt everything that can be doubted tends to affect 'not the underlying texture and fabric of the mind, but only the explicit judgments that issue from it,'[44] a reference to the very real presuppositions that underlie Descartes's approach (and indeed any approach to the problem of knowledge). The method Descartes wishes to apply to all knowledge is what he understands to be the method of mathematics, whose most basic operation is 'intuition.' Though in itself infallible, Cartesian intuition is not discursive but single and momentary. It is important to grasp the characteristics of intuition in Descartes. He distinguishes between 'clear and distinct ideas,' which yield the certainty shared by the mathematical grasp of the properties of extension and mobility, and 'confused ideas' such as colour and sound, which derive from sense. Descartes then muddles the issue by describing intuition as analogous to sensation – it is momentary, fleeting, 'simply vision.' Thus, Descartes forges an alliance between intellect (understood as analogous to sensation and specifically to an act of vision) and that which is the object of intellect, namely, the clear and distinct ideas emanating from the mathematical properties of what is extended in space. This in effect marries the ocular metaphor for understanding to Galileo's primary qualities. Not for the last time, however, this marriage causes the philosopher who subscribes to it no little difficulty.

44 *Insight* (1957), 410; CWL 3: 436.

Descartes realizes that an act of intuition, either recalled later or forming part of a chain of reasoning, is unable to yield the certainty it enjoys at the moment of its occurrence. For this reason Descartes's method (based supposedly on the procedures of mathematics) needs the further authentication of knowledge claims supplied by metaphysics; this point Descartes considers to have been overlooked by Galileo. Metaphysics supplies the grounds for ascertaining that certainty in knowledge is attainable.[45] Descartes bridges the chasm between the thinking thing and the extended thing by an elaborate piece of metaphysical reasoning. He advances from the *cogito* to the self to God to God's veracity as underwriting the validity of the 'clear and distinct ideas' by which nature is known. Knowledge for Descartes is always a private possession, akin to sensation, privately striven for but 'divinely vouchsafed.'

Descartes's metaphysical reasoning is the first but by no means the last attempt to bridge the gap between *res cogitans* and *res extensa*. From there it is but a short step to the dualism of mind of body. If the world of bodies is understood as extension then the mind is easily understood in opposition to this. Positing two completely disparate attributes, namely, spatiality and consciousness, Descartes assigns the body to one and mind or soul to the other. Galileo's fault line now runs between these two substances and mind-body dualism is established. Philosophy is primed to follow the routes such dualism will allow.

Newton intervenes between Descartes and the British empiricists, and the ideal of philosophy changes from the method of mathematics to the method of science.[46] Epistemology, however, remains central, and mental events retain their priority over knowledge of the world. As Anthony Kenny observes, 'Ideas, impressions, and sense-data are all, by Cartesian standards, mental entities; and for the British empiricists they are all epistemologically prior to the physical substances of the problematic external world. For Locke, Berkeley and Hume, no less than for Descartes, mind is better known than body in the sense that the internal is more certain than the external, the private prior to the public.'[47]

Locke's attempt to reassure us that the ideas of the mind deliver the real results in not a little confusion and illustrates the enduring influence of Galileo's distinction between primary and secondary qualities. Muddle arises from Locke's simultaneously entertaining that simple ideas are particulars

45 S.V. Keeling, *Descartes* (London University Press, 1965), 81–2.
46 For a helpful discussion of this and related matters see Ernst Cassirer, *The Philosophy of the Enlightenment* (Princeton University Press, 1932), chap. 1.
47 Anthony Kenny, *The Anatomy of the Soul* (Basil Blackwell, 1973), 114.

that 'enter by the senses simple and unmixed,'[48] and his depiction of simple ideas as solidity, extension, figure, and so forth. The latter are, of course, Galileo's primary qualities, and once again we see them invested with strong talismanic properties, guaranteeing that knowledge is veridical. The problem, however, is that such general ideas as solidity, extension, and so forth cannot be the basic building blocks of sensation, which by nature has particular smells, sounds, tastes, and so forth as its proper objects. Descartes, at the verbal level at least, avoided this confusion by casting primary qualities as the object of intellect, but Locke, accounting for knowledge in terms of sensation, cannot escape so easily. Locke creates a mismatch between the sensory receiver and what is claimed to be received. As W.J. Sorley says, 'Locke severs, instead of establishing, the connection between simple ideas and reality. The only ideas which can make good their claim to be regarded as simple ideas (particulars) have nothing resembling them in things. The others ... have only a doubtful claim to rank as simple ideas.'[49]

Lonergan makes the interesting point that Hume applies methodical doubt with greater rigour than Descartes.[50] In organizing claims around sense perception, Hume is a good deal more rigorous and ruthless than Locke or Berkeley in ridding his account of everything that cannot be reconciled with the bare presentations of sense. Out goes Locke's material substance as well as Berkeley's spiritual substance. Out too goes causality understood objectively as anything except temporal succession. The substantial ego or self is replaced by the flux of events. As a provider of the real, sense perception yields only sensations that are particular and fleeting.

A world view that flattens everything into fleeting sensations is lacking in pattern and permanence. To explain why we feel that we inhabit a reasonably stable and predictable world, Hume invokes a set of beliefs and habits bestowed on us by a beneficent Nature. These beliefs and habits explain such features as causal relations or the permanence of objects, which cannot be explained by mere fleeting impressions. Nature for Hume is an occult entity that makes up for what cannot be explained by the only 'cement' he will allow, the association of ideas. Most notably, Nature provides the bridge between the knower and the existence of bodies, a belief that no amount of 'cement' can possibly account for.

A discernible pattern has emerged in the philosophies so far considered. Descartes, Locke, and Hume have recourse to compensatory devices to

---

48 John Locke, *An Essay Concerning Human Understanding*, II.ii.1.
49 W.R. Sorley, A *History of English Philosophy* (Cambridge University Press, 1920) 118.
50 *Insight* (1957), 411.

bridge the gap between the knower and the known in order to provide assurance that what is claimed to be known is either real or (in the case of Hume) has the appearance of reality. But Hume is not sufficiently sensitive to the fact that the beliefs and habits he utilizes in this way are not themselves readily accessible to sense perception. On what basis, therefore, can he assert that they exist? In short, Hume is rigorous up to a point. He is less rigorous when accounting for the psychological mechanisms with which he props up his account of knowledge.

If Hume brings empiricism to a certain extreme, Kant makes a new beginning by attempting a synthesis of rationalism and empiricism. By wedding the a priori categories of the understanding to the a priori forms of the sensibility Kant tries to heal the fault line running from Galileo's distinction. Sense and intellect appear to have been brought into harmony once more, and the Galilean bifurcation appears to have been overcome. The empiricists had experimented along the sense-perception side of the Galilean divide, culminating in Humean scepticism. Now Kant has effected a reconciliation of what we *think* (the understanding) and what *is given* through the intuitions of sense. True scientific knowledge is constituted by this double synthesis: 'Thoughts without content are empty; intuitions without concepts are blind.'[51]

Where his predecessors relied on the talismanic powers of primary qualities (Rorty's 'privileged representations') or hidden mechanisms to cope with scepticism, Kant's Copernican revolution apparently outmanoeuvres the problem. For Kant it is not necessary to show how the ideas of the mind correspond with the objects in the world 'out there,' since both are constructs of the mind. In this way the a priori system of thought itself is made foundational. But the price of Kant's a priori is that we can never know the thing-in-itself because all our knowledge is a synthesis of a priori forms and categories. Rorty notes that appeal to privileged access is a move not open to Kant in the way it was to Descartes; for Kant is stuck with the fact that what we know are appearances. The price paid for making the a priori structure of knowledge foundational is that, far from overcoming the problem of representationism, it ensures that we are entirely enclosed within the phenomenal world of appearances.

Lonergan's central criticism of Kant's philosophy concerns the role of the unconditioned in Kant. For Kant, the unconditioned is a regulative ideal lying beyond experience and the phenomenal world. Its function is to systematize and unify human rationality, bidding us seek ever greater syntheses of phenomena. As merely a regulative ideal it is not constitutive of the real; nor could it be. For Lonergan, by contrast, the unconditioned is

51 Immanuel Kant, *Critique of Pure Reason*, B 75.

required for verification; and since the verified is the real, the unconditioned is constitutive of the real. The unconditioned is attained when a direct act of understanding is reflectively understood as a conditioned whose conditions have been fulfilled. The unconditioned is known when reflective understanding grasps that the data (or some of the data) 'fit' direct understanding. Far from being privileged, the fit between the data and understanding has to be checked out. Once this fit has been grasped the subject can legitimately proceed to make a judgment. In judgment the data of sense and the intelligible grasped by understanding are affirmed and posited as a unity. The unconditioned is the real and the real is the unconditioned. The gap between sense and understanding is overcome in judgment. The split between noumenon and phenomenon means that Kant's unconditioned cannot function in this way.

The reason Lonergan makes much of this is because it indicates Kant's failure to reconcile and overcome two forms of realism: the realism of animal extroversion and the realism of rational affirmation.[52] Ultimately, Kant's synthesis of the empiricist and rationalist strands in his philosophy fails to produce an effective bridge between sensibility and understanding. The gulf dividing the unknowable noumenal world from the knowable phenomenal world ensures that the synthesis of understanding and sensibility cannot deliver the 'really real,' and so the synthesis is never securely posited. For this reason the Galilean fault line remains open, with important consequences for the subsequent history of philosophy. It is as if the two strands in Kant's philosophy float free of one another, and philosophy bifurcates into positivism and pragmatism on the one side and idealism and immanentism on the other.[53] In the final analysis, Kant represents a heroic but failed attempt to close the gap between sense and intellect. As they move further apart, each becomes more entrenched in its own exclusivity, with positivism and pragmatism affirming the triumph of the physical sciences, while idealism becomes lost in the immanentism of thought thinking itself in human history.[54] Analytic philosophy has been drawn to the former, while the German philosophical tradition has dwelt on the latter.

52 *Insight* (1957), 414; CWL 3: 439.
53 *Insight* (1957), 414–15; CWL 3: 440.
54 *Insight* (1957), 415; CWL 3: 440–1. This helps explain what Lonergan has termed the 'naturalism' of the Anglo-Saxon philosophical tradition, which prizes scientific knowledge, and the 'historicism' of the German tradition, which prizes meaning. See *Topics in Education*, Collected Works of Bernard Lonergan, vol. 10 (University of Toronto Press, 1993), 12. Rorty might be seen to be attempting a reconciliation between these two philosophical movements. Whether or not he succeeds is not at issue here, but my view of the matter can be gathered from the conclusion of this chapter.

A Radical Comparison of Rorty and Lonergan

There is genuine and significant agreement between Rorty and Lonergan about the tradition running from Descartes to Kant. Where many conventional histories of philosophy emphasize the differences between the various camps – rationalism, empiricism, idealism – Rorty and Lonergan agree that they are simply variations on a theme. That theme is the epistemological priority of the mental, the 'veil of ideas,' with its attendant scepticism. This is the source of the many devices invoked to overcome scepticism, ranging from Descartes's appeal to God to more recent solutions to the same problem, such as the Naturally Given, Privileged Representations, and the like. Lonergan, like Rorty, rejects each and all of these devices because he rejects the view of knowledge that creates the need for them (based on the metaphor of the mirror or eye).

In their critiques of central features of the dominant epistemological tradition, both philosophers, therefore, are in extensive agreement. Rorty's response is to abandon the epistemological enterprise altogether, flawed as it is by the visual metaphor. Lonergan's response, however, distinguishes between the dominant tradition and another tradition that is free of any trace of representationism because it does not equate *ousia* (being) with 'idea' in the Platonist manner. Where Rorty, in his discussion of universals, simply lumps Plato and Aristotle together,[55] and refers to medieval scholastic philosophers somewhat indiscriminately (several 'asides' notwithstanding), Lonergan firmly distinguishes between the conceptualists, whose major spokesperson is John Duns Scotus in the fourteenth century, and the intellectualists, whose major spokesperson is Thomas Aquinas in the thirteenth century. The roots of the representationism that has momentous consequences for the history of philosophy lie in conceptualism.

The Roots of Disagreement

Here is Lonergan's account of the Scotist analysis of cognition:

> [O]bjective knowing is a matter of taking a look at what actually is there to be seen. If then intellect apprehends the intelligible in the sensible and the universal in the particular, its apprehension must be illusory, for it sees what is not there to be seen. None the less, we do know what is intelligible and universal. To account for this fact without violating his convictions on extroversion as the model of objectivity, Scotus distinguished a series of steps in the genesis of

55 See PMN 60–1, 125.

intellectual knowledge. The first step was abstraction; it occurs
unconsciously; it consists of the impression upon intellect of a
universal conceptual content. The second step was intellection:
intellect takes a look at conceptual content. The third step was a comparison of different contents with the result that intellect saw which
concepts were conjoined necessarily and which were incompatible.
There follows the deduction of the abstract metaphysics of all
possible worlds and to it one adds an intuition of the existing and
present as existing and present to attain knowledge of the actual
world.[56]

For conceptualists concepts come first and understanding consists in grasping the relations between concepts by mental looking and the link between
concepts and experience by intuition. Concepts are intermediary between
the knower and the real.

Lonergan considers that there is a less precise and more pervasive form
of conceptualism, which reaches far beyond the Scotist school. The objective universals of Platonist thought seem to owe their origin to the notion
that, as the eye of the body looks upon colours and shapes, so there is a
spiritual eye of the soul that looks at universals or, at least, recalls them.[57]

The eye metaphor is not just rooted in particular historical movements; it
appears to be an extremely difficult metaphor for men and women to
resist. The intellectualism of Aristotle and Aquinas contrasts with conceptualism. According to Lonergan's intellectualism, concepts derive from
understanding, and not the other way around. Intellectualism subverts the
metaphor of the mind as eye or mirror.

> For the intellectualist, it is impossible to confuse the Aristotelian
> form with the Platonic idea. Form is the *ousia* that is not a (Platonic)
> universal, but a cause of being ... Form is what causes matter to be a
> thing. On the cognitional side, form is known in knowing the answer
> to the question: 'Why are the sensible data to be conceived as of one
> thing, of a man, of a house?' But knowing why and knowing the
> cause, like knowing the reason and knowing the real reason, are
> descriptions of the act of understanding. As then form mediates
> causally between matter and thing, so understanding mediates
> causally between sensible data and conception. By a stroke of genius
> Aristotle replaced mythical Platonic *anamnesis* by psychological fact

56 *Insight* (1957), 406; CWL 3: 431; emphasis added.
57 *Insight* (1957), 413; CWL 3: 438.

and, to describe the psychological fact, eliminated the subsistent ideas to introduce formal causes in material things.[58]

Aristotle and Aquinas do not consider form to be 'just Plato's ideas, plucked from their noetic heaven, and shoved into material things.'[59] There is then a huge difference between the Aristotelian and Thomistic notion of form and the Platonic notion of universal ideas. For Aristotle and Aquinas the intelligible is grasped in the particular as that which makes sense of the particular. The idea of a 'chair,' for example, is neither parasitic on some Platonic ideal 'Chair' nor simply a convenient shorthand for many similarly shaped things: it is the form that causes this matter to be a chair. Because Aristotle and Aquinas specify form as *ousia*[60] and not as *idea* (understood as a mental entity), their epistemologies are free from representationism and 'veil of ideas' scepticism.

Furthermore, our notion of the structure of knowledge brings in its train a notion of the relation between the knower and the known. If knowing is regarded as a confrontational encounter, then the mind can easily be cast as that which stands over against the world 'out there,' and a dualistic universe ensues. Correlative to this dualistic arrangement will be certain notions of objectivity, of the real, and of the relations of mind to matter, and of mind to body. If knowing, however, is not by confrontation but by identity, so that the form causally present in matter is the form intentionally grasped by the mind, then the way is open for a radically different conception of the structure of knowledge and, along with this, of objectivity, the real, and the relation between mind and matter and between the mind and body.

Rorty and Mind

A major charge that can legitimately be brought against Rorty is that he draws conclusions that exceed the scope of his argument. Having shown that Platonist, Cartesian, and more recent accounts of knowledge are contaminated by the virus of representationism, he concludes that all epistemology is similarly vulnerable and should be put behind us. Rorty

58 Lonergan, *Verbum: Word and Idea in Aquinas* (London: Darton, Longman & Todd, 1968), 187–8. My understanding of Lonergan on this point is indebted to Geoffrey Price, 'Confrontation and Understanding in the Foundations of Political Philosophy,' *METHOD: Journal of Lonergan Studies* 1/2 (Fall 1983); and to Matthew Lamb, 'The Notion of the Transcultural in Bernard Lonergan's Theology,' *METHOD* 8/1 (Spring 1990).
59 Lonergan, *Verbum*, 187.
60 *Verbum*, 82–8.

never truly engages with the tradition with which Lonergan is associated. While Lonergan does not share the views of Rorty's opponents, he nevertheless gets caught up in Rorty's denials. A similar situation develops in respect of Rorty's reflections on 'mind,' mainly in the second chapter of *Philosophy and the Mirror of Nature*, entitled 'Persons without Minds.' I have deliberately left a consideration of his argument to this stage where it more conveniently leads on to the concluding sections of this chapter.

What is at first glance surprising to Lonergan's students is Rorty's apparent reduction of the issue of whether or not we have minds to the question Do we have sensations? Sensations and 'raw feels,' particularly in relation to pain, are taken as potential evidence that we have minds. For Rorty the agenda for this debate in the philosophy of mind was set by Gilbert Ryle's *The Concept of Mind*, in which 'raw feels' were almost the sole survivors from Ryle's behaviouristic account of the mind.[61] 'Raw feels' offer the only toehold on the mind some modern philosophers can muster, in as much as more long-standing beliefs and desires are equated with Rylean dispositions to behave in particular ways. In essence, Rorty's argument against mind as based on raw feels is yet another sustained attack on representationism as grounded in a variety of raw feels: raw feels as 'incorrigibly knowable' and hence the foundation of knowledge;[62] raw feels are equated with the Naturally Given to which all other known entities are somehow reducible;[63] hence raw feels are intermediary between the person and the object he is talking about.[64] In this argument, 'raw feels' are yet another version of 'veil of ideas' representationism, and so Rorty believes he has eliminated 'mind' by defeating representationism.

The view that Rorty supports, but cannot provide a clinching argument for because of problems of reference,[65] maintains that statements such as 'My C-fibers are firing' can be substituted for statements like 'I am in pain.' That is, reports of sensations are in fact not reports of *mental* events but reports of *neural* events. This is a position Rorty had once argued for on the grounds that 'the development of due respect for cerebroscopes would mean the discovery that there had never been any mental events.'[66] He cannot quite affirm the identity of mind and brain in his book but this is, in fact, the position he conveys. In chapter 5, where he tightens and toughens his position, he says, '[I]f the body had been easier to understand, nobody

61 PMN 66–7.
62 PMN 80–1.
63 PMN 104–5.
64 PMN 101.
65 PMN 119.
66 PMN 120 note 24.

would have thought that we had a mind.'[67] The 'Antipodeans,' to whom Rorty artfully attributes the beliefs he is supporting, claimed that 'talk of mental states was merely a placeholder for talk of neurons.'[68] It is not so much that the 'physical' has triumphed over the 'mental' as that an outmoded way of speaking, handed down from the seventeenth and eighteenth centuries, has been superseded. Rorty's basic argument is that '[n]o predictive or explanatory or descriptive power would be lost if we had spoken Antipodean all our lives.'[69]

Part of the admiration Rorty elicits from us stems from his brilliance in making the implausible plausible and the plausible implausible. For surely we must ask if Rorty has come anywhere near showing that mental events are the equivalent of neural events. Simply put, neural events are not conscious whereas mental events are conscious. Cerebroscopes do not make the firing of neurons in my brain conscious any more than microscopes make the crystal formation of salt conscious. In both cases the objects of my scrutiny become, by virtue of the scientific instruments I employ, objects of conscious study and investigation. But they do not thereby become any more conscious, whereas the mental operations I employ in learning about these objects would not exist without consciousness. Mental events are constituted by consciousness. Moreover, Rorty never explains how it is possible to say, without consciousness, 'My C-fibers are firing.'[70] How did *my* get into this sentence? My ownership of the C-fibers in question is not revealed by the cerebroscope. And how could the assertion 'It's just awful' have any import as a follow-up to the statement 'It's my C-fibers again ...'[71] unless some subjective conscious experience is presumed? Even the brief examples offered by Rorty tell against his conclusion.

Lonergan and the Subject

Rorty's brief against consciousness is based on his wish to get rid of the Cartesian notion of mind. But in order to get rid of the Cartesian notion of mind, it is not necessary to go to such lengths! Consciousness properly explored, in fact, shows us the way out of the Cartesian impasse. Consciousness is not in the first instance the presence of something to me but the presence of myself to myself. It is necessary for me to be present to

67 PMN 239.
68 PMN 81.
69 PMN 120.
70 See PMN 74.
71 Ibid.

myself for anything else to be present to me. I am constituted by my consciousness.

Now the metaphor of knowing as looking to which Rorty and Lonergan are both opposed is founded on an inadequate view of consciousness – namely, consciousness as perception, as a cognitive act that reveals the object as it was prior to the occurrence of the act.[72] This notion of consciousness is based on the ocular metaphor that suffers from all the problems Rorty uncovers at such length in his book. While Lonergan does not equate consciousness with knowing, he does hold that each of the activities I perform in coming to know is conscious – conscious as experienced. I do not discover myself as conscious by peering inside to see what is there – this would be a repetition of the fallacy of knowing as looking – but I can enlarge my awareness, and in doing so, attend to my conscious activities and attempt to understand them. I might note, for example, that were it not for the striking fact that by human consciousness I am present to myself when something else is present to me, I would not know that I know something when I know something. And if that were the case, I would not be able to encode my knowledge in symbolic forms and pass it on to others, including succeeding generations. Human culture is only possible because of the nature of human consciousness.

Rorty's rejection of consciousness is a consequence of his rejection of verification as an appeal to inner process or to immediate acquaintance with the Naturally Given. Lonergan is at one with the latter rejection: what he means by data is quite distinct from the notion and function of the Naturally Given attacked by Rorty. The function of the Naturally Given is to overcome the problem of verification, which afflicts all notions of knowing as looking; and it achieves this by claiming that something given is *imposed* on the mind. By contrast, the function of Lonergan's notion of data is not to solve the problem of verification – data are not uninterpreted facts imposed on the mind. Data as Lonergan conceives them do not play a foundational role. Method, the invariant and conscious three-step pattern of coming to know, is foundational. This is not the Enlightenment search for an ahistorical, presuppositionless, neutral standpoint outside of time. Rather, it is a normative pattern of concrete conscious operations rooted in time and history: and method is an analysis and thematization of what we do in any human context when we come to know something. Moreover, consciousness is heightened with each step of knowing: by understanding we move towards the attainment of meaning; by verification we make a judgment, taking a stand on what is so. And when we move beyond knowl-

72 *Collection* (Darton, Longman & Todd, 1968), 176; Collected Works of Bernard Lonergan, vol. 4 (University of Toronto Press, 1988), 164–5.

edge claims to decision and action, consciousness becomes self-conscious as we constitute and reveal what we stand for. Consciousness is heightened at each step because the area of conscious control expands at each step as we move from the frequently unavoidable contingency of sensation through to the free, deliberate, and responsible process of choosing, deciding, and acting on the basis of knowledge attained.

In contrast to both Cartesian dualism and Rorty's unitary physicalism, Lonergan posits an integrative view of the human subject in which body and mind interlock to make a single person. The laws of physics, chemistry, biology, and neurology are not negated in any way; but they do open up ever higher integrations. Just as the laws of physics and chemistry are not negated in plants but encompassed within the higher integration of botany, so in human beings lower levels are integrated into the higher levels of the conscious operations of human thinking, deciding, and acting. Through the activation of these conscious operations men and women not only make the world around them but also make themselves.

In this talk of human beings making themselves by their choices and actions, Lonergan touches on an area of agreement with Rorty who, while rejecting the notion of the mind, retains the notion of person:

> Even if the problems of consciousness and reason are both dissolved, however, that of personhood might seem to remain intact, since this notion draws on our moral intuitions, intuitions which seem unlikely to be merely the results of misguided Greek or seventeenth century attempts to construct models of knowing or of the mind.[73]

However, the notion of 'free choice' that Rorty advocates is not at all like Lonergan's; nor could it be. Rorty denies any constant framework of inquiry, any distinction between scheme and content, and so accepts – quite proudly – the notion of the incommensurability of knowledge claims. From incommensurability it is but a short step to intellectual consumerism. Try this on for size; see how it feels; test its fit. 'Fit' here cannot, of course, mean 'fit' with independent evidence or a more basic description, since these are ruled out. Criteria are internal. 'Fit' in a moral context can only be a matter of choice and taste. For Rorty 'free' can only mean 'at will,' because he has repudiated the epistemological subject and denied epistemic authority to the subject's conscious processes. Rorty's moral subject – his notion of 'person' – floats free, is able to choose her lifestyle at will or arbitrarily. The norms inherent in responsible subjectivity (be attentive, be

73 PMN 127.

intelligent, be rational, and be responsible) are never attended to, and we are left with Rorty's detached private-enterprise ego.[74]

The Basic Objection to Rorty

This brings us to a central question raised in relation to Richard Rorty's philosophy. Does it or does it not uphold the rule of reason, particularly in respect of how human beings conduct themselves? Or is it bereft of any criteria of reasonableness and hence unable to condemn the most brutish and traditionally despicable behaviour imaginable? Positions have been taken up on either side of these questions.[75] No one would suggest that Richard Rorty himself condones barbaric behaviour; and he himself insists that beliefs have to be 'justified' and 'warranted.' It all depends on what is meant by 'justified' and 'warranted' in the context of Rorty's philosophy – what does he deem to be *the* criterion that settles whether a belief is 'justified' or 'warranted'? Is it evidence, argument, reason, or is it that epistemic authority is solely invested in society? If it is the former, one would need to ask what kinds of reason or evidence 'justify' or 'warrant' a belief. But Rorty is clearly opposed to that line of questioning, because he believes it implies what he most heartily repudiates: (1) a constant element in the structure of human reasoning, (2) a neutral matrix of investigation, and (3) the continuity between generations of certain rational criteria rather than the provisional, temporary, and ever-changing methods and criteria he supports.[76] As a behaviourist Rorty's option is the view that societal approval or consensus confers legitimacy on our affirmations. As he puts it himself:

> [A]ssertions are justified by society rather than by the character of the inner representations they express ... Explaining rationality and epistemic authority by reference to what society lets us say, rather than the latter by the former, is the essence of what I shall call 'epistemological behaviorism.'[77]

In Rorty's book the final arbiter of legitimacy is society, and society's authority cannot possess any enduring criteria of rationality. The conclu-

74 Rorty's views on these and related issues are repeated with even greater force in his later work *Contingency, Irony and Solidarity* (Cambridge University Press, 1981).
75 Notably by Hugo Meynell, whose articles (referred to in note 2 above) argue that Rorty's position offers no defence against brutish and cruel behaviour.
76 PMN 392, 270.
77 PMN 174.

sion cannot be avoided that agreement among a bunch of thugs or bigots bestows as much epistemic authority as agreement among responsible scholars and scientists.

Conclusion

There is a fundamental contradiction at the heart of Richard Rorty's more general position that is instructive because it reveals where his position is situated within the history of philosophy. It is an existential contradiction between Rorty's conclusions and the argument that supports those conclusions. For Rorty recounts the tale of philosophy as a series of accidents, a fortuitous sequence of events and ideas that appear to be heading in no particular direction. Indeed, the sequence of events succeeded only in leading Western philosophy into a series of blind alleys such as universals, the inner eye, epistemology, and the mind. Strangely, this apparently directionless series of historical blunders somehow arrived at a remarkable destination to which, in retrospect, it appears to have been heading all along. Rortyan pragmatism is both the critic of history and its beneficiary, indeed its creation. The historical process that blindly and erratically witnessed the construction of so many false ideas also provides, amazingly, the tools both for its own deconstruction and the construction of Rorty's epistemological behaviourism. He presents his position as the logical outcome of the long Western philosophical conversation.

At the end of *Philosophy and the Mirror of Nature* Rorty adverts to this 'Whiggishness' in his account. He offers an apology for it, saying that he hopes to have shown 'the issues with which philosophers are presently concerned, and with which they Whiggishly see philosophy as having always (perhaps unwittingly) been concerned, as results of historical accident, as turns the conversation has taken.'[78] But this is disingenuous. The basic structure of Rorty's argument is twofold: the history of philosophy is a series of accidents; epistemological behaviourism is a product of history and is correct. The contradiction resides in the two guiding principles of Rorty's argument, the notion of historical contingency, on the one hand, and the notion of chronological supersession, on the other. The former asserts that philosophy is heading nowhere; the latter holds that progress is inevitable.

While the history of philosophy might appear to lack direction and purpose, Rorty's argument does not. Rorty is extremely confident of his position and of its modernity, a modernity that has strong scientistic overtones. Rorty quotes with approval Sellars's dictum that science is the mea-

---

78 PMN 391. This view is reinforced and expanded by Rorty in *Contingency, Irony and Solidarity*.

sure of all things.[79] The notion of person he advocates is a unitary physicalism, whose associated vocabulary, he feels confident, will gradually overtake
outdated references to the mind. All of these considerations lead us to
place Rorty's pragmatism clearly alongside positivism on the philosophical
map. For a major thesis of this chapter is that Rorty's position, far from
being the accidental turn in the conversation he stages for us, is intelligible
only in the light of previous movements in philosophy under the sway of
Galileo's distinction. But Rorty appears, at least momentarily, to challenge
any confident placement on the philosophical map. After all, in the
penultimate section of his last chapter, behaviourism and materialism
coexist forcefully with a set of 'existential doctrines.'[80] He has no ambition
to deny the cognitive status of pronouncements about the arts, for example, or to make the physical sciences the paradigm of true knowledge.
All of this is true. Rorty is not a positivist but a pragmatist and his doc-
trine of incommensurability underwrites the validity of a multiplicity of
discourses.

However, this does not negate the direction given to the history of
philosophy by Galileo's distinction. If my earlier remarks about the vulnerability of the notion of the subject under the influence of Galileo are
sound, then Rorty's position can be seen to fulfil that influence. For, as I
have already argued, Rorty's free-floating existentialist is only a consequence of the elimination of the epistemological subject and of the
normativity inherent in the subject. The elimination of the knowing subject
creates the conditions for Rorty's definition and celebration of modernity,
unrestrained as it is by any abiding norms of rationality.

Rorty's existentialism, in short, rests on his positivism. The subject is
dropped and consciousness methodologically excluded from philosophical
discourse because, he argues, the mental is indistinguishable from the
neural, the mind from the brain. The epistemological quest is abandoned
for physiological psychology, which should tell us all we need to know about
the mind, provided it abandons questionnaires and relies instead on Rorty's
beloved cerebroscopes. Where the philosophers Rorty attacks had attempted
to reconcile subjectivity and objectivity within the dualistic Galilean framework and had inevitably failed, notwithstanding their use of some inge-
nious devices, Rorty solves the problem of dualism by the simple expedient
of eliminating the cognitional subject altogether. Rorty's endeavours run
alongside those of the tradition he criticizes, in so far as he too attempts to
overcome the anomalies that arise from dualistic schemes. His 'solution'
may be more drastic and unequivocally one-sided, but even here Rorty

79 PMN 124.
80 PMN 379.

follows an established tradition. For both Hume and Russell have shown that empiricism and positivism have always had problems with identifying and locating the subject or ego.

Rorty's argument is novel in the measure that it splits the ocular metaphor from the Galilean distinction, which has been its natural historical ally. As Lonergan's historical explorations make clear, the assimilation of knowing to looking was current long before Galileo. But the metaphor of the eye, the image of knowledge as confrontation, and the assumption that the 'really real' consists of the mathematical properties of matter 'out there,' are quite compatible and often cohabit. By arguing against the eye metaphor so powerfully and convincingly while retaining the distinction between primary and secondary qualities, Rorty's book marks a significant and possibly historic shift in Western philosophy. Once Galileo's non-scientific distinction has been so decisively wrenched apart from the metaphor of the eye, it may be difficult for the two to be put back together again.

The historical approach taken in this chapter has prevented me doing justice to the way Lonergan meets the Galilean distinction head-on,[81] nor have I set out how he envisages the relationship between philosophy and science.[82] I trust that I have been able to suggest something of Lonergan's interpretation of the history of philosophy. In particular, I hope that this chapter has shown

1 that Richard Rorty's position in fact has a fully intelligible place within the tradition that he partially deconstructs, and is less deviant and less accidental than he believes;
2 that Rorty's critique is confined to the dominant epistemological tradition and seriously overlooks another tradition for which Lonergan is a major representative (perhaps *the* major proponent); and
3 that, whereas Rorty fails to come to grips with the tradition with which Lonergan is associated, Lonergan's understanding of the development of the epistemological conversation throws a good deal of light on Rorty. In particular, it reveals how it is the elimination of the subject and its immanent and operative normativity that conditions Rorty's definition of 'modernity' and 'post-Philosophical culture.'

---

81 See, for example, *Insight* (1957), 252, 294, 345: CWL 3: 277, 319, 368–9.
82 See, for example, *A Third Collection* (London: Geoffrey Chapman, 1985) 44–7, 146ff.; also *Method in Theology* 93–9. At a time when many philosophers are busy legislating philosophy out of existence, Lonergan's account of the place and functions of philosophy looks increasingly like the best offer around.

PART THREE

Some Applications

8

Hume's 'Is-Ought' Problem: A Solution

David Hume first raised the 'is-ought' problem in this famous passage from *A Treatise of Human Nature*:

> I cannot forbear adding to these reasonings an observation which may perhaps, be found of some importance. In every system of morality, which I have hitherto met with, I have always remark'd, that the author proceeds for some time in the ordinary way of reasoning, and establishes the being of a God, or makes observations conerning human affairs; when of a sudden I am surpriz'd to find, that instead of the usual copulations of propositions, *is* and *is not*, I meet with no proposition that is not connected with an *ought*, or an *ought not*. This change is imperceptible, but is, however, of the last consequence. For as this *ought*, or *ought not*, expresses some new relation or affirmation 'tis necessary that it shou'd be observ'd and explain'd; and at the same time that a reason should be given for what seems altogether inconceivable, how this new relation can be a deduction from others, which are entirely different from it. But as authors do not commonly use this precaution, I shall presume to recommend it to the readers; and am persuaded, that this small attention wou'd subvert all the vulgar system of morality, and let us see, that the distinction of vice and virtue is not founded on the relations of objects, nor is perceived by reason.[1]

---

1 D. Hume, *Treatise of Human Nature*, ed. L.A. Selby-Bigge (Clarendon Press, 1888), 467–70.

Behind Hume's quietly persuasive comments lie at least two questionable assumptions. The first is that the way language is ordinarily used is wrong; rather than take note, in an empirical fashion, of how moral discourse is normally conducted, Hume chooses to be negatively prescriptive in respect of 'all the vulgar system of morality.' This is ironic in so far as it indicates a performative contradiction in Hume: that is, a contradiction between what he is saying and what he is, in effect, doing. For the clear implication of what Hume 'recommends to the readers,' based on his empirical observations of how moral discussion is normally conducted, is that we *ought not* to talk in certain ways! A clear *ought not* can be inferred from Hume's empirical observations on the way *ought not* propositions are apt to follow on the heels of *is* and *is not* propositions, with the result that he is clearly failing to follow his own recommendation.

The second assumption – and in technical terms the more telling – is that the transition from *is* to *ought* is or could only be in the form of a 'deduction'; such a deduction he argues to be erroneous since there is no way in which 'this new relation can be a deduction from others, which are entirely different from it.' As a statement of the restrictions imposed by logic, Hume's comments here are unassailable, for in logic we can only take from our premises what is already there, and there is no way in which *ought* is implied by or entailed in *is*. What is open to question is Hume's assumption that the relationship obtaining between *is* propositions and *ought* propositions in ordinary moral discussion is or is intended to be one of logical deduction. It is this second assumption that I wish to address in this article. The first assumption has been challenged by Wittgenstein, who encourages us to test the meaning of words in the contexts that are their usual homes. The second – technical – assumption has been challenged most powerfully by Bernard Lonergan through his notions of sublation and the four levels of consciousness.

The best way of grasping what Lonergan means by the terms 'sublation' and 'four levels' is to see the process by which we arrive at a value judgment as comprising four distinct but related stages of conscious operations. The first three of these stages are the steps by which we reach cognitional judgments or knowledge claims – experience, understanding, and judgment. The fourth stage – the stage at which we arrive at value judgments – and hence moral judgments – was a position Lonergan arrived at some time after writing *Insight: A Study of Human Understanding* (published 1957) and before completing *Method in Theology* (published 1972). Lonergan himself did not address the 'is-ought' problem directly in his later writings, but he indicated in interviews that he was aware that his notion of four levels was pertinent to the problem. It is my belief that Lonergan's notion of the four levels of consciousness and how they relate to each other is a major contribution to the debate that has surrounded the 'is-ought' and the related fact/value controversy since the Enlightenment. What then does Lonergan mean by the four levels of consciousness?

Let me summarize briefly the position I have set out at greater length in chapters 1 and 2. Lonergan contends that as human beings we operate naturally and spontaneously at four different levels of consciousness. The first level is the experiential or empirical level, the level of conscious awareness we enjoy through our senses – through hearing, seeing, smelling, tasting, touching. We move to the second level of consciousness when something catches our attention and we ask What is that? With the arrival of a question our mind is aroused, it stirs itself and begins to probe. The subject has begun to inquire, to exercise intelligence, as her mind is trained on a question and straining for an answer. What should be noted here is that the transition from the first, experiential, level of consciousness to the second, intellectual, level is effected by a question. It is the question that has raised the level of my conscious awareness; I have, so to speak, passed through the gate of the question to a higher level of consciousness – 'higher' because with each new kind of question there is a higher degree of personal involvement. Having embarked on the pursuit of an answer to the question, for instance, I cannot just spin ideas and hypotheses out of the air, but am obliged to measure my ideas and suggested meanings against the data of sense – against the available evidence. This requires an exercise of my personal freedom not required at the level of mere sensory experience. The concentration and control required by intellectual effort, as we attempt to find meaning in the data of sense, will be recognized by most of us.

Should an answer to the question What is that? be forthcoming – if I form a hypothesis or guess – another question arises, Is that so? This new question raises a whole new set of considerations, looking for confirmation or disconfirmation of the hypothesis or guess. This question raises the stakes, putting me onto a higher level of consciousness, for it seeks a definite affirmation or negation. To move from the merely hypothetical level of consciousness to the level of making ontological claims about the universe is to heighten one's personal involvement because it requires one to take a stand on what is or is not so. Once more, the transition from one level of consciousness to the next is effected by the question Is that so? Can this hypothesis be verified?

But besides questions for understanding (What? Why? When? How? Where? How often?) and questions for reflection (Is that so? Is it probably so?) leading to verification and a knowledge claim, there is another type of question, the question that is preparatory to action: Is that right? Is it good? How good is it? These are the questions that shift the subject from the third to the fourth level of consciousness. With the arrival of value questions, it is not merely a matter of taking a stand on a knowledge claim; it is a matter, in addition, of determining what *I stand for*. Lonergan sees this fourth level of consciousness as comprising evaluation, choice, decision, and action. The heart of the fourth level is action, since the other operations of evaluation, choice, and so on are the means by which the subject determines which action would be most appropriate in the circumstances. The fourth level is characterized as a level of deliberation, freedom, and responsibility, and because of the deep level of involvement of the subject, Lonergan considers that at this level consciousness becomes self-conscious. Consciousness at this level becomes conscience.[2]

These are the four levels of consciousness depicted by Lonergan. Each level builds on and subsumes – or, to use the technical term, *sublates* – the previous level or levels. The subject passes beyond the previous level through the question gate and enters the new, higher level. It is the question that introduces and *governs* the new level. For example, because of the value question asked at the fourth level, the *facts* established at the third level become *standards* by which an answer will be formed at the fourth level – the athlete's times taken to complete a series of races, for instance, will become the standards by which he or she is assessed against the performance of other athletes. This in turn will determine which athlete will be selected, say, for a country's Olympic team, and so on. It is not simply the case that at the fourth level of consciousness the facts established at the third level are evaluated and assessed, but rather that at the fourth level these facts are put to new uses in the business of evaluation and assessment that the subject carries out at the fourth level under the impetus and direction of the new value question. Value judgments are cognitive: in making a value judgment we are asserting that something is the case. But value judgments are not merely cognitive because they are geared to action. By means of the value question, facts are transmuted into standards and become relevant to the decision that needs to be made to bring a specific course of action about. The *absolute quality* of facts is retained in the sense that at the fourth level the facts become the fixed reference points by means of which an answer to the question Is this good? can be found, or a measured response can be made to the question How good is it? For unlike facts, the issue of value is not an either/or affair; values admit of degrees and value judgments have an elastic quality that factual judgments do not share. In answering the question How Good? it will be the rigid nature of the facts-as-standards taken to the

2 For a clear account by Lonergan of the notion of the four levels of consciousness, see his article 'The Subject' in *A Second Collection* (Darton,
   Longman & Todd, 1972), 69 f.

fourth level that will provide the measuring rod by which a precise answer will be determined. The athlete's recorded times may be such as to put him in a class by himself, away out in front, or, on the other hand, they may be so close to those of other athletes as to suggest that he is only marginally better.

Questions are easily overlooked, and it is noticeable, for example, that while Wittgenstein asks a lot of questions in his philosophical writings, he has very little to say about the function of questions. Lonergan places great importance on the function of questions. For the question determines the answer we are looking for, and the answer we are looking for determines the area of discourse we find ourselves in. Hume was right in claiming that we cannot deduce *ought* from *is*; but he was wrong in assuming that the transition from *is* to *ought* could only be effected by means of a logical deduction. Hume overlooked the role of the question.

Lonergan's notion of sublation does not only hold that each succeeding level passes beyond the previous level or levels. It also holds that what is normative at each level connects up with the levels above it. So, as I have said, the absolute quality of the facts established at the level of cognitional judgment is shared by the standards in light of which an answer is found to the value question at the fourth level. To take another example, if someone asks if X is a 'good school,' we immediately attempt to *justify* our answer – It is, or It isn't – by reference to a whole series of facts: its record of academic attainment, the proportion of pupils achieving higher grades in national examinations, how its results in national tests compare with the national average, its record in respect of pupils' behaviour, the number of exclusions in the past three years, how many of these were permanent and how many fixed term, etc. etc. So by reviewing a broad range of factual information – often in the form of statistical data – answers to value questions are found. The facts of cognitional judgments provide the evidence for supporting or subverting value judgments. And this goes to show that value judgments are genuinely cognitive as well as evaluative.

Again, the binary structure of logic, which is operative at the second level of consciousness, the intellectual level – the *yes/no* character of logic that Wittgenstein explores at some length in the *Tractatus Logico-Philosophicus* – is carried forward into succeeding higher levels: into the affirmation or negation required at the level of cognitional judgment (*It is so* or *It is not so*) as well as into the affirmation or negation required at the level of evaluation (*It is good* or *It is not good*). Because the lower levels are built into the higher levels, not only do value judgments have genuine cognitive content, they are also required to be logically coherent: there are truth conditions attached to value judgments and, as such, they can be meaningfully affirmed or denied. The notion of sublation is rather a beautiful notion, drawing out as it does the nature and structure of the process by which value judgments are achieved.

Lonergan claims that the four steps by which value judgments are achieved are normative – not in the sense that to go through these four steps will ensure a true value judgment, but in the sense that no true value judgment can be reached unless one goes through these four steps. For there can be no true understanding unless the data of experience are attended to, since it is the data that have to be understood (described, interpreted, explained); nor can there be true knowledge without prior understanding, since knowledge is the affirmation that one's understanding is true; likewise, there can be no true value judgment without knowledge, since the facts of the matter will provide the standards by means of which a true value judgment can be made. The point of any value judgment is to determine whether a certain end is being achieved or will be achieved by the entity in question. So to say that something is a good chair is to say that it serves its purpose as a chair; to say that something is a good watch or clock is to say that something serves well the end of telling the time. It is because Hume – and in this he set the fashion for generations to come, provoking a reaction from the later Wittgenstein – developed a blind spot for propositions that do not state facts or result from logical deductions that he could find no place for *ought* in normal discourse. *Ought* statements do not 'fit in' to statements of fact, but they do 'fit in' to statements about ends; that is their natural home and habitat.

Because the four-stage process by which true value judgments are achieved is invariant and normative, Lonergan calls it *transcendental* and the method by which we achieve such judgments he calls *transcendental method.* It is a structure or process of thinking and reasoning that we follow spontaneously and irresistibly when working out practical problems or dealing with everyday situations. (Because this is the case, Lonergan's solution to the problem posed by Hume has much in common with Wittgenstein's. But Wittgenstein recommended that we pay close attention to how words are actually used in a variety of contexts. Lonergan's solution is the more technical, *explaining why* Hume's assumptions regarding the relation between *is* and *ought* are wrong.) Another way of understanding *transcendental* in Lonergan's use of the term, which differs from Kant's, is to say that a denial of this structure of knowing and valuing is tantamount to a performative contradiction. For to support such a denial, the denier would have to appeal to fresh data or propose a new interpretation of the data, would be required to demonstrate that his interpretation was true, and in this way justify his value judgment that we *ought not* to uphold the notion of transcendental method. In other words, the denier would have to appeal performatively to the very process he is denying in order to uphold his denial, so that what he was doing would be in contradiction with what he was saying.

Moral Judgments

Having explored the nature and structure of value judgments, I shall now attempt to say something about the distinctive nature of moral judgments. My argument will be that moral judgments are a species of value judgment, that they have the same structure as value judgments but differ from mere value judgments in respect of their content. As it happens, there is an interesting passage in Wittgenstein that brings out well the difference between moral and other types of value judgment:

> If for instance I say that this is a good chair this means that the chair serves a certain predetermined purpose and the word good here has only meaning in so far as this purpose has been previously fixed upon. In fact the word good in the relative sense simply means coming up to a certain predetermined standard ... and if I say that this is the right road I mean it is the right road relative to a certain goal. Used in this way these expressions don't present any difficulty ... But this is not how Ethics uses them. Supposing that I could play tennis and one of you saw me playing and said, 'Well, you play pretty badly' and suppose I answered, 'I know I'm playing badly but I don't want to play any better,' all the other man could say would be 'Ah, then that's all right.' But suppose I had told one of you a preposterous lie and he came up to me and said, 'You're behaving like a beast,' and then I were to say, 'I know I behave badly, but then I don't want to behave any better,' could he then say, 'Ah, then that's all right'? Certainly not; he would say, 'Well you ought to want to behave better.' Here you have an absolute judgment of value, whereas the first instance was one of relative judgment.[3]

Wittgenstein at the time he gave this lecture (around 1930) still held the view he had expressed in the *Tractatus*, that ethical judgments take us 'beyond significant language.' Nevertheless, the passage does tell us something about the distinctiveness of moral judgments. Whereas in judgments such as 'This is a good chair' or 'This is a good clock' the goodness in question is relative to an end we have *chosen* to adopt – and may well be quite objective relative to that end – in the case of human happiness or well-

---

3 L. Wittgenstein, *Lecture on Ethics*, ed. Rush Rhees, in *Philosophy Today* (Macmillan, 1968).

being, I shall argue, there can be no question of choice. There is simply no choice about it. Human happiness or well-being or flourishing or prosperity or thriving – I use all these terms collectively in order to convey Aristotle's notion of *eudaimonia* – is an absolute end, acting as a fixed standard, one we cannot play around with. It stands above all human conventions. Why this is the case now needs to be explained.

If we accept that the structure of value judgments is transcendental in the way previously explained, then we have to accept the consequence that this structure is inviolable. To violate the structure is to violate the basic set of norms to which appeal can be made to justify any value judgment whatsoever. The structure of value judgments relates to evaluating as a process, the process we go through in order to reach a true value judgment. But this transcendental structure is not limited to cognitional and evaluative process. For by relating the steps we go through with the four levels of consciousness, Lonergan has linked his position with the structure of human personality. Consciousness is that which constitutes human personality: we are persons by virtue of the consciousness we enjoy. While it may be the case that in the order of knowing we come to grasp the structure of cognitional and evaluative process before grasping the structure of the human personality, in the order of being it is the fact that a person's nature is transcendental that forms the basis for transcendental method. *Esse* precedes *agere: it is because we are as we are that we can act as we do.* That is the crucial step in my argument: from transcendental method to the structure of human personality, from process to person.

From this it follows that human personality constitutes a fixed and absolute standard in the realm of moral behaviour. For to violate the norms of the human person is equivalent to violating the norms of transcendental method, and that, we have seen, is always an illegitimate move, indeed one that is involved in self-contradiction. A similar contradiction is incurred by any attempt to dispute the fact that the integrity and prosperity of the human person constitute an absolute standard of right conduct. For any moral argument against human well-being would have to propose some advantage to humankind as grounds for changing or abolishing this standard. No reason could be proposed for changing the standard that did not appeal to the standard in justification for the proposed change. It is because they are concrete realizations of transcendental method that persons are special, ends in themselves, free agents, what Lonergan terms 'ontic values.' Moral judgments are moral precisely because they are tied to the end of human well-being, human flourishing, human prosperity. For this reason, moral judgments stand at the apex of the various conscious operations we perform as human beings, for their subject matter and their standard is humanity itself. In moral discourse, it is our humanity that is at stake.

Some very interesting consequences follow from this definition of the human person by reference to the structure of transcendental method. The subject who makes a moral judgment is also constituted as a person by the norms inherent in the conscious operations she performs when making the judgment. It follows that in being true to these norms, the person making the judgment or taking the action is being true to herself. In other words, when I make a true moral judgment, I am fitting myself to myself, I am making myself whole, I am upholding and promoting my human integrity, I am developing myself as a person. By contrast, when I knowingly make a morally wrong judgment, the norms of transcendental method are violated and by that very act I am being untrue to myself and I fail to retain my human integrity. There is a complete coincidence of impact made by moral judgments on myself and on the others whose well-being is the content or the subject matter of the moral judgment. In being true to the humanity of others, I uphold my own; in betraying their humanity, I betray my own.

Another consequence of the absolute standard of human flourishing is that moral judgments require a quite peculiar self-transcendence on the part of the subject or agent, for they cannot be in the subject's or anyone else's self-interest. Unlike other value judgments, where I often decide that something is good because it serves my interests or the interests of my company or my friends, moral judgments stand above all partial self-interests. The reason is the absolute standard of human well-being. Therein lies the reason for Lonergan's constant repetition in his later writings that the subject's self-transcendence is the criterion of objectivity in moral judgments.[4]

Bernard Lonergan did not apply his notion of transcendental method to moral philosophy in any systematic way. But I believe his position can be developed along the lines I have indicated to provide the basis for a natural-law approach to moral argument. Because Lonergan's transcendental method yields an absolute conception of the human person, it provides the basis for a philosophy of rights and obligations founded on this notion of person. But to develop that thesis is beyond the scope of this chapter, which must confine itself to demonstrating just how effectively Lonergan answers Hume on the precise technical issue of how we can move legitimately from *is* propositions to *ought* propositions.

Intuitionism, emotivism, and prescriptivism were all approaches taken to moral philosophy in mainstream twentieth-century English-language philosophy, with implications for the status and nature of moral propositions.

4 See, for example, *Method in Theology* (Darton, Longman & Todd, 1972), 121–2.

It would be true to say that each was developed in view of the perceived difficulties, first voiced by Hume, surrounding the interface between judgments of fact and judgments of value. It has been my argument here that Lonergan's notion of the four levels of consciousness together with his notion of sublation go a long way towards dispelling these long-standing difficulties. In so doing (I believe it could be argued) they provide a basis for a natural-law approach to morality in which moral judgments could be accepted as both objective and as saying something real about the world.

It should perhaps be added here that Lonergan himself did not advocate a 'natural law' approach to moral reasoning, but rather developed a basic or foundational position on ethics along the lines of intentionality analysis. Those wishing to learn more about Lonergan's approach to ethics should consult the pages on ethics in *Method in Theology*. A full and balanced commentary on Lonergan's analysis of moral judgment can be found in Mark J. Doorley's *The Place of the Heart in Lonergan's Ethics* (University Press of America, 1996). A wide-ranging discussion of Lonergan's approach to ethics is available in the chapter on ethics in Joseph Flanagan's *Quest for Self-Knowledge* (University of Toronto Press, 1997).

9

Lonergan and Wittgenstein on Logic

Lonergan: From Logic to Method

The basic position on logic of Lonergan and Wittgenstein is that both greatly esteemed logic and considered logic important BUT ... It is limited in certain respects or its limitations came to be recognized ... One of Lonergan's refrains in *Insight* is 'logic is static, science is dynamic.'

Logic is static. It can bring clarity to definitions, it can help towards a precise grasp of terms, it can aid in exploring the presuppositions and implications of a particular intellectual position, it can establish the validity of inference, and so forth. But logic is not the principle of movement, of development, of intellectual growth. Method is required for that. Whereas in the twentieth-century analytical tradition there was a strong tendency to see philosophy as a branch of logic, almost a subdivision of logic, or as the application of logical techniques to questions and issues, Lonergan takes the bold stance of putting logic into method. It is by means of method, under the impetus of the pure, disinterested desire to know the truth, that we achieve new understanding and new knowledge. Logic is a special development of aspects of understanding, but it cannot account for the 'breakthrough' aspect of understanding, the moment of 'insight,' the sudden flash of illumination. Method embraces experience, understanding, and judgment, and accounts for science's 'moving viewpoint,' the fact that the true scientist never sits back and says, 'There it is, finished, complete.' Logic aspires to completeness, intellectual tidiness, and finality. Science cannot because the method of science, which is an important instantiation of Lonergan's *generalized empirical method*, reaches conclusions only to find that new questions arise, leading to further investigation. And so the wheel of method turns once more. *Logic is static, method is dynamic.*

Wittgenstein: From Logic to Forms of Life

Wittgenstein also came to see the limitations of logic. Indeed, the major change in Wittgenstein's philosophy from the position of the *Tractatus Logico-Philosophicus*, published in 1921, to that of the *Philosophical Investigations*, published posthumously in 1953, is essentially a change in his stance towards logic. In the *Tractatus*, it is the apparatus of logic that enables language to be meaningful. The structure of my language is the structure of my world, and the structure of logic determines the structure of language. In other words the *Tractatus* posited an isomorphism between reality and logic. Logic determines the structure, it fixes only the structure; it does not actually tell us about anything we might find in the world, it only indicates the *structure* of what it is we might find, just as the system of Newtonian mechanics tells us the kinds of systems verifiable in the physical world. However, logic determines the structure not of all reality but of that reality of which we can speak. Towards the end of the *Tractatus*, Wittgenstein moves on to the question of ethics and religious issues, and his position is that these are matters beyond the limits of legitimate language. The very last sentence of the *Tractatus* is 'What we cannot speak about we must pass over in silence.' By this he means that the *most important things in life* are beyond mathematics and science and philosophy – but the logical positivists in Vienna and in England chose to interpret his words as indicating that ethical and religious statements were beyond meaning – quite literally, meaningless.

What caused Wittgenstein to change his mind about the relation of logic to language and to life was encapsulated in a conversation he had with his Italian friend Piero Sraffa. Sraffa was a brilliant economist, of a broadly Marxist character, who had jeopardized his career in Italy by publishing an attack on Mussolini's policies. He was invited by John Maynard Keynes to come and work at King's College in Cambridge; and so he met Wittgenstein. They became close friends, and arranged to meet semi-formally once a week. One of the famous stories about these meetings concerns the occasion when Wittgenstein was explaining to Sraffa how a proposition and that which the proposition is about must have the same *logical form*. Sraffa is supposed to have brushed his chin with his fingertips in Neapolitan style and said, 'What is the logical form of *that*?' Sraffa in large measure influenced Wittgenstein to start viewing things from a sociological viewpoint, and this led the philosopher to abandon his logical view of language and to begin to see language as a social institution. In the *Tractatus* Wittgenstein had viewed logic as the seat and source of meaning; in the *Investigations* he switches to 'forms of life' as the philosophical ultimates, because they are the matrix within which meaning is generated. Language grows and develops within the communal institutions and economies to which our basic human needs – our need for food, drink, and shelter, for example – give rise. Language is a social phenomenon before it becomes an individual possession. From this springs the Wittgensteinian attack on the notion of a private language and, by implication, his historically important disowning of much of the Western philosophical tradition stemming from Descartes. Much of this, he believed, was due to the influence of his Italian friend Sraffa. In the preface to *Philosophical Investigations*, it is not to his prestigious English friends – Bertrand Russell, G.E. Moore, or Maynard Keynes – that Wittgenstein acknowledges an intellectual debt, but to his friend Sraffa. He says quite bluntly, 'I am indebted to *this* stimulus for the most consequential ideas of this book.'

So that is the big picture regarding these two philosophers. In Lonergan, logic is part of method, and reality is isomorphic not with logic but with method – with experience, understanding, judgment, and evaluating. In Wittgenstein the movement is from logic to forms of life; the sharp antithesis of logic, its 'either/or' character, gives way to Wittgenstein's proposal of 'family resemblances,' the notion that the meanings of words often overlap, being in some ways the same but different in others. We move away from formal logic towards what was called 'informal logic' – working out what Wittgenstein calls the 'grammar' of words, the roles they play in language as a social institution. A child who knows how to use the word 'red' appropriately has learned the 'grammar' of colour vocabulary, the rules that make the language game possible. It makes sense to ask of some object, 'Is that green or blue?' but not to say, 'Is that green or hard?' 'Is that green or round?' It is not so much a matter of knowing how language relates to reality, conceived of as standing over there, but of knowing how to use words: 'The meaning of a word is its use in language' (PI 43). Language is a tool kit and words are tools whose use we learn by taking part in 'forms of life.' In this way the later Wittgenstein overcomes the narrowness and rigidity of his earlier investment in formal logic.

Nothing is out of bounds any more. The languages of ethics and of religion and, for that matter, of philosophy itself can all be viewed as of forms of life. Hence, for example, the importance that some philosophers of religion have attributed to the dominance of Wittgensteinian philosophy in England. After the wasteland of logical positivism in the 1940s and 1950s, which stripped theology of any proper role and religious language of any meaning, the arrival of the later Wittgenstein was a huge liberation.

F.H. Bradley

To understand the influence exercised by logic and stances towards logic in British and Anglo-American intellectual life in the course of the twentieth century and into this century, we have to go back to the late nineteenth century. This should reconnect our story with Lonergan. In the late Middle Ages logic had been a thriving discipline. It fell into neglect in English philosophy in the seventeenth and eighteenth centuries. Although Hume said some important things about the relations between ideas in contrast with the relations between things in the world, he and the other British empiricists were epistemologists rather than logicians. In the nineteenth century John Stuart Mill attempted to work out an empiricist logic in his famous work *A System of Logic*. Empiricists placed their emphasis on sensation rather than intellection, and Mill was faced with the uphill task of devising an *inductive logic* to explain how the generalizations and laws of science can be built on individual acts of sensation. For sensation regards only the particular – particular sounds, smells, tastes, and sights. How can empirical science talk of laws and principles? The empiricist is faced with the problem of how we get from the particular to the general. Mill's efforts represent the old empiricist recourse to constant repetition inducing in us a belief in the uniformity of nature. This approach stirred up some resounding comments from the British idealists who came to the fore before Mill's death. The British idealists were the dominant philosophical group in England for the second half of the nineteenth century and on into the twentieth century. In particular, F.H. Bradley's brilliant attacks on empiricist psychologism and associationism were deeply influential, as were his attacks on Mill's attempts to conjure universals out of particulars.[1]

In his *Principles of Logic* Bradley says things on the topic of universals that are to prove influential with Lonergan. For example, when we say, 'All animals are mortal,' (he argues) we are not making an empirical statement but a hypothetical statement. We are saying, 'Whatever is an animal will die,' and that is the same as saying that 'If something is an animal, then it is mortal.' Propositions that speak of all things – like 'All animals' – are only categorical if their reference is to existing animals, otherwise they are hypothetical. This is a distinction Russell takes up with approval in his well-

---

1 See Philip Ferreira, 'Bradley's Attack on Associationism,' in James Bradley, ed., *Philosophy after F.H. Bradley* (Thoemmes Press, England, 1996). I have drawn on this volume for several of my comments on F.H. Bradley.

known essay *On Denoting*, claiming that Bradley is right and that statements like 'All men are mortal' are usually hypothetical rather than categorical: 'If anything is a man, then it is mortal.' Lonergan, as we shall see, adopts a similar position.

The Influence of H.W.B. Joseph

Lonergan took a keen interest in the nature of logical inference. When speaking of early influences on his philosophical development, he mentions, in virtually the same breath as Newman's *Grammar of Assent*, H.W.B. Joseph's *An Introduction to Logic*. Lonergan says he read this book with great care when a student at Heythrop College, the Jesuit house of studies near Oxford; and even that he made a detailed study of it. Now Joseph was a Fellow and Tutor at New College, Oxford, and a disciple of the Oxford philosopher John Cook Wilson, who published very little but exercised considerable influence as a gifted teacher. We usually associate the origins of the British analytical movement with Cambridge rather than Oxford, and with names like Moore and Russell, who were Cambridge men; yet the first reactions against idealism and the new move towards realism in twentieth-century British philosophy were in fact made by Oxford Aristotelians like Cook Wilson and Joseph.[2] Lonergan says that Joseph's *Introduction to Logic* introduced him to modern science.[3]

Joseph's book was first published in 1906 and in a second, revised edition in 1916. (There is an apology for the delay in the publication of the revised edition, caused by the 'War.') It was, in fact, a standard work of logic for some time, used in schools as well as in universities, and Joseph was an influential teacher. To pick it up is to enter into another world. The chapter headings have a certain old-fashioned quaintness: 'Of immediate inferences,' 'Of the intension and extension of terms,' 'Of Induction,' 'Of the proposition or judgment,' 'Of explanation,' 'Of the methodology of the sciences,' and so forth. But it is full of good things, comprehensive and detailed – a teacher's book, crammed with examples. It gives a very clear account of a wide range of logical terms, explores the nature of judgment and of explanation, and examines the nature of logical inference.

We also read such things as this statement: 'The natural man thinks much about things, and asks and answers questions about them; but it is by an effort

---

2 One of the lasting monuments of this period in English philosophy was the publication of the handsome edition of Aristotle's works in English translated by Sir W.D. Ross, who was provost of Oriel College, Oxford.
3 B. Lonergan, *A Second Collection*, ed. William F.J. Ryan, SJ and Bernard J. Tyrrell, SJ (Darton, Longman & Todd, 1974), 276.

that he comes to see how these things are only known to him in his perceptions of them and his thoughts about them, and so comes to turn his attention inward upon the nature of the acts of perceiving or of thinking.'[4] Joseph also says, '[W]e must have experience of thinking about things, before we can investigate the principles of thinking; only this means, in the case of thinking, that we must *ourselves* think about things first, for no one can have experience of thinking except in his own mind.'[5] He continues: 'Nor can these new objects of his study be preserved and dissected like a material thing; a man cannot catch a thought and bottle it; he must create it by thinking it, if he wishes to think about it; and the task will be found difficult while it is strange, and not altogether easy when familiar.'[6] These quotations represent the general theme of Joseph's opening chapter, entitled 'General Character of the Enquiry.' They also foreshadow and state clearly one of the basic methodological principles enunciated by Lonergan in *Insight*, when he invites the reader to appropriate her own cognitional processes.

Joseph shows himself an Oxford philosopher of this time by his belief that logic is concerned with forms of thought; it is a system into which judgments can fit. He says that logical terms live in judgments, and he is opposed to the new symbolic logic associated at that time with Russell and Whitehead. Broadly speaking, Oxford's strong connection between logic and judgment is, of course, what we find in Lonergan's *Insight*. At Cambridge there was a different emphasis. There logic was coming to be seen first and foremost as system, as a calculus. Curiously perhaps, Lonergan was interested in both of these positions, and he followed closely the developments in symbolic and mathematical logic that took place throughout the twentieth century.

The Form of Inference

The link between logic and judgment comes to the fore in an important early paper of Lonergan's, published in 1943, 'The Form of Inference.'[7] What we find there is Lonergan's reduction of all the traditional scholastic figures of syllogism – Barbara, Celarent, Darii, Ferio, and so on – to one form, which he calls 'the simple hypothetical argument': If A, then B; but A; therefore B. For Lonergan that is the basic valid form of inference, a form that is purely logical in character but is found in every movement from

---

4 H.W.B. Joseph, *An Introduction to Logic* (Clarendon Press, 1906; rev. ed., 1916), 8.
5 Ibid., 2.
6 Ibid., 8.
7 B. Lonergan, 'The Form of Inference,' in *Collection*, ed. F.E. Crowe (Darton, Longman & Todd, 1967).

understanding to judgment. For the movement to judgment according to Lonergan is achieved when the conditions attached to the intelligibility grasped in understanding are fulfilled, so that the intelligible becomes virtually unconditioned – a conditioned whose conditions are fulfilled. No matter how empirical the judgment might be, no matter how matter-of-fact the judgmental proposition, the movement from understanding to judgment has for Lonergan the cogency of logic and is not just empirical: If A, then B. But A, therefore B. As he points out, it is not the implication of one or some in all (a purely quantitative matter of fact), but the fulfilment of the conditions attending the intelligible grasped in understanding. In making this clear, Lonergan is implicitly declaring his philosophical continuity with Joseph, Bradley, and early twentieth-century Oxford philosophy. He is talking about inference as the basis of judgment and repudiating mere dependence on what he called 'denotational coincidence' – on the way things happen to be in the world.

Lonergan was not, however, indifferent to what was happening at Cambridge and in Europe at that time. When he speaks of logic in later life, he usually makes the distinction between formal logic and mathematical or extensional logic. Formal logic is the kind of logic associated with Aristotle, which seeks to establish what the cause of something is. It is the explanatory syllogism, the syllogism that helps us understand something. In this type of syllogism, the middle term is supplied by the cause that makes something what it is. If the cause exists, its consequent necessarily exists. To take what Lonergan calls Aristotle's 'stock example,' we might say that if the moon is darkened, then the earth intervenes between the sun and the moon; but the moon is darkened; therefore the earth intervenes. Here we understand the nature of an eclipse by grasping what causes an eclipse.

Lonergan usually distinguishes that kind of logic from what he calls mathematical or symbolic logic, which is sometimes called 'class logic' or 'extensional logic.' As he puts it in *Understanding and Being*,[8] extensional logic is concerned with 'all men' and 'all horses,' but not with what Lonergan calls 'distracting insights.' It is concerned with the process of getting consequences out of premises, and for this to happen you have to set up your premises with great accuracy and set down clear rules of implication. Once these are in place, symbolic logic can be done by a machine, or a computer. The key idea is that conclusions are truth-functions of the premises; and it

8 B. Lonergan, *Understanding and Being*, vol. 5 of Collected Works of Bernard Lonergan, ed. Elizabeth A. and Mark D. Morelli (University of Toronto Press, 1990). For a fuller treatment of mathematical logic see vol. 18 of the Collected Works, *Phenomenology and Logic: The Boston College Lectures on Mathematical Logic and Existentialism*, ed. Philip J. McShane (University of Toronto Press, 2001).

is perfectly possible to draw up truth tables that set out the truth and falsity of the conclusions that can be drawn from certain premises. Once the truth tables are established, the validity of conclusions can be checked routinely or mechanically.

Perhaps Lonergan's interest in developments in extensional or class logic was due as much to his interest in mathematics as to his interest in philosophy. He was a gifted mathematician who was also interested in questions about the foundations of mathematics. He discusses his own ideas about the foundations of mathematics in the Boston lectures on mathematical logic; as a student of mathematics, he was capable of understanding the twentieth-century debates on the relations between mathematics and logic. As a student of Aristotle he also understood the kind of self-imposed restrictions the recent symbolic logic chose to work within as well as the type of inference that Aristotle in syllogistic logic had in mind, the kind of inference that operates in cognitive judgment, whenever we assert that something is the case.

The Impersonal Objective

Let us now move back to Wittgenstein and Russell and to the cultural and philosophical impulse that underpinned the development of a symbolic logic at the beginning of the twentieth century. It is important to grasp 'the impersonal objective' behind the new focus on logic in England at the start of the twentieth century. The objective was to establish the impersonality and objectivity of judgment. In cultural terms, the British analytic school of Moore, Russell, and Wittgenstein aimed at clearing away the metaphysical clutter of the Victorians, so that knowledge could be re-defined in the epistemologically more secure terms of linguistic logic. In order to overcome both the subjectivism of the personal idealists, some of whom reverted to Berkeley's 'esse est percipi,' and the scepticism of many of the absolute idealists, some of whom contended that what could be known was highly uncertain, since we can only know the part through the whole, the analytic philosophers had recourse to logic as the standard by which truth would be measured. It was taken for granted that language was not logical and needed to be purged of its illogicalities. If a logically perfect language could be manufactured – and that was the aim of Russell and Wittgenstein in the movement known as logical atomism – then judgments would be more measured and more certain. The continental ally of the Cambridge philosophers in this quest was the German mathematician and philosopher of mathematics Gottlob Frege.

The language of objectivity came to be characterized as impersonal. In the literary critical theory of the time, T.S. Eliot and I.A. Richards sought to underwrite critical judgments grounded in this quality of impersonality and

hence, they believed, of objectivity. The quest for a logically perfect language is at one with Wittgenstein's abandonment of the philosophical
importance of the subject. In the *Tractatus* the subject does not belong to
the world but is the limit of the world (5.632). Russell too came to deny the
substantial reality of the 'I,' of the subject. And while the later Wittgenstein
abandons logic for forms of life, he still makes little place for the individual
subject and her contributions to the sum of human knowledge, because the
matrix of language is social and not personal. Hence the impersonality of
so much philosophical discourse today and the confusion of objectivity with
the absence of subjectivity.[9]

It is Lonergan's genius to hold on both to a proper estimation of logic
and objectivity, on the one hand, and to a proper understanding of the
indispensability of the subject, on the other. He says that objectivity is the
consequence of authentic subjectivity. He contextualizes logic in *Insight*:
'Upon the normative exigencies of the pure desire [to know] rests the
validity of all logics and all methods ... Logic and methods ... are to be
accepted insofar as they succeed in formulating that dynamic exigence; and
they are to be revised insofar as they fail.'[10]

Wittgenstein appears to have shared the common view at the time that
the objectivity of logic depended upon the elimination of the subject.
Lonergan repudiated that view and demonstrated the opposite. That is the
reason for the focus on the subject in much of his philosophy, his stress on
transcendence and conversion and on the need for the development of the
subject if a worthwhile ethics is to be achieved. To pursue those matters
here would take me very far from the focus of this volume. It remains that
Lonergan's emphasis on the subject's role in knowing, while upholding the
possibility of objective knowledge, is the main difference between him and
members of the analytical tradition. By the same token, it is this reflection on the subject that could supply the missing bridge between British-
American philosophy and Continental philosophy.

9 Lonergan comments on this point in his lectures on mathematical logic:
   '[T]here is quite a harmony between the symbolic, technical approach to logic
   and the empiricist, pragmatic viewpoint in philosophy. This business of not
   using your head as you go along eliminates or makes irrelevant the human
   subject. And the fundamental issue, as we will see, with regard to mathematical
   logic is the opposition between mind, on the one hand, and technique, on the
   other. In Aristotle, logic is an assertion of rationality against sophistry or
   against mere rhetoric. But the modern opposition is not "rationality versus
   sophistry," "rationality versus rhetoric." It is rather the fundamental opposition
   that arises between mind and its own creation. Will the creation take the place
   of mind, eliminate it, shoulder it out of the way? There is more than a little
   danger along those lines.' See *Phenomenology and Logic*, 16.
10 B. Lonergan, *Insight* (Longmans, Green & Co., 1957), 373.

10

Education, Psychology, and Philosophy

Bernard Lonergan is one of those thinkers whom it is difficult to define and pin down with exactitude, a feature that does not serve him well in an age when we like to pigeon-hole our celebrities. Lonergan is usually referred to either as a theologian or as a philosopher and sometimes he is called a philosopher-theologian. He is also with good reason referred to as a methodologist. But there is a very good case to be made for the claim that he is – perhaps first and foremost – an educationist. By calling Lonergan an educationist I am not just referring to the fact that he was for most of his life a teacher, though he would not have been the educationist he was if he had not known education from the inside – in the classroom, the seminar room, and the lecture hall, at what is sometimes called 'the chalk face.'

In this chapter I want to say something about Lonergan the educationist and to link these comments to some about Lonergan the neglected philosopher. In the Introduction I make the observation that if one is looking around for intellectual allies of Lonergan, one is more likely to find them on the education shelves of the library or bookshop than on the philosophy shelves. The reason for this has something to do with the rejection or, more commonly, the neglect of Lonergan in philosophical circles within the analytical tradition.

Education

Education is about learning and Lonergan was fascinated with, and fascinating on, the topic of how children – and all of us – learn anything. The notions we find in *Insight* about the 'known unknown' and how we use the known to attack the unknown by creating a 'heuristic structure' (see chapter 1) are among the best things that have been written on the nature of learning. One of the things the good teacher does is to use what the pupils already know to help them discover what they do not yet know; to provide them with the clues that will enable them to reach the answer; to furnish them with the skills that they then use to solve the problem. The way we see the world, the way we interpret it, and the way we cope with it – all depend on what we already carry around with us in our heads. Conversely, Lonergan was also well aware of the fact that whatever new or original understanding we achieve has to be fitted into the body of knowledge and understanding we have already acquired and that this may cause a shift – which can be more or less fundamental and radical – among the beliefs we have entertained, perhaps for the best part of a lifetime. Learning is not a mechanistic or static thing but a dynamic, living activity, and sometimes a bloody and messy business, that grows and develops and is driven and propelled by *asking and answering questions.*

Teachers are always asking questions, and they begin to feel they are getting somewhere when their students begin to ask questions of their own. Lonergan is quite eloquent on the role of the question in driving inquiry forward and making knowledge possible. So within his cognitional theory, it is questions for intelligence that promote us from the experiential level to the level of understanding; and it is questions for reflection that promote us from the level of understanding to the level of judgment. He points out how our realization that our understanding and knowledge are incomplete commonly generates further questions; the questions identify the 'known unknown' and so move us to further insights. Insights coalesce into viewpoints and lower viewpoints are raised by further questions to higher viewpoints. In the area of intellectual development, Lonergan terms the question 'the operator,' the principle that moves us onwards and upwards. As he says, in one of his deceptively simple statements in *Insight:* 'Thus, unless one asks the further questions, one remains with the insights one has already, and so intelligence does not develop.'[1] For the same reason, it is when the stream of questions dries up, when there are no further relevant questions to be asked, that we know we have reached the end of our investigations of a particular situation.

This emphasis Lonergan places on questioning and answering helps to illustrate not only the dynamic, living character of learning but also its *subjective* character. The questions are asked by the subject; the answers to the questions are proposed by the subject. It is not only the case that inquiry is an anticipatory activity – we ask questions because we anticipate finding answers to them; and hence we move inquiry along by means of

1 *Insight* (Longmans, Green & Co., 1957), 471; CWL 3: 495.

predicting and hypothesizing. But this dynamic aspect, in turn, brings out the inescapable *subjectivity of* knowledge, since the proximate sources of meaning are in the subject. The fruit of knowledge grows on the tree of the subject.[2] And here – as we touch on the vexed issue of subjectivity – is where we arrive at the cross-over point between Lonergan the man of educational vision and Lonergan the neglected philosopher.

For there can be no doubt that the ascendant philosophical tradition in Britain and the United States has great problems in handling the subjective – or even in acknowledging it. Hence Lonergan's strong focus on the subject is bound to create philosophical barriers between him and most – but not all – members of the analytical tradition. Yet in education few would deny that a strong focus on the subject is inescapable. This is not only because teachers are all too aware of the subjectivity of knowledge, seeing every day as they do the difference between students of different levels of ability as well as the differences between students from different social backgrounds. It is also because education – in the Western tradition deriving from Greece and Rome, at least – is concerned with the whole person. In England, the government has set up a system requiring every school in the land to be inspected every so many years. We inspect schools under many categories relating to learning – such as standards of attainment, the quality of teaching and learning, the curriculum, and so forth. But we also inspect under the heading of the school's provision for the personal development of the students. We look at provision for their spiritual, moral, social, and cultural development. Those are the headings or categories we inspect under and the reason is simple: schools are not just exam factories where students are graded according to the academic scores they achieve; they are also places in which human beings mature, grow, and develop. What is more, such is the widespread recognition of the subjectivity of learning in education that academic attainment cannot be separated neatly from personal development. A strong correlation is usually found to exist between academic success and failure and social and personal development or failure to develop. The causes of academic failure in our schools are more often on the nurture side of the nature/nurture debate than simply on the nature side.

The radical compatibility between Lonergan's philosophy and educational thinking is centered, I believe, on the focus of that philosophy on the subject. This was a focus that was sharpened and deepened as Lonergan moved from *Insight* to *Method in Theology*. In *Method* the first three levels of consciousness – the centre of attention in *Insight* – are seen to be pen-

2 Lonergan, *A Second Collection* (1974), 71.

etrated and sublated by the fourth level of consciousness, the level of freedom and responsibility, the level of action and values. In *Method* the subject's self-transcendence is considered to be the ultimate criterion of cognitive and moral objectivity, because objectivity is sharply defined as the consequence of authentic subjectivity.[3] With such a notion of objectivity in play, it becomes very clear that the quality of the human subject in the humanities, the humane disciplines – their authenticity and capacity for self-transcendence – is central to accurate understanding and balanced judgment. Understanding and knowledge can never be neatly severed from the human authenticity of the subject who claims to understand and to know. Hence the notion of *conversion* that lies at the heart of *Method*.

It is this emphasis on the role of the subject in knowing, and on subjectivity more broadly understood in the area of moral and social development, that creates the bond between Lonergan's thinking and much contemporary educational thinking; and it is the very same emphasis that sets Lonergan apart from – and makes him suspect in the eyes of – most contemporary analytic philosophers. I would like now to turn to the reasons for the embarrassment that analytic philosophers have over the notion of the subject and of how this came to affect broad philosophical tastes and preferences in the course of the twentieth century and on into the twenty-first century.

The Flight from the Subject

To understand this distaste for the subject in modern analytic philosophy, we might look first at the thinking of the German mathematician and philosopher Gottlob Frege.[4] Frege radically segregated the subjective and the objective domains of reality. He assigned all aspects of human subjectivity to psychology, which he ruled had no place in philosophical discussion. The reason for Frege's strong way with psychology was related simultaneously to his desire to ensure the universal validity of science and his fear that empiricist notions of perception, set out in psychological terms, would undermine this universal validity. For, with some justification, Frege believed that if all knowledge claims – including those of science – are based on nothing more than the subject's inherently private impressions and ideas, as empiricism maintains, it becomes impossible to claim that meaning and truth can be truly objective. The shared meanings and concepts to which everyone has access in scientific discussion would be impossible. So

---

3 Lonergan, *Method in Theology* (Darton, Longman & Todd, 1972), 265 and 292.
4 My comments on Frege are indebted to Michael H. McCarthy, *The Crisis of Philosophy* (State University of New York Press, 1990), 251f.

Frege set out criteria of objectivity that, he believed, would ensure the universal validity of science – to be objective an entity must be intentionally accessible to all cognitive subjects and causally independent of subjective operations.[5] Furthermore, Frege adopts something approximating to conceptual realism, the notion that abstract concepts and thoughts exist even if there are no thinkers who conceive them or think them, just as the moon or the mountains or the North Sea exist even if there is no one to perceive them. By making the logical order independent of the intentional operations of the mind, Frege believed he had stated the conditions that made scientific discourse possible. What is ironic almost in Frege's espousal of a kind of Platonic conceptual realism is that it hinges on an acceptance of the empiricist conception of objectivity as what is 'already-out-there-now-real' and – at the same time – a rejection of the empiricist account of how we achieve an understanding of what is out there now. Rejecting the idealist response to empiricism, which made reality dependent on the mind, Frege attempted to make reality totally independent of the operations of the mind. Objectivity and subjectivity were incompatible and the only way to safeguard objectivity was to get rid of subjectivity as being unworthy of philosophical interest. Consideration of the subject and the operations of the subject were not the proper concern of philosophy at all, but of psychology, and psychology had no place in philosophy.

This rigid separation of philosophy from psychology was powerfully reinforced by Wittgenstein, a fellow logician, who was a friend and correspondent of Frege. In the *Tractatus Logico-Philosophicus* Wittgenstein wrote:

> Psychology is no more closely related to philosophy than any other natural science. Theory of knowledge is the philosophy of psychology. Does not my study of language correspond to the study of thought-processes, which philosophers used to consider so essential to the philosophy of logic? Only in most cases they got entangled in unessential psychological investigations.   (TR 4.1121)

Again, in the so-called Blue Book, written in the early 1930s, Wittgenstein says,

> Supposing we tried to construct a mind-model as a result of psychological investigations, a model which, as we should say, would explain the action of the mind. This model would be part of a psychological theory in the way in which a mechanical model of the ether can be a part of a theory of electricity ... We may find that such

5 Ibid., 252.

a mind-model would have to be very complicated and intricate in order to explain the observed mental activities ... But this aspect of the mind does not interest us. The problems which it may set are psychological problems, and the method of their solution is that of natural science.[6]

One only needs to hear these powerful words from some of the dominant figures in the analytical tradition, and then think of Lonergan, to realize the kind of reaction they are likely to have to an epistemology and ontology grounded on a cognitional theory. The psychological basis of Lonergan's philosophy is a major reason for its neglect and rejection by members of the analytical tradition. It is also a major reason why Lonergan's thinking is more cognate with the thinking of many of the thinkers who influence educational thinking in Europe and the USA. Some of those mentioned by Lonergan would readily be on the syllabus of most education departments: Piaget, Maslow, Rollo May, Carl Rogers, all mentioned in *Method*, not to mention Stack Sullivan from *Insight*.

The reason is that education is open to psychology in ways in which contemporary Anglo-Saxon philosophy is not. That is why one will find in contemporary theories about reading and the reading process an underlying theory of comprehension that has much in common with what Lonergan has to tell us about learning in *Insight*. As the twentieth century progressed, reading came to be seen less and less as a mechanistic process of converting print into sound and more and more as a thoughtful process of grasping meaning in words and sentences, a process of interrogating the text, of predicting and hypothesizing, and of checking provisional guesses by reading on and seeing how things hung together.[7] Reading for meaning was held up as an ideal in contrast to what came to be known as 'barking at print' – the simple decoding of marks on the page into sound.

Cognitive psychology lies at the heart of modern theories of learning and modern reading theory, and while one will find traces of empiricism, idealism, and pragmatism in the theories of cognitive psychologists, for the most part they are simply interested in coherent and credible accounts of how children – and all of us – learn or make sense of the world or of print. It is hardly surprising then that one will find that many in education hold theories of learning and theories explaining the reading process that bear a close resemblance to Lonergan's theory of cognition.

6 Wittgenstein, *The Blue and Brown Books* (Basil Blackwell, 1972), 6.
7 V. Southgate, H. Arnold, S. Johnson, *Extending Beginning Reading* (Heinemann Educational Books, 1981), 222–3. See also Frank Smith, *Understanding Reading*, 2nd ed. (Holt, Rinehart and Winston, 1978).

There is, however, one important difference between the philosopher's approach to cognitional theory and the psychologist's or the educationist's, and that is the issue of normativity. Normativity is the business of the philosopher. It does not really concern or interest the psychologist, who is more concerned with giving an accurate account of the process we go through – in reading, in learning – than in attempting to explain the *validity of knowledge claims.*

This brings us to the heart of the matter. The kind of psychology against which both Frege and Wittgenstein were reacting and which they wished to exclude from philosophy was empiricist psychology – the psychology of associationism, what Hume called 'the cement of the universe.' Frege rejected empiricist psychology because it could provide no basis for the enduring validity of science; it could not explain the public and enduring meaning of scientific terms. Wittgenstein rejected associationism because it was free of norms and rules that might explain how words mean and how language works; associationism knows no rules, it is its own rule, since it depends on the purely contingent connection of one thing with another. Wittgenstein's exclusion of psychology from philosophy is of a piece with his rejection of a private language. In the case of a strictly private utterance there can be no criterion of right and wrong: 'One would like to say: whatever is going to seem right to me is right. And that only means that here we can't talk about "right"' (PI 258). The same can be said about associationism: it provides no rules explaining how language hooks onto the world: rather it makes the link between word and object a chance and contingent thing bereft of rules.

The exclusion of psychology from philosophy is given a new twist by Richard Rorty in *Philosophy and the Mirror of Nature,* when he urges philosophers to abandon the epistemological quest altogether and to pass epistemology over to the experimental psychologists, who are much better equipped than philosophers to discover and explain the neurological 'wiring' by means of which we are hooked onto the world.[8] In other words, epistemology should be abandoned by philosophers and handed over to the scientists. This is yet another way of saying that philosophy and psychology are two different disciplines and represents an attempt to drop epistemology from the philosophical agenda by placing it in the hands of the physiological psychologists.[9]

8 Richard Rorty, *Philosophy and the Mirror of Nature* (Basil Blackwell, 1980), 163. See also *Consequences of Pragmatism* (University of Minnesota Press, 1982), 16–17.
9 *Philosophy and the Mirror of Nature,* 254–6.

While Rorty's position might seem extreme to some, its roots are well established in the American philosophical and psychological traditions. This is well brought out in Louis Menand's fascinating *The Metaphysical Club*,[10] where we learn how the emergence of pragmatism in the nineteenth-century United States was accompanied by the division of traditional philosophy into philosophy proper and psychology, identified as physiological psychology, with 'mental acts' being assigned to the latter.[11] A rather long quotation will indicate the nature of this historical development:

> The reason many Americans attended German universities was to do laboratory work, and the notion of science they brought back with them when they returned to the United States was empirical and positivist ... 'Pure science' meant an unsentimental effort to reduce the explanation of phenomena to the physical laws of cause and effect, to restrict the scope of knowledge to things that can be measured ... Physiological psychology was founded on a distinction between the mind (consciousness) and the brain (an organ of the body), and its premise was that all mind processes are correlated with brain processes, that every conscious event has a physical basis. 'Mental science' therefore meant experimentation rather than introspection. It meant measuring the reactions of the nervous system in a laboratory rather than speculating on the universal laws of reason in a library ... The consequence was that what we now call psychology established itself as an academic discipline in the modern sense – that is, a field with a distinctive program of research – well before what we now call philosophy did. If the mind could be studied scientifically, and if what could not be studied scientifically was not knowledge, what exactly was the research program of philosophy?[12]

A few comments on this historical development are called for here. First, to equate objectivity with what can be measured is to accept as correct the empiricist notion that the real is what lies 'over there,' spread out in space and time, as the object of an act of ocular vision – for only what is spread out in space and time can be measured. Second, to accord meaning or validity to that only which can be measured is to imply that, in the case of

10 Louis Menand, *The Metaphysical Club* (HarperCollins, 2001). The edition referred to here is the Flamingo edition of 2002.
11 Ibid., 258–69.
12 Ibid., 257–60.

the subject, only the subject as object can ever be a legitimate object of inquiry. For the subject as subject – as the one who sees, hears, understands, weighs the evidence, asserts, claims, knows, and so on – cannot become an object of measurement without changing from subject as subject to subject as object. In other words, the methodological principle that only that which is capable of being measured or subjected to some form of numerical calculation can be considered a legitimate object of knowledge runs the risk of excluding subjectivity from the outset. Finally, it cannot be gainsaid that the fruit of knowledge grows on the tree of the subject or, to put it more simply still, it is subjects who know and there can be and is no knowledge without knowing subjects. The implications of that simple proposition are that until it is shown how objectivity can be reconciled with subjectivity the issue of objectivity is not being properly addressed. In other words, to attempt to establish objectivity without reference to subjectivity, by some methodological principle that simply excludes subjectivity from one's consideration, is not a solution to the problem but is an act of evasion.

If the above reasoning is sound, it follows that an exploration of the subject as subject is an important philosophical requirement. One of the main themes of this book is that only such an exploration of the subject, paradoxically, will restore the belief that the objects affirmed in judgment exist independently of our minds because only a systematic exploration of the subject's conscious operations when coming to know something can yield the norms that make such a claim credible. This exploration of the subject's conscious operations in respect of cognitional and volitional acts is what is meant here by *intentionality analysis*.

Intentionality

To speak of acts as intentional is to say that there is a certain direction to them, that they are pointed or aimed in a particular way, that they have behind them a specific purpose or intention. To ask questions is intentional, since questions have the purpose of achieving answers and different kinds of questions have the purpose of achieving different kinds of answers. To attempt to answer questions is also intentional, since this too is an activity aimed or directed at bringing something about. Intentional activities can be distinguished from other activities that are not directional, such as 'passing' feelings of irritability or amusement or those feelings of 'vividness' or 'feebleness' on which traditional empiricist philosophy (under the sway of the ocular metaphor) used to place a great deal of reliance.

Intentional activities are also spontaneous activities: we do not normally decide to ask the questions What is that? or Is that so? Such questions are not usually the object of preliminary debate and decision but occur naturally. To say that something occurs spontaneously is to say that it follows naturally: it is in the nature of this organism to behave or react in such and such a way when such and such occurs. Spontaneity need not be the enemy of freedom and may be, as it is in humans, the precondition for free action. We are rational creatures for whom to ask questions and to act for a reason are spontaneous, natural activities.

What Lonergan is saying is that these spontaneous intentional activities are also structured, they follow a definite pattern. This pattern is not something we determine from without or by our own volition; it occurs spontaneously and irresistibly and is self-assembling, self-constituting, one stage or part summoning forth the next, as it heads for completion. It is a basic intentionality aimed at achieving the truth and what is right. It is a conscious process and as such can become the object of reflection and analysis. At the fourth level of consciousness intentionality becomes self-conscious, and we find people using the word 'intentional' explicitly, saying, 'I intend (to keep my promises),' 'You intentionally (set out to kill him),' and so on. At the fourth level of consciousness we take possession of our intentionality and become consciously responsible for it, saying, 'I intended it' or 'I meant it.' The four stages or levels of consciousness stretch from sensory experience to action, but always they are to do with meaning – with its discovery (through inquiry) or with its creation (through planning and action): such is the native dynamism of our intelligence that we are meant for, or ordered for, the discovery and creation of meaning. While the analysis of intentionality may legitimately be termed a psychological activity, it is totally different in its outcomes from empiricist psychology. Empiricist psychology gives birth to associationism, with all the problems it holds for epistemology, which have been brilliantly exploited by Wittgenstein. By contrast, intentionality analysis uncovers the norms by which the legitimate discovery and creation of meaning are governed.

Let me summarize what I have said so far in this chapter.

Lonergan has more natural allies among modern educationists than he tends to have among modern philosophers. The reason is that education places a strong emphasis on the cultivation of the individual subject and on psychological theories of learning and personal development.

Analytic philosophy in the twentieth century developed an antipathy towards psychology and sought to exclude psychology from having any legitimate role in philosophy. American pragmatism shared this sentiment.

One reason for this antipathy was that empiricist psychology failed to account for the rules or norms that made language a public possession accessible to all. Another was that philosophy sought to model itself on scientific methods of inquiry that relied on the investigation of objects by means of measurement and numerical calculations.

Lonergan's cognitional theory differs profoundly from associationism and is better described as intentionality analysis. It also differs from science in that it seeks to investigate the subject not as object but precisely as subject. Properly handled, intentionality analysis uncovers the normative procedures by which the legitimate discovery and creation of meaning are governed.

A corollary of this argument or reasoning is that, if we wish Lonergan's philosophy to penetrate the thinking of today's analytic philosophers, we need to explain how he can be both psychological in his approach and yet account for normativity. How Lonergan has done that has been in large measure the burden of this book.

Trying to Do Without the Subject

The loss of subjectivity, the abandonment of the subject's role in knowing and valuing is a huge loss to analytic philosophy because it means that it has great difficulty in having anything worthwhile to say about those areas of human life and those intellectual disciplines in which the role of the subject is a basic assumption or a central focus of attention. Without any adequate understanding of the subject, what can modern analytic philosophy say not only about education and learning but about art or history or ethics, for example? It is simply not possible to talk about art without talking about the artist. In painting we refer to works of art by referring to the name of the artists – it's a Picasso, a Van Gogh, a Caravaggio. And a history that leaves out the achievement of men and women, their sayings, decisions, and actions, whether acting individually or in cooperation with others, would hardly merit the name. Even the histories of logic, mathematics, or science – the disciplines the analytical tradition most admires – are unintelligible if we leave out the subjective element, the intellectual struggles and breakthroughs of great logicians, mathematicians, and scientists and the intersubjective occasions and influences that led to those breakthroughs. Subjectivity is the key to history because it is only by treating the individual subjects that we can place them in their times and even see them as part of a cultural movement. As for ethics, it is not easy to see how we can begin to speak of rights, duties, and responsibilities unless we have some notion of what constitutes a person, nor, furthermore, of how we can begin to speak of persons unless we have some understanding of subjects. An exploration of subjectivity would seem to lie at the heart of any intellectual inquiry into the nature of ethics.

Yet perhaps the area that most profoundly illustrates the absurdity of attempting to account for human attainment and knowledge while leaving the subject out of account is human language itself. Paradoxically, the interest taken by many contemporary analytical philosophers in language might also provide the occasion for some kind of rapprochement between Lonergan's critical realism and analytic philosophy.

Language

Most modern analytic philosophers have abandoned Bertrand Russell's attempt to explain the meaning of words by claiming that this meaning is derived unmediated from the objects the words denote. We have already seen the difficulties Russell encountered when he attempted to explain the meaning of words in this way (see chapter 5) – such difficulties as having to account for the meaning of words denoting fictitious entities like the King of France or a golden mountain, not to mention the meaning of such terms as 'nobody,' 'nowhere,' or 'everybody.' The root cause of these difficulties lies in the empiricist assumption that reality is the 'already-out-there.' From this it would appear to follow that the words that are presumed to reveal this reality, to speak about it, must do so by referring, first and foremost, to things 'out there,' to 'facts in the world.'

For Lonergan, by contrast, the primary reference of words is not 'out there,' but rather inwards to acts of understanding, acts of judgment, and acts of valuing, choosing, and deciding. Speaking and writing are instrumental acts of meaning: they express or mediate the primary acts of meaning, which consist of understanding, judging and deciding, and acting. So there is continuity and discontinuity between understanding, for example, and language. There is continuity in so far as the language I speak expresses my understanding; there is discontinuity in so far as the hearer who understands my meaning can express it in the same or in quite different words.

This understanding of language is quite liberating for it frees us from the absurdities into which empiricist assumptions led someone as intelligent as Bertrand Russell and expands our understanding of how meaning can be created and communicated. The distinction between primary and instrumental acts of meaning, for example, allows for meaning to be expressed in non-linguistic modes such as music, sculpture, painting, gesture, dance, and mime. And where empiricism prized something called 'literal language' above 'poetic language' or 'metaphorical language,' deeming the former to relate directly to sense data or objects in the world and the latter to be little more than 'flowery adornments' or devices designed to achieve particular emotional effects,[13] the fact that language means in so far as it is

---

13 See A.J. Ayer, *Language, Truth and Logic* (Gollancz, 1946), 45.

the expression of the more basic understanding or judgment of the subject and not in so far as it points to things in the world makes such a demotion of metaphorical language absurd. So long as they are grounded in acts of understanding, judging, and valuing, the metaphors, images, and various mimetic devices used by poets and other literary artists are quite legitimate carriers of meaning. Poets are free to claim that they have at their disposal a range of means for the expression of certain meanings with a precision outside the scope of ordinary, so-called 'literal' language. There is no attempt here to reduce metaphorical language to some 'literal language' that is considered to be somehow more basic. Nor, according to this theory of language, are words especially privileged as carriers of meaning. Strictly speaking words and sentences do not mean but rather subjects mean – through their acts of understanding, their knowledge claims, their acts of valuing, and their deeds and actions. Sentences and propositions are true only in so far as they express true acts of judgment and the accurate reference of the nouns used in sentences is determined by the truth of the sentences.

In fact, the distinction between primary acts of meaning and language as only instrumentally meaningful enables us to appreciate more fully how it is that language develops and what in fact so-called 'literal' language actually is. Any empirical investigation of how a historical language, such as English, has evolved and developed over time will discover that, contrary to empiricist assumptions, metaphorical expression came before literal expression. As Vygotsky says of primitive language: 'The primary word is not a straightforward symbol for a concept but rather an image, a picture, a mental sketch of a concept, a short tale about it – indeed a small work of art.'[14] It is only with the passage of time, Vygotsky notes, that 'the image that gave birth to the name,' and the feelings originally tied to it, lose out and conceptual meaning becomes uppermost. Susanne K. Langer is in agreement claiming, with some caustic force, that with time 'speech becomes increasingly discursive, practical, prosaic, until human beings can actually believe it was invented as a utility, and was later embellished with metaphors for the sake of a cultural product called poetry.'[15]

The emergence of linguistic philosophy under the influence of the later Wittgenstein has led many analytic philosophers to ponder language more deeply and to reintroduce the role of the speaker or writer – the subject – via the notion of intentionality. So, for example, the American philosopher John Searle, accounting for the meaning of spoken words, says this:

14 L.S. Vygotsky, *Thought and Language* (Massachusetts Institute of Technology Press, 1962), 75.
15 S.K. Langer, *Philosophy in a New Key* (Harvard University Press, 1942), 126.

The key to understanding meaning is this: meaning is a form of derived intentionality. The original or intrinsic intentionality of a speaker's thought is transferred to words, sentences, marks, symbols, and so on. If uttered meaningfully, those words, sentences, marks, and symbols now have intentionality derived from the speaker's thoughts. They have not just conventional linguistic meaning but intended speaker meaning as well. The conventional intentionality of the words and sentences of a language can be used by a speaker to perform a speech act. When a speaker performs a speech act, he imposes his intentionality on those symbols.[16]

Reading Searle and his philosophical precursor and mentor, J.L. Austin, I have often been struck by the probable fruitfulness of a dialogue between Searle and the followers of Lonergan. There is, I believe, scope for mutually beneficial exchanges on the nature of intentionality and the nature of language, and on the role of the subject in respect of each. One of the insights of Austin's, which Searle has expanded in his own writings, is the distinction he makes between illocutionary acts and perlocutionary acts. As explained by Searle, the illocutionary act is 'the minimal complete unit of human linguistic communication,' something we perform whenever we talk or write to each other.[17] Perlocutionary acts, by contrast, are speech acts that bring about certain consequences. So orders, promises, jokes, entreaties, insults are, in Austin's terms, perlocutionary acts since they are speech acts that bring about some particular consequence over and above mere understanding or knowledge.[18]

This distinction, which reflects the influence of Wittgenstein on Austin and Wittgenstein's repudiation of the empiricist tendency to reduce language to simple declarative sentences or propositions, is useful as far as it goes. It is certainly not intelligible without the notion of intentionality and, hence, of the subject's role in the speech act. But it seems to me that it would gain in depth and flexibility if it could be allied to Lonergan's division of human consciousness into four levels or stages – the empirical, the intellectual, the rational or critical, and the deliberate or responsible. As the reader will recall, the fourth level of consciousness is concerned with valuing, choosing, and acting. Clearly the speech acts that Austin terms perlocutionary are those that Lonergan would assign to the subject operating at the fourth level of consciousness. For at this level the subject is not just communicating meaning – understanding or knowledge achieved at

16 John Searle, *Mind, Language and Society* (Phoenix, 1999), 141.
17 Ibid., 136.
18 Ibid., 137f.

the second and third levels of consciousness respectively – but she is getting things done, bringing about results in the world. To say 'I do' in a marriage ceremony or to draw up a will or to pronounce sentence in a court of law or to sign a promissory note or to issue a summons or even to tell a joke are perlocutionary acts, in Austin's terminology, or acts at the fourth level of consciousness, in Lonergan's.

What is more, Lonergan's four levels of consciousness provide a means for distinguishing and classifying human utterances and speech acts in such a way that it becomes relatively easy to assess the meaning of each. So moans and groans, 'ohs' and 'ahs,' screams and roars, and the like can be readily assigned to the experiential level of consciousness, as spontaneous expressions of pain and pleasure, delight and sorrow, fear and aggression, unmediated by understanding or anything resembling a knowledge claim. They contrast with the more carefully crafted expressions with which we attempt to communicate our understanding and our knowledge, expressions of what the subject achieves at the second and third levels of consciousness. And finally, as we have seen, the notion of the fourth level of consciousness enables us to see the difference between simple communication and what Austin called 'doing things with words.' In short, Lonergan's four levels of consciousness, in addition to helping us solve long-standing problems like the 'is-ought' problem, could serve as a useful way of classifying and ordering different kinds of utterance and speech act. And given the links between the levels of consciousness, the role of the subject, and the light thrown by the four levels on the notion of intentionality, the scope for mutually enriching dialogue between critical realists and analytic philosophers must surely be immense.

Glossary of Key Terms

This list of key terms in Lonergan's philosophy is not meant to be exhaustive. It might help the reader to a clearer understanding of some central notions as well as clarify how his philosophy differs from other philosophies. Words in bold italics can also be found in this glossary.

Cognition   This is synonymous with knowledge. Hence 'cognitive' means pertaining to knowledge and 'non-cognitive' means not pertaining to knowledge. The term is technically useful because it connotes the notion of knowledge as understood and explained by the philosopher, as opposed to more commonsensical understandings of the word.

Consciousness   This is a difficult term to define since it is so close to us that it is not easy to find simpler experiences or terms with which to explain or describe it. But in this book it refers to the awareness that accompanies various acts, including the various components of the act of coming to know something, such as *experience, understanding,* and *judgment.* However, it is important to realize that consciousness is not coterminous with cognition and that there are many non-cognitive acts as well as emotional states that are conscious – such as desiring, loving, wanting, hating, loathing, and suffering (acts) and sadness, joy, and gratitude (emotions). Consciousness may be distinguished from awareness if we think of the latter as facing outwards to the world 'out there' and consciousness as facing inwards to one's own experiences. Indeed, the primary meaning of consciousness in this book is self-presence, and it is maintained that unless I am present to myself through consciousness nothing else can be present to me. The kind of self-presence being referred to here is simply experiential; it is non-reflexive, non-introspective, but something we simply experience when we are conscious. There has been a tendency in empiricist philosophies to assimilate consciousness to perception but Lonergan is keen to avoid this. By presenting consciousness as basically *experiential*, he sees it as something we experience whenever we do something we would term a conscious act as opposed to an unconscious act. Lonergan speaks of different levels of consciousness and sees the human subject as acting at, and being constituted by, *four levels of consciousness*. Not only is consciousness cognitive and emotive, it is also constitutive: human beings are constituted by human consciousness.

Culture   Culture is only possible because human consciousness is not basically perception but self-presence. It is because I am present to myself when I see something that not only do I see something but I am aware of myself as seeing something. For this reason, at the level of cognition, not only do I know something but I know that I know it. And because I know that I know something when I know it, I am able to take hold of my knowledge, encode it in speech and other forms, and communicate it to others. Self-presence also makes possible self-questioning and self-examination and the ability to reform and improve myself. But fundamentally it makes it possible for a community to hand on the knowledge, wisdom, and values that it has accumulated to future generations – and hence makes possible human culture. Lonergan makes a valuable distinction between two understandings of culture. First, there is the classical understanding of culture. This is a conservative, traditional outlook that holds to a normative definition of culture as a unique and permanent achievement of universal validity into which 'outsiders' – such as barbarians or the young – have to be inducted if they are to escape the charge of being uncultured. Classicism holds up models to be imitated, ideals and virtues to be emulated, eternal verities to be known, and universal laws to be applied to particular circumstances. This is the notion of culture entertained in ancient Greece and Rome, which endured throughout the centuries, at least in the notion of 'high culture,' and perhaps reached its peak in Europe of the eighteenth century. It remains widely influential today.

But there is another, more recent understanding of culture. This is the empirical notion of culture as the set of meanings and values that happen to inform a way of life. Rather than culture being considered unique, the empirical approach finds that there are many cultures; rather than culture being considered a permanent achievement, the empirical approach finds that cultures shift and change over time. Longergan finds that behind the classical notion of culture stands the Aristotelian notion of science as true, certain knowledge of things through their causes. By this definition, what is discovered in science is true, invariant, permanent, and closed to revision. By contrast, the modern notion of science is of provisional knowledge based on a dynamic, open-ended method of inquiry that yields cumulative and progressive results. Rather than knowledge, modern science speaks of opinion – the best scientific opinion of the day; it is not fixed or permanent but radically open to change and development. The overthrow of established scientific opinion in the modern era is not a cause for despondency but for celebration, since it is in this way that science advances. Modern historical consciousness has redefined what is meant by science and this redefinition of science has contributed in turn to the reconception of culture. It is the modern understanding of science that lies at the heart of the empirical notion of culture and that has given rise to modern historical consciousness, to what Lonergan also calls 'historical mindedness.' According to historical consciousness, science is an ongoing normative process of inquiry resulting in a continuing succession of theoretical systems.

This distinction between the classical notion of culture and the empirical notion of culture is valuable in illustrating and explaining the difference between the mentality of the past and the mentality of today, between a conservatism that clings to the past and a modern outlook that can appropriate the past and also look to the future. The distinction can be fruitfully applied to the history of philosophy, seeing past attempts at finding foundations for philosophy in so-called incorrigible atomic propositions or eternal axioms as doomed to failure, because in conflict with basic scientific method. The alternative, however, need not be chaos and anarchy or some form of extreme relativism. On the contrary, Lonergan proposes a *method* of inquiry that combines the invariance required in foundations with the pattern of sensitive, intellectual, and rational operations that generates the changes and developments required for scientific advancement. The search for foundations in philosophy should not be abandoned, but should be reconceived as the need for cognitive integration.

Existence   Empiricists tend to equate what exists with what we experience directly with our senses. Betrand Russell might be seen as refining this fairly crude understanding through his notion that existence is a property of propositions. According to this notion, existence is something added to a concept, when a concept is said to 'have application' in sensory experience. The concept is said to be 'satisfied,' to 'apply,' to be 'instantiated' in experience. Existence in this way of thinking is a brute fact – something we bump up against with our senses. It is not to be grasped by means of thought or intelligence but by an event that is, quite literally, mind-less and meaning-less, since it consists of nothing more than palpable sensory contact with that which is said to exist: we confirm that a concept is instantiated by coming into contact with such an instantiation through our senses. Critical realists share with empiricists the idea that existence refers to the real – the real is what exists, the unreal is what does not exist. But they disagree fundamentally about how we arrive at the real, at what exists. For critical realists claim that what exists is what is affirmed as being the case in true *judgments*. And true judgments are based on the verification of the meaning of the data put forward at the second level of knowing, the level of *understanding*. Hence judgment (of what is or of what is not) is an intelligent and rational process, not something executed at the first level of knowing, the level of sensory experiencing. Existence in critical realism is identical with being when being is understood to refer to what *is* or *is not* affirmed in judgment.

'Being' is a word that English-language philosophers tend to shun or to be uneasy about (perhaps afraid of being slipped a Supreme Being), and for this reason in this book I have tended to refer instead to 'the real' or 'reality,' words which mean the same as 'being,' To grasp that being or existence is what is affirmed in judgment is to grasp how 'existence' or 'being' differs from mere concepts. For to entertain a concept is different from affirming that something belongs to the real world, that something *is*; and to say that something exists is to move beyond the merely conceptual level – the level of understanding – to the level of knowledge, the level at which ontological claims are made. For this reason, while it is possible to have a concept of existence, existence can never be reduced to a concept. It reaches beyond any mere concept to the end point of intellectual inquiry when we gain a full increment of knowledge. Hence the basic human desire to know the truth is, in effect, a basic *intentionality* towards grasping the real, towards knowing what is, to knowing being. Being is that to which our intentional apparatus tends; it is the unknown that is intended in all our questions. Thomistic philosophers are fond of urging their readers to think of being or existence not as a noun (which has the appearance of a concept) but as a verb, just as Aquinas frequently used the Latin verb 'esse' (to be) to mean 'being.' Existence means 'to exist' and the claim that something exists depends on intelligent understanding and rational judgment: hence anything that exists has the unity and pattern of intelligibility, the absoluteness and concreteness of fact, and the actuality of the verb 'to be.'

Experience This is the first stage in coming to know something. It is that about which we ask questions in order to achieve *understanding* and knowledge. At the most obvious level it is what we do when we apply our senses – when we see, hear, touch, taste, or smell something. These are operations at the experiential level. Experience by itself does not yield meaning but rather the data for inquiry. Inquiry occurs in response to such questions about the data as 'What is that? How often does it happen?' and so forth. Another source of data is *consciousness*, the consciousness that accompanies subjective acts of seeing, understanding, judging, valuing, deciding, and acting. Such consciousness is another type of experience. The data of consciousness can also become a focus for our questioning. The scientist systematically investigates the data of sense, the philosopher systematically investigates the data of consciousness.

Four levels of consciousness   The human person is constituted by human consciousness and human consciousness comprises four levels corresponding to the four distinct sets of operations we perform at each level – the level of sensory activity, also known as the level of experience; the level of understanding, also known as the level of intelligence; the level of judgment, or the rational or critical level. These three levels are the three levels of *cognition*, and Lonergan sees them as constituting a *generalized empirical method*, since it is by means of these recurrent operations that we develop our knowledge of things in the world, of empirical matters of fact. But beyond these three levels there is another level, one characterized by freedom and responsibility, the level at which we deliberate, choose, decide, resolve, and act. This is the level at which, motivated by value and guided by our knowledge, we live our lives and interact with each other. It builds on the other levels of consciousness and, in turn, frequently penetrates and directs them.

To say that an action is free is not to say that it is done at will or arbitrarily. Human freedom cannot be uncoupled from reason. The actions of those who have not reached the use of reason or of those who, in whatever way, have lost the use of reason are considered to be unfree. We say that they are not responsible for their actions. To be free is to be capable of taking responsibility for what we do or say; to be responsible is to know and understand what we are doing. We are free to be responsible. The responsible exercise of human freedom builds on the understanding and knowledge achieved at the second and third levels of consciousness. Indeed, it is not possible even to speak of inquiring or reasoning without presuming a context of personal freedom. For the process of inquiry or of reasoning – interrogating the data, the play of intelligence on a problem or issue, turning over possible answers to a question, attempting to follow the argument wherever it may lead – presumes that the pursuit of the truth is a free and open-ended activity. (The concept of truth is not compatible with the denial of free will.)

But reasoning by itself does not get things done. Reasoning can present different courses of action and suggest the reasons for pursuing one course rather than others. But for the job to be done there is needed deliberation, evaluation, choice, and decision, and these are a distinct set of operations leading to action. As such they belong to the fourth level of consciousness. Lonergan gives the name of Transcendental Method to the fourfold set of operations we perform in line with the fourfold division of consciousness. See also *consciousness, experience, judgment, method, sublation,* and *understanding.*

Idea   In this book an idea is the intelligible form or plan or design that makes something the thing that it is. So the intelligible form of a house makes a collection of stones, bricks, tiles, wood, and glass into a house. Without this intelligible form, or idea, there would be no house and hence the idea is an essential part of the being of the house, of the fact that the house exists. When we understand what something is we grasp what is intelligible about it and that is the form or idea that makes it what it is. When there is true understanding – when our understanding has been verified (see *verification*) – there is an identity between the idea that I grasp and the idea that exists in the materials I see, touch, hear, smell, or taste. In traditional empiricist philosophy the idea is often thought of as an internal copy in the mind of an object 'out there' in the world, a purely mental entity. Hence the idea is said to represent the real object, to stand proxy for it, to be a sign of the reality to which it points. In epistemology this idea of the idea gives rise to the problem of representationism, namely, the notion that we can never know the real in itself since all we know are ideas, which are simply mental representations of reality; there is always a 'veil of ideas' between the knower and the real. This in turn can give rise to further problems such as scepticism, the view that I can never legitimately claim to know anything, or subjectivism, the view that I can never know objective reality but only the ideas that are subjectively present to me. But this notion of idea is repudiated by Lonergan. When we know something, he is saying, we do not know an idea but rather it is through the idea, by means of the idea, that we know it. And the idea we grasp in coming to know something – the idea that enables us to know it – is the idea that makes the thing the thing it is. See also *understanding.*

Intentionality   The process we go through in coming to know something is not an aimless process but one that is highly directed and purposeful, albeit this direction and purpose are built into the structure of inquiry itself and are not something deliberately imposed by the subject. Inherent in the notion of intentionality is the notion that our cognitional operations are about something – they are designed to bring about results, to achieve answers. They are shaped and purposeful and, what is more, as one part of the process is completed it summons forth the next: so, for example, questions generate attempts at understanding and proposed understandings generate questions about their accuracy and validity. We check our understanding spontaneously to ensure that it is secure before we pronounce that we know with some degree of certainty. Knowledge, in turn, often presents us with further questions such as 'What is to be done about this?' In common speech 'intentional' means with foreknowledge and deliberation, but this is not always the case when the word is used philosophically. In Lonergan's philosophy acts and actions that are 'intentional' in the sense that they are done with deliberation and foreknowledge are acts and actions carried out at the fourth level of consciousness, they are acts we perform self-consciously. At this level we, as it were, take responsibility for our intentions and hence intentionality becomes explicit, becomes self-conscious. But the cognitive acts we perform at the earlier levels are also intentional. Acts that are intentional are always conscious acts but they are not always self-conscious acts. However, because they are conscious they can become the object of inquiry.

Introspection   In this book this term denotes the process of knowing oneself, usually as a subject who knows and does things. Just as Lonergan repudiates the notion of knowing as looking, so he repudiates the assimilation of introspection to a kind of inward looking, a kind of peering into the 'black box' of one's mind to see what is there – a notion encouraged by the word's etymology. Not unnaturally, he assimilates introspection to his own understanding of what knowing is, and hence he considers that, because coming to know something is a conscious and not an unconscious act, we experience consciously what we are doing when we come to know something and that, by reflecting on this experience, attempting to understand it and affirming it as knowledge, we can discover ourselves as knowers.

Judgment   This is the third and final stage in coming to know something, when we judge that something is or is not the case. Knowledge comprises *experiencing, understanding,* and judging. At judgment we are done with hesitation and confirm or disconfirm our understanding. We give our understanding a 'yes' or a 'no,' affirming that something is or is not the case or is probably so or probably not so. With judgment we are making a knowledge claim and hence affirming something we believe to be true. It is through the truth claims we make in judgments that we assert what is really so in the world, that we affirm reality, that we assert that something exists (see *existence*). The true is what is intelligently understood and reasonably affirmed in judgment. Likewise, the real is isomorphic with the structure of knowing: as experienced, the real is given; as understood, the real is intelligible; as known, the real is an absolute, a fact. Hence, the real is something that exists independently of the subject affirming it, but at the same time it has to be interpreted or understood in order to be discovered. There is no such thing as an uninterpreted fact. See also *existence.*

Language   Bertrand Russell ran into difficulties when he proceeded on the assumption that words get their meaning from their reference to things 'out there' or 'over there.' This conflation of meaning and reference made it difficult for him to account for the meaning of words with 'no' in front of them, like 'no one' or 'nowhere,' or words denoting fictitious entities like the King of France or, for that matter, words formulating the laws of science or the principles of mathematics. Lonergan avoids this problem because he does not consider the primary reference of words to be to things 'out there' but rather to be inwards – to acts of understanding and acts of judgment. Words that are not grounded in acts of understanding are meaningless and words that are not grounded in acts of judgment have no meaningful reference. The distinction between understanding and judgment means that in Lonergan's epistemology there is no danger of conflating meaning with reference – understanding comes from the subject and not from the object understood, and it is quite possible to understand what a golden mountain is without judging that there is or must be such an entity. In the same way, it is possible to judge that there is no one in the room because judgment, which mounts on understanding, is nothing more than the affirmation that something is or is *not* the case. What is more, judgments can be meaningful but wrong, so it is clear that meaning is not dependent on reference.

Understanding and judgment are the primary acts of meaning, while speaking and writing are instrumental acts of meaning that express or mediate the primary acts of meaning. This explains how what we normally call 'language' is not the sole repository of meaning and how meaning can be encoded in a broad range of non-linguistic media such as dance, music, gesture, mime, sculpture, painting, photographs, images, signs, symbols, mathematical formulae, scientific laws, or hieroglyphics. It also explains how it is that, historically, poetry is prior to prose and literal language results from the sedimentation of metaphorical language. Words and sentences do not, strictly speaking, mean but rather subjects mean through their acts of understanding and judgment. But because language is so closely tied to understanding it is difficult to differentiate between accurate understanding and the expression of this in language; between true propositions, on the one hand, and true judgments, on the other. That is why genuinely new understanding – intellectual breakthroughs of whatever kind – require new words or terms to be coined or old words or terms to be stretched to accommodate new meanings. While we might *distinguish* truly between meaning and language – and such a distinction is important if we are not to get into some of the difficulties mentioned – it is in point of fact virtually impossible to *separate* meaning and its expression in language. Wittgenstein was right about that. (However, it should be noted that Lonergan is not vulnerable to Wittgenstein's attacks on the notion of a private language. That is because the transition from 'in here' to 'out there' that the conception of language as primarily private requires does not arise for Lonergan, who does not conceive of knowing as akin to a private act of sensation nor of reality as what already lies out there. The major transition for Lonergan is not from 'in here' to 'out there,' but rather from sensory experiencing to understanding. Once understanding has been achieved, expression becomes possible and, with expression, communication.)

Tying language to understanding and judgment also brings in the notions of *subjectivity* and *intentionality*, since both of these notions are intrinsic to the notions of *understanding* and *judgment*. Lonergan's notion of the *four levels of* intentional *consciousness* goes a long way towards explaining the different functions of different kinds of sentences or different linguistic genres and, in particular, can explain how some utterances simply convey meaning while others – called by Austin and Searle 'perlocutionary acts' – bring about real changes in the world. See also *intentionality, judgment, subjectivity,* and *understanding.*

Method   This refers to a pattern of recurrent and related operations yielding cumulative and progressive results. Lonergan refuses to identify knowing with a single act or action, such as looking or hearing, thinking or intuiting. Rather, knowing consists of a set of operations that form a pattern. The pattern is recurrent since any further act of knowing will consist of exactly the same operations. The fruits of these operations are not repetitious but cumulative and progressive. Lonergan's basic achievement is to uncover and analyse this basic pattern and to illustrate how it is applied in the various disciplines of mathematics, science, history, and common sense. Considered in itself, however, the method is transcendental in the sense that it transcends any given field of inquiry and is commensurate with the workings of the human mind itself. As in Kant, transcendental method is the necessary but not sufficient condition of any method of inquiry. It is a *metamethod* that is both foundational and universally significant and relevant. All other methods of human inquiry, be it in mathematics, history, geography, or any other discipline, are but extensions and adaptations of transcendental method. It is for this reason that an intelligent person who may know little or nothing about a situation or subject can sometimes bring clarity to it by seeing how far the methods being employed conform with the procedures of transcendental method – or conform with what Lonergan terms the 'transcendental precepts': Be attentive, Be intelligent, Be reasonable, Be responsible. Because it relates to the free and spontaneous workings of the human mind, Lonergan's method is not the repetition of some mechanical process in the way that the operations of my car engine or the workings of my computer are. Rather it touches on the basic and spontaneous operations of the human mind in its inquisitive mode, as it goes about trying to find out what is the case or what should be done. It is profoundly human and, when combined with the notion of *self-transcendence*, humanly profound. For Lonergan, transcendental method becomes a guide and compass that helps us to find our way in the human and natural sciences. By its means he endeavours to show what the human sciences have in common with the natural sciences as well as how they differ from the natural sciences. As a method underlying human inquiry in all fields, transcendental method has the potential to bring unity and coherence to human knowledge and to answer the problem of the fragmentation of human knowledge that many complain of today.

Objectivity   The basic meaning is 'pertaining to the object' and, if by 'object' one means what lies 'out there' as the object of one's seeing or hearing or touching (sensing), then objectivity in knowing might be considered to reside in seeing and hearing, and so on, what it there and not seeing or hearing what is not there. If cognition is equated with sensation, then objectivity will consist of successfully reaching out with one or more of one's senses to what lies out there. But in addition to the basic meaning of 'pertaining to the object,' objectivity in knowing frequently connotes the accurate knowledge of the object of our inquiry, our knowledge of it as it truly is, valid or successful knowing. That is what is usually meant by 'objectivity' in this book. At the level of experience, Lonergan's position is that it is true that objectivity resides in the givenness of the data and as part of the knowing process consists in seeing, hearing, touching (sensing) what is given and not seeing, hearing, touching (sensing) what is not given. But if knowing is more than sensing, other criteria of objectivity come into play. At the intelligent and rational levels, objectivity resides in the norms of intelligence and rationality and is achieved when the subject complies with these norms. That means, at the intellectual level, complying with the criteria of clarity, rigour, and coherence; and, at the critical or rational level, with the criterion of sufficient reason. The overarching criterion of objectivity is the detached, disinterested desire to know: it is this overarching drive that combines the three movements of knowing into a single act of knowing. For this reason, Lonergan claims that objectivity is the consequence of authentic *subjectivity*. In analytic philosophy there has been an attempt to define objectivity as the absence of subjectivity, but this attempt is strongly resisted by Lonergan, who sees knowledge as necessarily comprising two poles, one subjective and the other objective. See also *subjectivity*.

Questions   We grow in understanding and knowledge by asking and answering questions. It is through questioning that we move from ignorance to answer. Questions drive intellectual and moral inquiry, and because of that we know we have reached the end of a particular inquiry when there are no further relevant questions to ask. Inquiry is set in motion by questions seeking understanding: What is that? How does it work? How often does it happen? Why? These are questions moving the subject to understand and, if understanding is successful, if we come up with an interpretation or explanation, another set of questions arises: Is that so? Is it true? Is it probable or improbable? These are questions bidding the subject to check out the interpretation or explanation to see if it is sound, if it is true, if it is reliable. This second set of questions is aimed at the answers to the first set of questions – hence Lonergan calls them 'questions for reflection.' They are aimed at bringing a certain closure to inquiry by attempting to place a 'yes' or a 'no' by the answers we have come up with to the first set of questions. If successful, they lead on to the *judgment* that something is or is not the case. With judgment we have reached an increment in our knowledge. We can stop at that, but frequently, because we are human, another set of questions arises at this stage: Is that right? Is it appropriate? Is it fair and just? What is to be done about it? These are 'questions for deliberation' when we are challenged to ponder possible choices, decisions, and actions.

Questions and answers are the staple of everyday life and are basic to getting things done in the world – by their means we gain in our understanding, control, and mastery of the world about us. But on the side of the subject, it is by asking and answering questions honestly, truthfully, and fearlessly that we grow intellectually and morally. Questions are an expression of the desire to know the truth, and it this desire, which is basic to our humanity, that propels inquiry from one stage to the next. Indeed, it is the different kinds of questions that we ask – questions for understanding or for reflection or for deliberation – that determine the type of discourse we are involved in and the level of consciousness we are operating in: we pass from one level of consciousness to another through the question-gate. We can, of course (and most of us do from time to time), ignore the desire to know, switch it off, so to speak, because we can't be bothered or it gets in the way of our own interests or wishes – and then we are being untrue to this basic human drive and will not make the gains in understanding and knowledge that we could. Lonergan is acutely alert to the fact that we are questing, searching, desiring beings and he wishes to thematize this dynamic element in human consciousness, since to rule it out or to ignore its existence is to end up with a truncated and impoverished understanding of who and what we are. See also *four levels of consciousness, intentionality, self-transcendence,* and *subjectivity.*

Self-transcendence   The subject who knows, decides, and acts can stay within the orbit of his or her own self-interest, wishes, or desires. On the other hand, the subject can, in terms of knowing, affirm something as true. In coming to know, not what appears, not what is imagined, but what is so, the subject is moving beyond his or her own self-interest and desires in an act of cognitive self-transcendence. For what is affirmed as being so is affirmed as being so independently of the subject's own wishes, or emotional preferences. What is so exists independently of the subject who affirms its existence. But cognition is not the only act of intentional self-transcendence performed by the subject. With moral choice and action, the subject moves beyond cognitional self-transcendence to moral self-transcendence by coming to know and to do what is truly good. Lonergan calls this 'real self-transcendence' since it is a moving beyond any merely personal satisfactions and interests to become, through one's actions, a centre of benevolence and goodness in the world. Moral self-transcendence takes place at the fourth level of consciousness and involves the subject self-consciously and deliberately opting for what is right, and in so doing not only making a change in the world but also making him- or herself the person he or she is. As such, moral choice, decision, and action are another step along the path of conscious intentionality, a step characterized by freedom and responsibility, and by the self-consciousness that accompanies our deliberate and considered activation of our own human freedom. Finally, Lonergan sees the state of being in love as the pinnacle of self-transcendence, since by being genuinely in love one's thoughts and commitments are with the beloved in preference to one's own likes and dislikes. Being in love is a dynamic state that transforms and transfigures the fourth level of human consciousness, becoming the supreme principle of all our acting and doing, and hence reorientating our thoughts and actions so that they are now at the service not of ourselves but of the one who is the object of our love. See also *four levels of consciousness, intentionality,* and *method.*

Subjectivity   The basic reference is to the subjective pole in knowing. Subjectivity refers to the various moves and acts performed by the subject in the process of coming to know something. The subject is constituted by consciousness and, because human consciousness consists of four levels, the structure of the subject is similarly fourfold. In common speech, views or opinions said to be 'subjective' are considered to be biased or partial in some respect, but in strict philosophical terms there can be no knowledge-claim that is not the claim of someone, and hence all knowledge is subjective; there simply cannot be knowledge that is not subjective in that sense. As Lonergan put it, 'The fruit of knowledge grows on the tree of the subject.' Lonergan's greatest contribution to philosophy has been to show how subjectivity and *objectivity* in knowledge can be reconciled. Such reconciliation depends on the subject complying with the criteria operating at each stage of cognition, as outlined under 'objectivity' above. Objectivity, in the sense of true or successful knowledge, is not the consequence of any kind of subjectivity but only of responsible subjectivity – that is, of subjectivity that is in accord with what Lonergan terms the 'four transcendental precepts': Be attentive, Be intelligent, Be rational, and Be responsible. The subjectivity that is normative in the attainment of objectivity is responsible subjectivity.

Sublation   This is a technical term used by Lonergan to indicate how, as we move towards knowledge and action based on knowledge, the later operations in the set subsume and build upon the earlier ones. The earlier operations are not discarded as we move onto the later operations, but are taken into the later ones, and their findings are put to new uses under the impetus of the questions directing the later operations. So, for example, the fourth level of intentional consciousness does not leave behind the previous levels of experiencing, understanding, and judging, but directs them to a new goal as we strive to build our actions on the knowledge we have accumulated by means of experiencing, understanding, and judging. Actions not built on knowledge and understanding are likely to result in blunders and to be described as stupid and irresponsible.

Thomism   The philosophy of St Thomas Aquinas as it has come down to us in history, often mediated by his major commentators. Neo-Thomism is a development of this philosophy under the impetus of the encyclical *Aeterni Patris* of Pope Leo XIII in 1879. Outstanding Neo-Thomist philosophers in the twentieth century were French scholars Étienne Gilson and Jacques Maritain. 'Transcendental Thomism' is a name attaching to the philosophy of the Belgian scholar Joseph Maréchal (1878–1944), whose treatment of Aquinas was deeply influenced by the perceived need to grapple with Kant. Lonergan is sometimes 'placed' as a 'transcendental Thomist' but, while acknowledging his debt to Maréchal, this description fails to take account of the British influences on his philosophy – not least that of John Henry Newman as well as that of some nineteenth-century British idealists and the Oxford Aristotelians of the early twentieth century – as well as of the influence of his familiarity with mathematical logic and the like. Lonergan's influences are many and varied, and he is too much his own man to be neatly pigeon-holed as a this or a that.

Understanding   This is the second stage in coming to know something. It is what occurs when we grasp the meaning, or possible meaning, of something. Perhaps understanding can be most easily understood from examples in mathematics – when, for instance, we grasp the fact that the sum of the angles of a triangle MUST equal 180 degrees. This MUST is clearly not something we ascertain with our senses, but it is nevertheless compelling and irresistible. It is something we understand. Not all understanding is so compelling, and frequently we express our understanding (of historical events, say, or of the physical universe) in the form of hypotheses or suppositions. Understanding seeks to describe or explain. By description we understand by relating the data to our senses. By explanation we understand by relating parts of the data to each other.

Verification   This occurs at the third stage in coming to know something and is the prelude to *judgment*. In the threefold process of coming to know, understanding occurs at the second stage in reply to such questions as What? Why? and How often? But understanding by itself does not constitute knowledge and has to be checked and verified before the judgment can be formed that something is or is not the case. Verification is the process of checking, and confirming or falsifying, our understanding. This is a critical epistemology, since what is not verified cannot be accepted as true. In this epistemology, the verified is the real.

Bernard Lonergan: Biographical Note

Bernard Joseph Francis Lonergan was born in Canada of Irish and English stock in 1904, the eldest of three boys. In 1922 he joined the Society of Jesus (the Jesuits). As part of his long intellectual preparation for the life of a Jesuit priest, he was sent in 1926 to study philosophy at Heythrop College, the Jesuit study centre a few miles north-west of Oxford. While studying scholastic philosophy at Heythrop – and pronouncing on what he perceived to be its decided limitations – he in fact spent some of his time preparing for a general degree at the University of London, his four subjects being Greek, Latin, French, and mathematics. He also supplemented his study of scholastic philosophy with the reading of Aristotle, Newman's *Grammar of Assent*, and H.W.B. Joseph's *An Introduction to Logic*. A certain ambivalence to the Jesuit Order and to Catholic scholarship in general was to be an abiding characteristic of Lonergan's life-long dedication to high-quality scholarship. When he later came to study Aquinas – and it is worth pointing out that his first real encounter with Aquinas came after he had studied Newman, Joseph, Aristotle, Plato, and Augustine – he was quite scathing about the current state of Thomistic scholarship: 'The current interpretation,' he wrote to a friend, 'is a consistent misinterpretation ... [W]hat the current Thomists call intellectual knowledge is really sense knowledge ...,' and so forth. A rather ruthless independence of mind and a determination to find things out for himself can be seen to have been strong characteristics from early on. He later went on to take a theology degree and, just before the outbreak of the Second World War, a doctorate in theology, at the Gregorian University in Rome.

Although most of his major teaching posts were to be in theology, it would be misleading to pigeon-hole Lonergan as merely a theologian.

Much of his interest in theology was methodological – the problematic he addressed in his book *Method in Theology* was how someone who is thoroughly modern, and in being modern is historically minded, can possibly subscribe to a theology that is dogmatic. This inevitably led him into issues of methodology, and his interest in methodology did not stop at theology but led into philosophy, the foundations of mathematics, economics, history, and the natural and social sciences. His basic position, which throws light on his interest in methodology, can be summed up in his saying, 'The human mind is always the human mind.'

Lonergan's teaching career was varied: at seminaries in Montreal and Toronto, at the Gregorian University in Rome, at Harvard as Stillman Professor of Divinity, at Regis College in Toronto and at Boston College as Distinguished Professor of Theology. While he was alive, he was best known in the English-speaking world for two books, *Insight: A Study of Human Understanding*, published in 1957, and *Method in Theology*, published in 1972. Other works published in English in his lifetime were a historical exploration of Aquinas entitled *Verbum: Word and Idea in Aquinas* and two collections of essays. Since his death in 1984 his literary executors have arranged for his major writings – including translations of those completed in Latin while at the Gregorian in Rome and many occasional courses, articles, and papers on topics as varied as economics, phenomenology, and mathematical logic – to be published by the University of Toronto Press as his Collected Works in some twenty-five volumes.

In one of the many anecdotes sprinkled throughout his *Memoirs*,[1] Frederick Copleston, the distinguished English Jesuit historian of philosophy who was Lonergan's contemporary on the teaching staff at the Gregorian, tells of meeting Lonergan on the Spanish Steps, a spot where their paths frequently crossed as each took his afternoon walk round Rome. 'I remember how on one occasion I tried to allay what I thought was a groundless anxiety on his [Lonergan's] part. Some people had been photographing an actress or fashion model on the Steps (a by no means rare occurrence), and Bernard was apprehensive that a photograph taken while he was passing up might have included him and might appear in some paper. I tried to reassure him that it was unlikely that a photo would be published with himself in it, and even if this did occur, it would not matter in the least. He would certainly look as though he were deep in thought, as doubtless he was.' Copleston speaks of finding Lonergan on social occasions 'always simple and humorous' and goes on to say, 'He was a very human person, besides being an outstanding theologian.' This was an impression many gathered from meeting Lonergan.

---

1 Frederick C. Copleston, S.J., *Memoirs* (Sheed and Ward, 1993).

In the mid-1960s Lonergan underwent a medical operation to remove a cancerous lung. This inevitably took its toll on his physical strength, and his convalescence was difficult and painful. For a time his career as a writer and academic was under threat just as he was coming to grips with *Method in Theology*, in many ways the life-long goal of his academic career, and moving into what we can see in retrospect to be the second major creative phase in his thinking. Throughout this period he was sustained by his strong faith and those who met him at this time believe that the experience, painful and threatening as it was, informed his thinking in his later period. In this phase of his thinking Lonergan moved beyond the powerful but somewhat cerebral intellectualism of *Insight* into a fuller, more concrete view of the human person and, alongside this, a fuller and more concrete grasp of what constitutes human development and change. Part of this major paradigm shift is his vision of philosophy – a vision that, with the advantage of hindsight, we can see was present in his thinking from early on – moving from the narrowness of logic to the fullness of method, mirroring the historical shift from the Aristotelian conception of science to that found in the modern practice of science.

Those who would like to learn from Lonergan the philosopher might be best advised to begin with *Understanding and Being* (volume 5 of the Collected Works) rather than plunge headlong into the more massive *Insight*, which requires unusual stamina to complete. Another good starting place would be 'Cognitional Structure,' a paper published in his first collection of essays entitled simply *Collection* (volume 4 of the Collected Works), although some readers might prefer the slightly longer but very clear summary of his basic position that Lonergan sets out in the first chapter of *Method in Theology*, entitled 'Method.' From any of these starting points the reader could be prepared to take on the formidable task of working through *Insight* (volume 3 of the Collected Works).

Index